DEADPOOL & CABLE
SPLIT SECOND

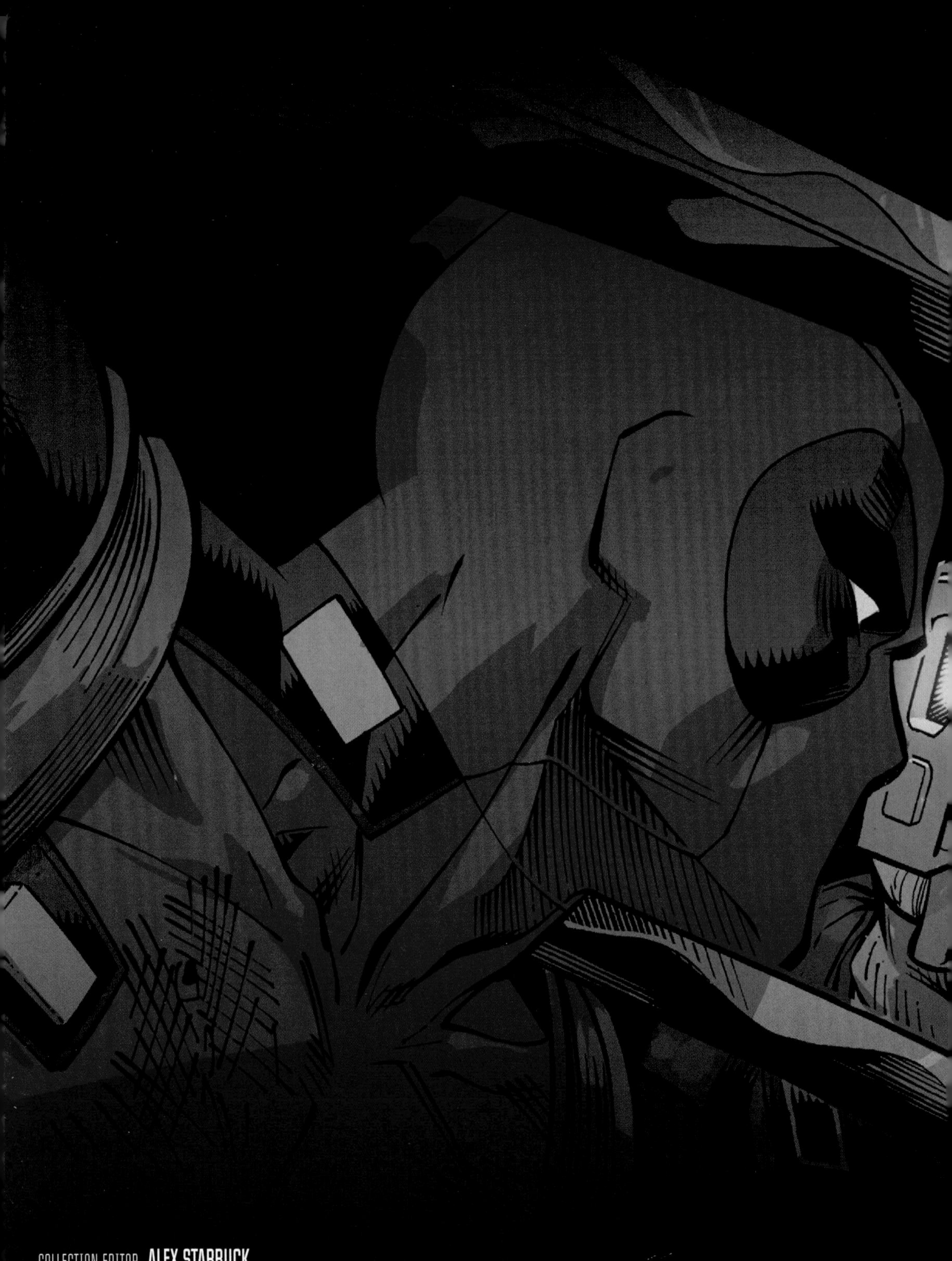

COLLECTION EDITOR **ALEX STARBUCK**
ASSOCIATE EDITOR **SARAH BRUNSTAD**
EDITORS, SPECIAL PROJECTS **JENNIFER GRÜNWALD & MARK D. BEAZLEY**
VP, PRODUCTION & SPECIAL PROJECTS **JEFF YOUNGQUIST**
SVP PRINT, SALES & MARKETING **DAVID GABRIEL**
BOOK DESIGNER **JOE FRONTIRRE**

EDITOR IN CHIEF **AXEL ALONSO**
CHIEF CREATIVE OFFICER **JOE QUESADA**
PUBLISHER **DAN BUCKLEY**
EXECUTIVE PRODUCER **ALAN FINE**

STORY **FABIAN NICIEZA & REILLY BROWN**

SCRIPT **FABIAN NICIEZA**   PENCILS **REILLY BROWN**

INKS **REILLY BROWN & JAY LEISTEN** WITH **JEREMY FREEMAN**   COLORS **JIM CHARALAMPIDIS**

LETTERER **VC'S JOE SABINO**   COVER ART **REILLY BROWN & JIM CHARALAMPIDIS**

PRODUCTION **ANNIE CHUNG**   PRODUCTION MANAGER **TIM SMITH 3**   ASSISTANT EDITOR **HEATHER ANTOS**   EDITOR **JORDAN D. WHITE**

DEADPOOL CREATED BY ROB LIEFELD & FABIAN NICIEZA; CABLE CREATED BY ROB LIEFELD & LOUISE SIMONSON

DPOOL & CABLE: SPLIT SECOND. Contains material originally published in magazine form as DEADPOOL & CABLE: SPLIT SECOND #1-3 and TRUE BELIEVERS: DEADPOOL VARIANTS #1. First printing 2016. ISBN# 978-0-7851-9514-6. shed by MARVEL WORLDWIDE, INC., a subsidiary of MARVEL ENTERTAINMENT, LLC. OFFICE OF PUBLICATION: 135 West 50th Street, New York, NY 10020. Copyright © 2016 MARVEL No similarity between any of the names, characters, ons, and/or institutions in this magazine with those of any living or dead person or institution is intended, and any such similarity which may exist is purely coincidental. **Printed in Canada.** ALAN FINE, President, Marvel Entertainment; BUCKLEY, President, TV, Publishing & Brand Management; JOE QUESADA, Chief Creative Officer; TOM BREVOORT, SVP of Publishing; DAVID BOGART, SVP of Business Affairs & Operations, Publishing & Partnership; C.B. CEBULSKI, VP of d Management & Development, Asia; DAVID GABRIEL, SVP of Sales & Marketing, Publishing; JEFF YOUNGQUIST, VP of Production & Special Projects; DAN CARR, Executive Director of Publishing Technology; ALEX MORALES, Director of shing Operations; SUSAN CRESPI, Production Manager; STAN LEE, Chairman Emeritus. For information regarding advertising in Marvel Comics or on Marvel.com, please contact Vit DeBellis, Integrated Sales Manager, at vdebellis@marvel. For Marvel subscription inquiries, please call 888-511-5480. **Manufactured between 2/26/2016 and 4/4/2016 by SOLISCO PRINTERS, SCOTT, QC, CANADA.**

8 7 6 5 4 3 2 1

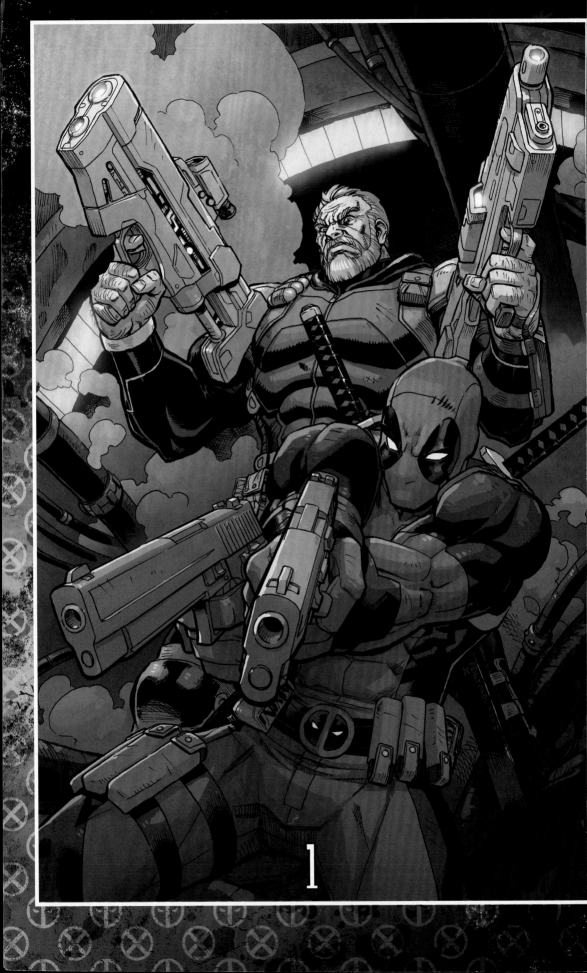

1

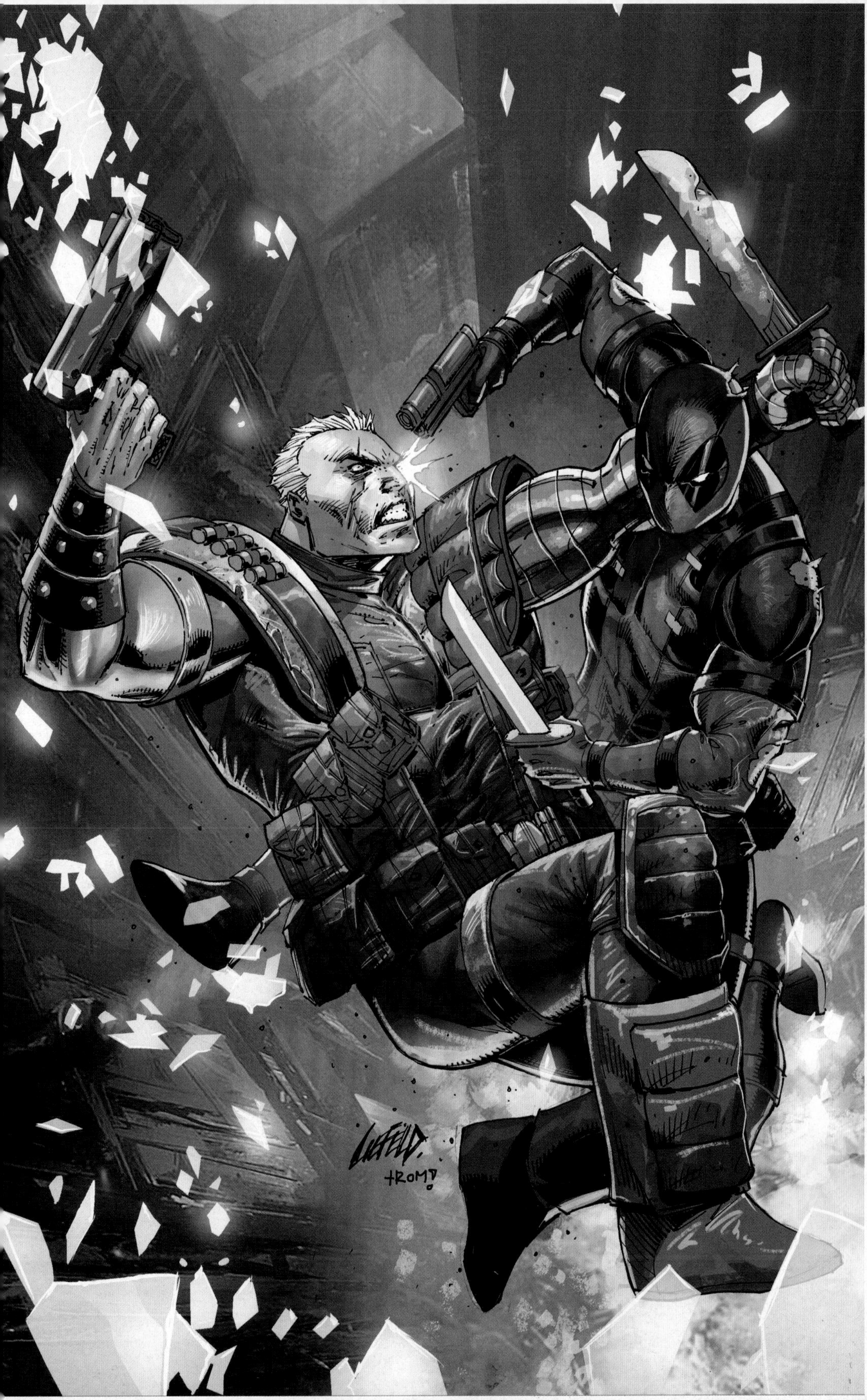

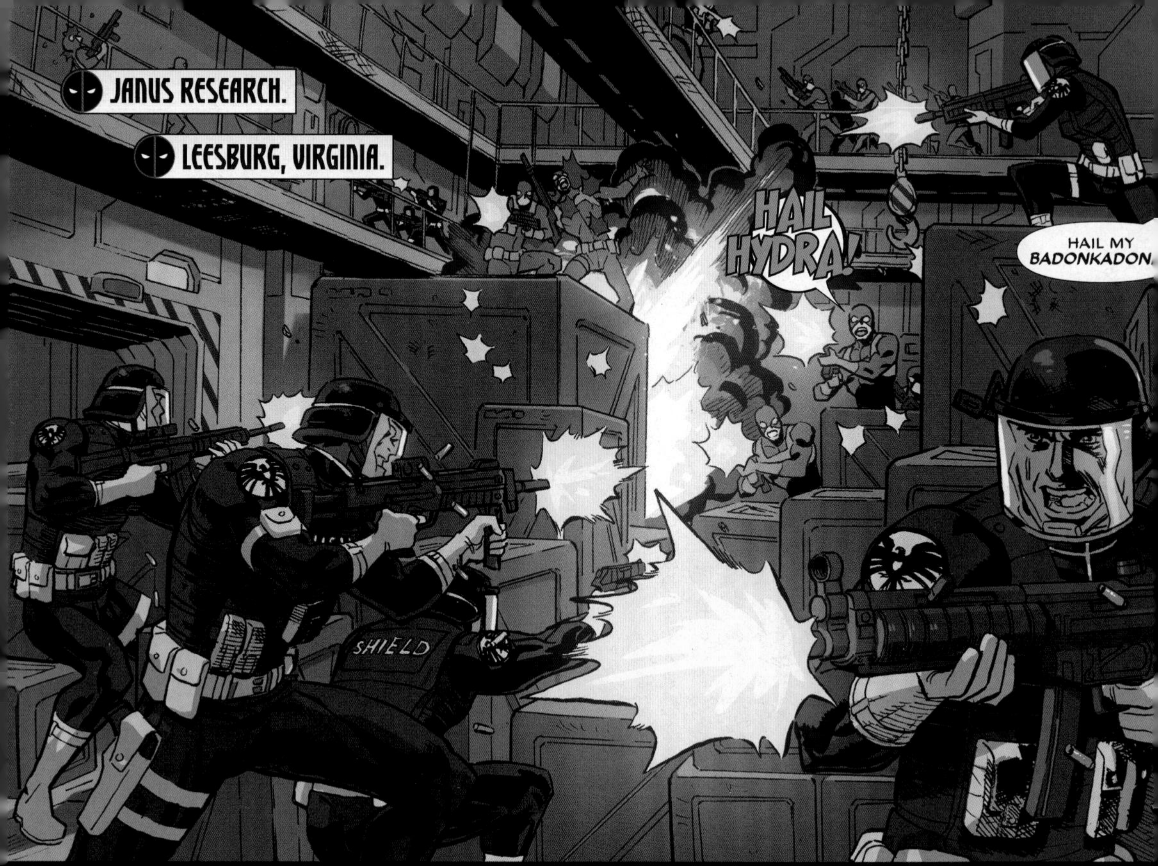
JANUS RESEARCH.
LEESBURG, VIRGINIA.
HAIL HYDRA!
HAIL MY BADONKADON
SHIELD

DEADPOOL & CABLE

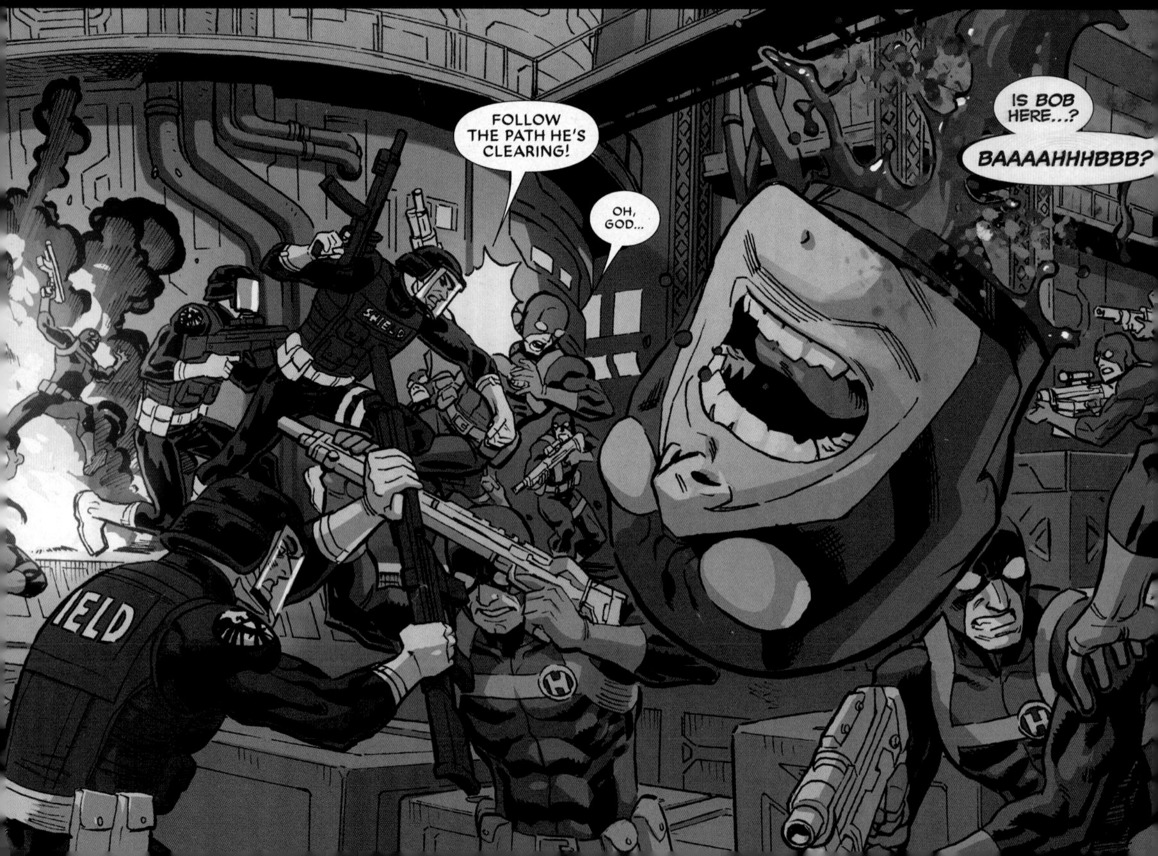
FOLLOW THE PATH HE'S CLEARING!
OH, GOD...
IS BOB HERE...?
BAAAAHHHBBB?

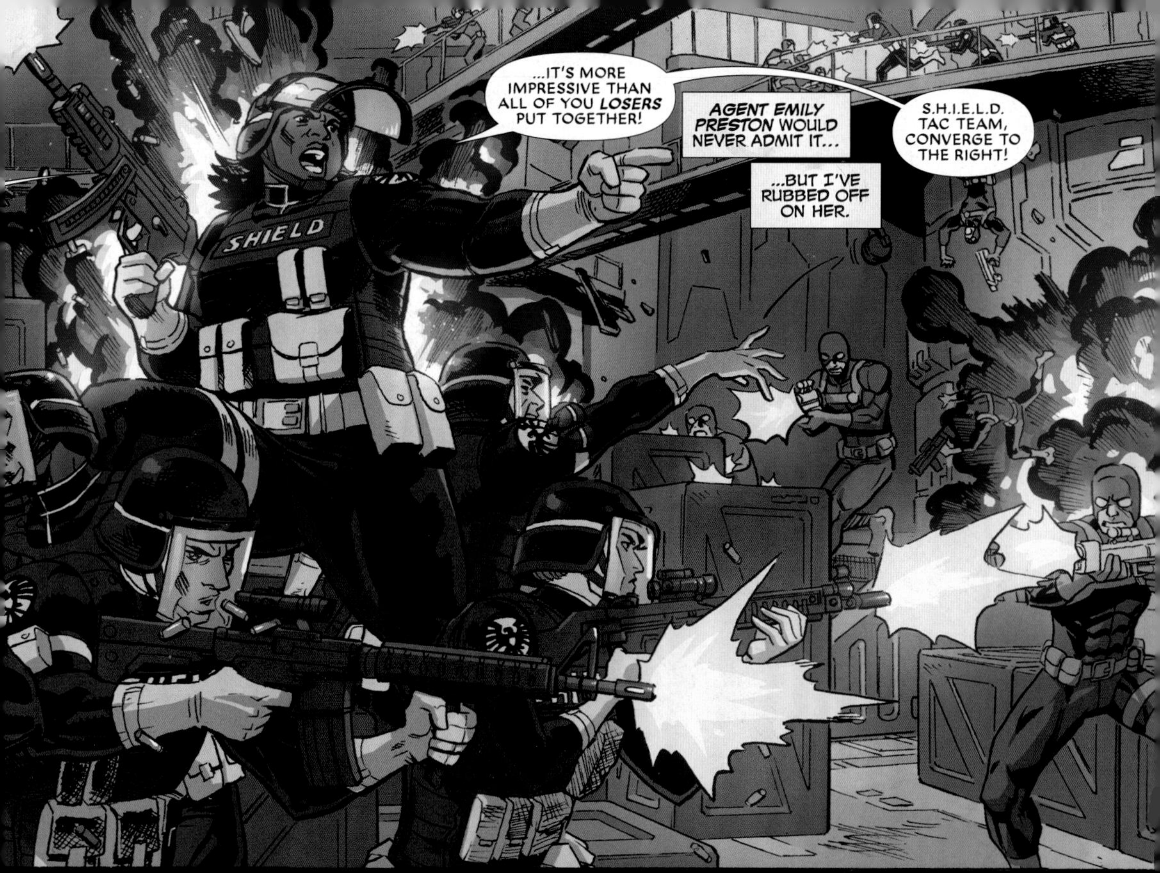
...IT'S MORE IMPRESSIVE THAN ALL OF YOU LOSERS PUT TOGETHER!
AGENT EMILY PRESTON WOULD NEVER ADMIT IT...
...BUT I'VE RUBBED OFF ON HER.
S.H.I.E.L.D. TAC TEAM, CONVERGE TO THE RIGHT!
SHIELD

SPLIT SECOND

CHAPTER ONE: NOT APOLLO CREED

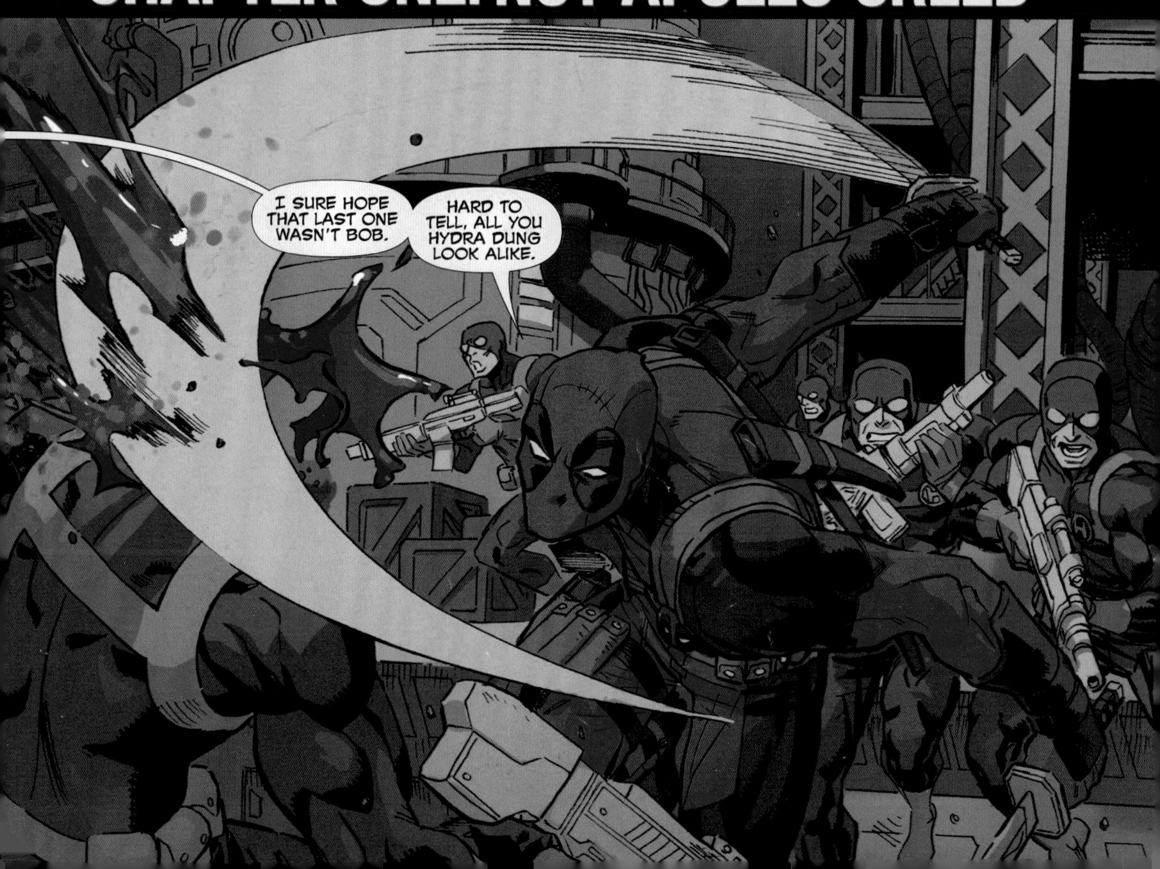
I SURE HOPE THAT LAST ONE WASN'T BOB.
HARD TO TELL, ALL YOU HYDRA DUNG LOOK ALIKE.

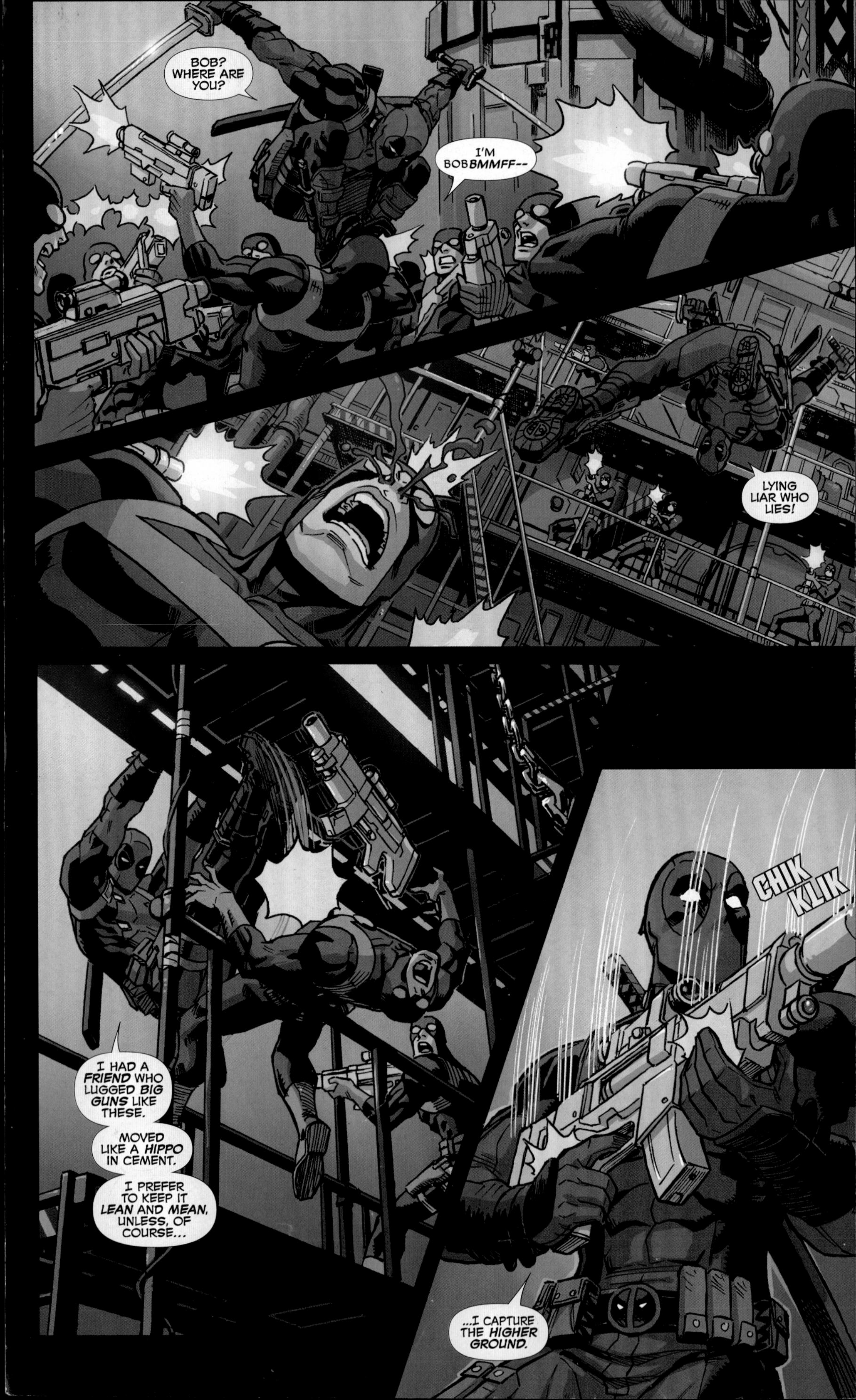
BOB? WHERE ARE YOU?
I'M BOBBMMFF--
LYING LIAR WHO LIES!
I HAD A FRIEND WHO LUGGED BIG GUNS LIKE THESE.
MOVED LIKE A HIPPO IN CEMENT.
I PREFER TO KEEP IT LEAN AND MEAN, UNLESS, OF COURSE...
CHIK KLIK
...I CAPTURE THE HIGHER GROUND.

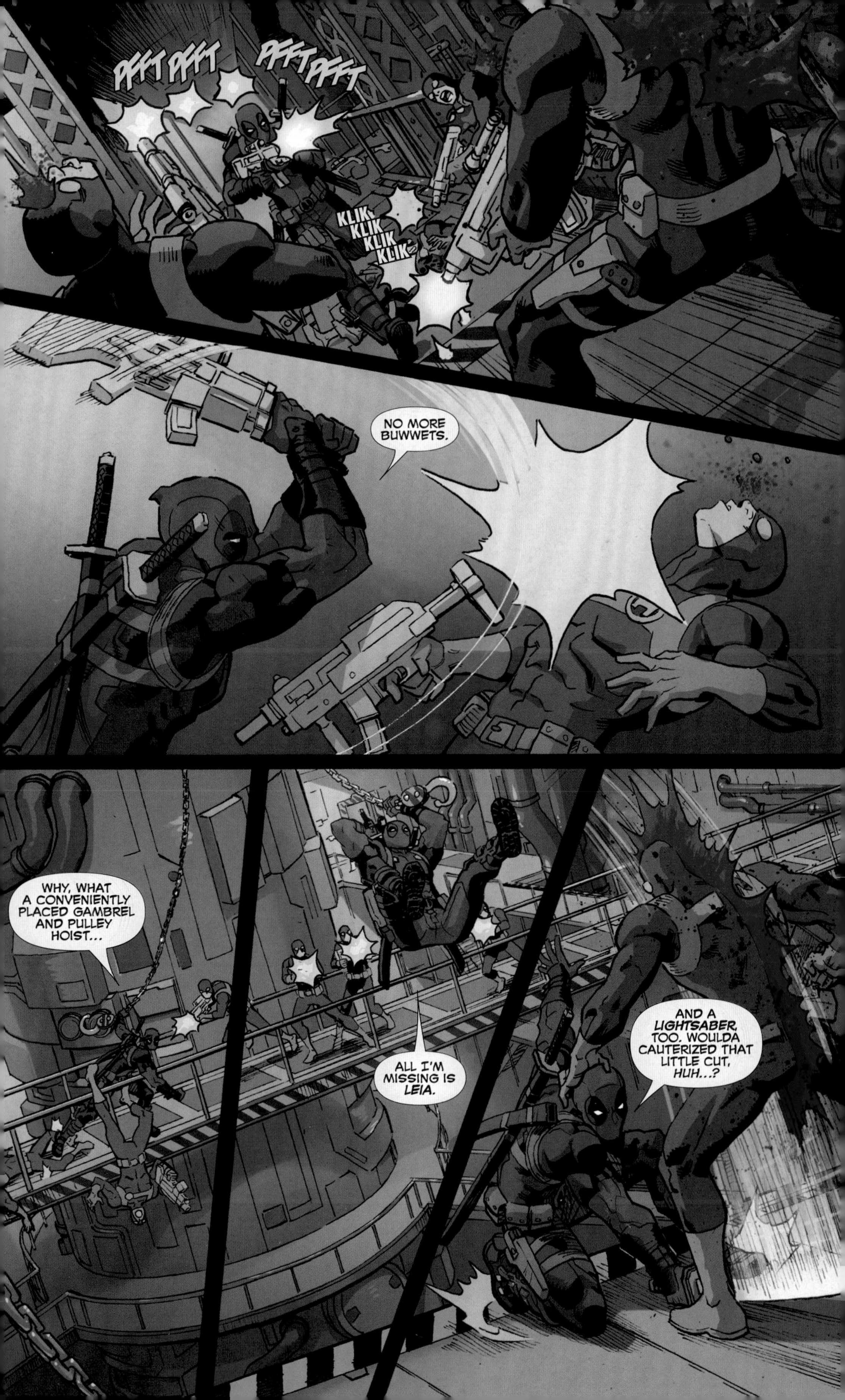
PFFT PFFT
PFFT PFFT
KLIK KLIK KLIK KLIK
NO MORE BUWWETS.
WHY, WHAT A CONVENIENTLY PLACED GAMBREL AND PULLEY HOIST...
ALL I'M MISSING IS *LEIA.*
AND A *LIGHTSABER,* TOO. WOULDA CAUTERIZED THAT LITTLE CUT, *HUH...?*

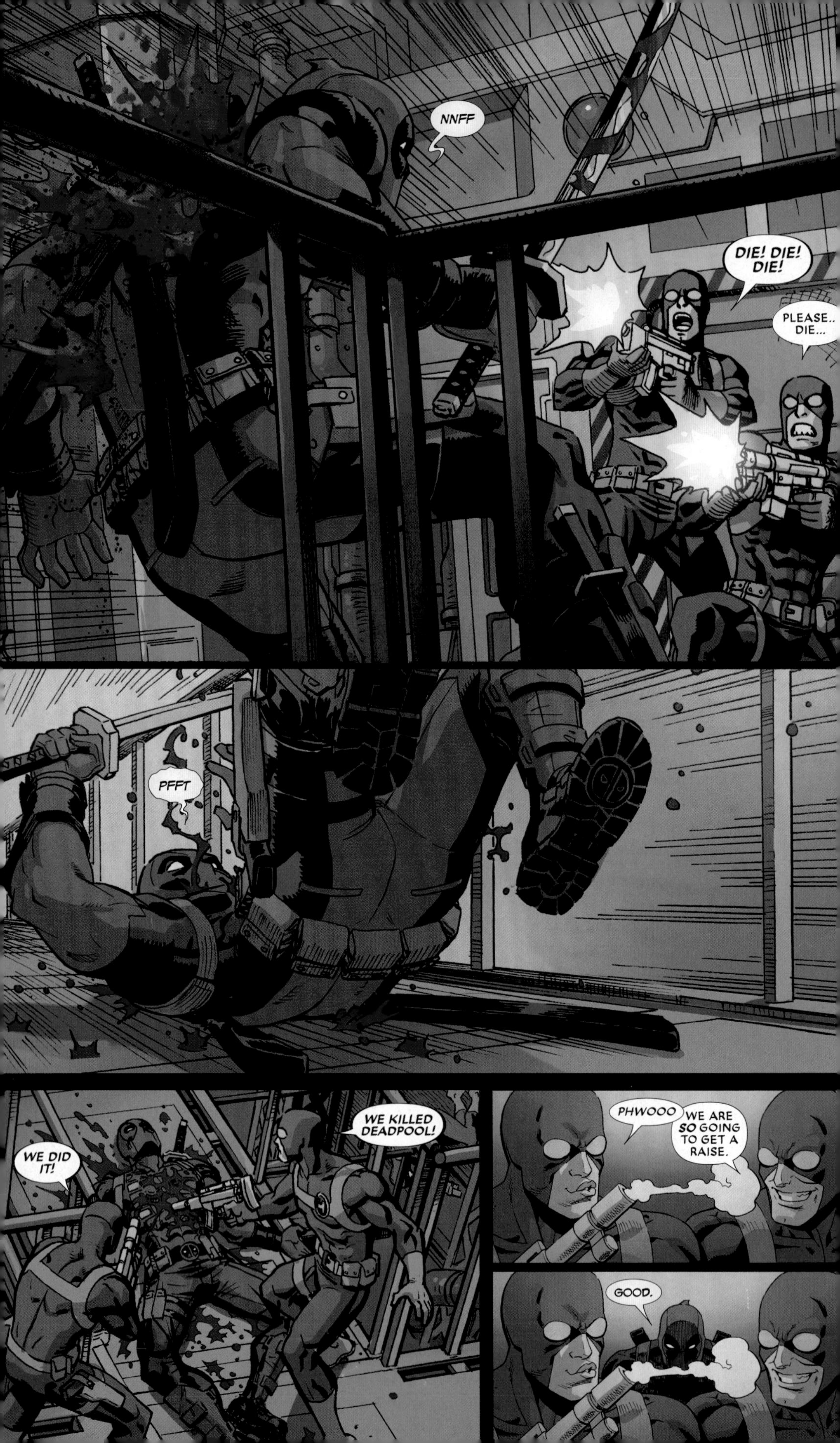
NNFF
DIE! DIE! DIE!
PLEASE.. DIE...
PFFT
WE DID IT!
WE KILLED DEADPOOL!
PHWOOO
WE ARE SO GOING TO GET A RAISE.
GOOD.

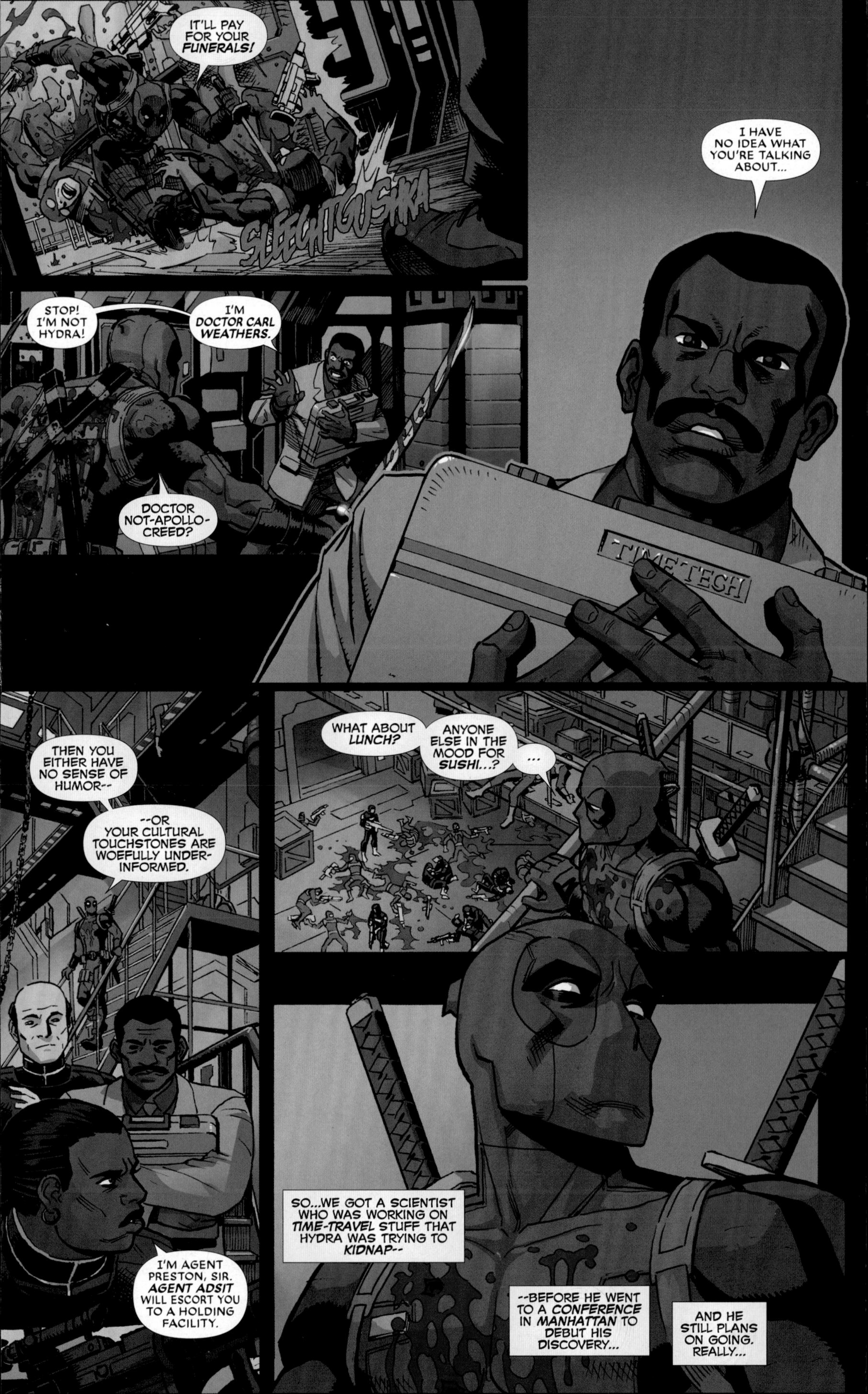
IT'LL PAY FOR YOUR FUNERALS!
SLEECHTGUSHKA
I HAVE NO IDEA WHAT YOU'RE TALKING ABOUT...
STOP! I'M NOT HYDRA!
I'M DOCTOR CARL WEATHERS.
DOCTOR NOT-APOLLO-CREED?
TIME TECH
THEN YOU EITHER HAVE NO SENSE OF HUMOR--
--OR YOUR CULTURAL TOUCHSTONES ARE WOEFULLY UNDER-INFORMED.
I'M AGENT PRESTON, SIR. AGENT ADSIT WILL ESCORT YOU TO A HOLDING FACILITY.
WHAT ABOUT LUNCH?
ANYONE ELSE IN THE MOOD FOR SUSHI...?
...
SO...WE GOT A SCIENTIST WHO WAS WORKING ON TIME-TRAVEL STUFF THAT HYDRA WAS TRYING TO KIDNAP--
--BEFORE HE WENT TO A CONFERENCE IN MANHATTAN TO DEBUT HIS DISCOVERY...
AND HE STILL PLANS ON GOING. REALLY...

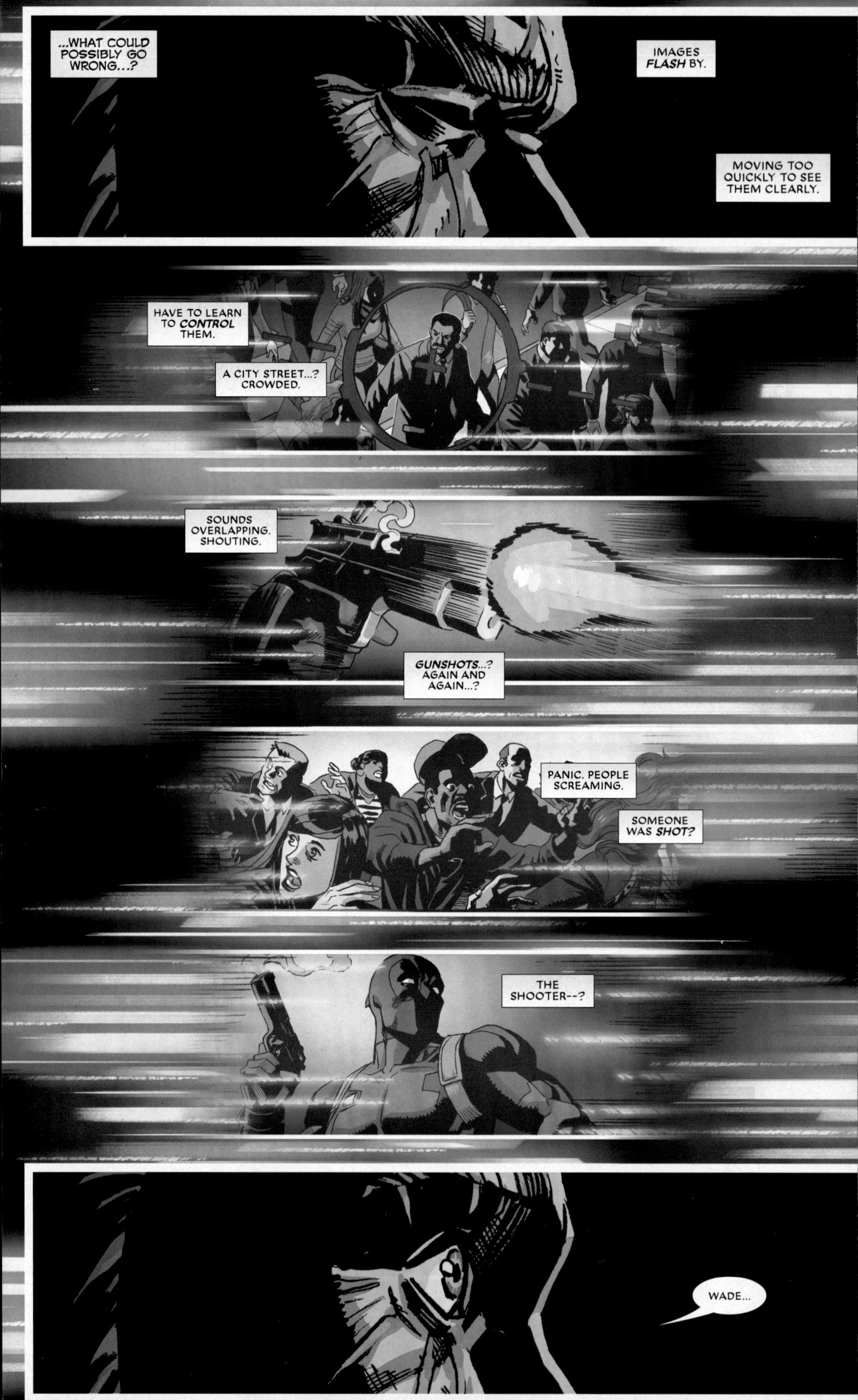

...WHAT COULD POSSIBLY GO WRONG...?
IMAGES FLASH BY.
MOVING TOO QUICKLY TO SEE THEM CLEARLY.
HAVE TO LEARN TO CONTROL THEM.
A CITY STREET...? CROWDED.
SOUNDS OVERLAPPING. SHOUTING.
GUNSHOTS...? AGAIN AND AGAIN...?
PANIC. PEOPLE SCREAMING.
SOMEONE WAS SHOT?
THE SHOOTER--?
WADE...

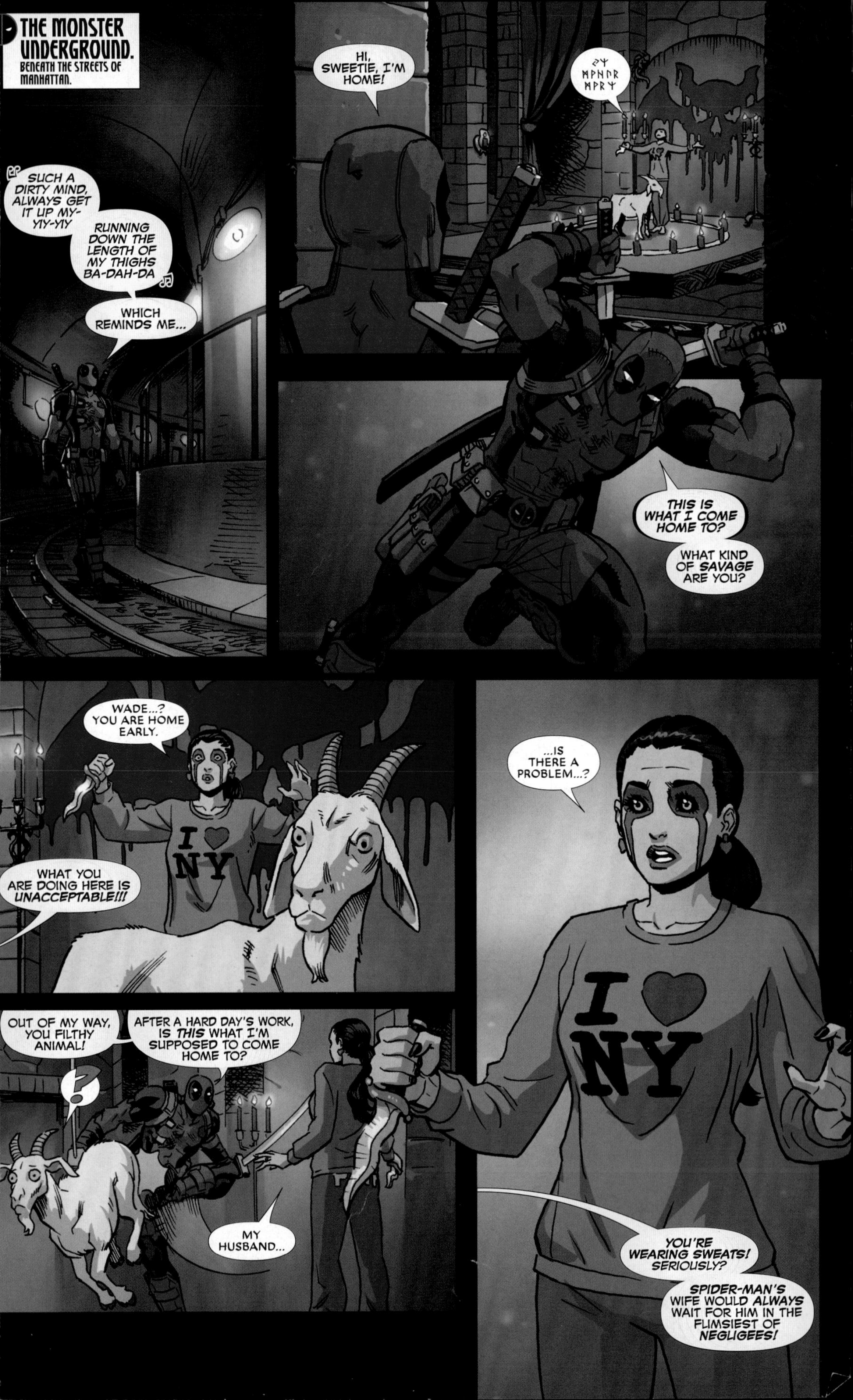
THE MONSTER UNDERGROUND.
BENEATH THE STREETS OF MANHATTAN.
SUCH A DIRTY MIND, ALWAYS GET IT UP MY-YIY-YIY
RUNNING DOWN THE LENGTH OF MY THIGHS BA-DAH-DA
WHICH REMINDS ME...
HI, SWEETIE, I'M HOME!
THIS IS WHAT I COME HOME TO?
WHAT KIND OF SAVAGE ARE YOU?
WADE...? YOU ARE HOME EARLY.
WHAT YOU ARE DOING HERE IS UNACCEPTABLE!!!
...IS THERE A PROBLEM...?
OUT OF MY WAY, YOU FILTHY ANIMAL!
AFTER A HARD DAY'S WORK, IS THIS WHAT I'M SUPPOSED TO COME HOME TO?
MY HUSBAND...
YOU'RE WEARING SWEATS! SERIOUSLY?
SPIDER-MAN'S WIFE WOULD ALWAYS WAIT FOR HIM IN THE FLIMSIEST OF NEGLIGEES!

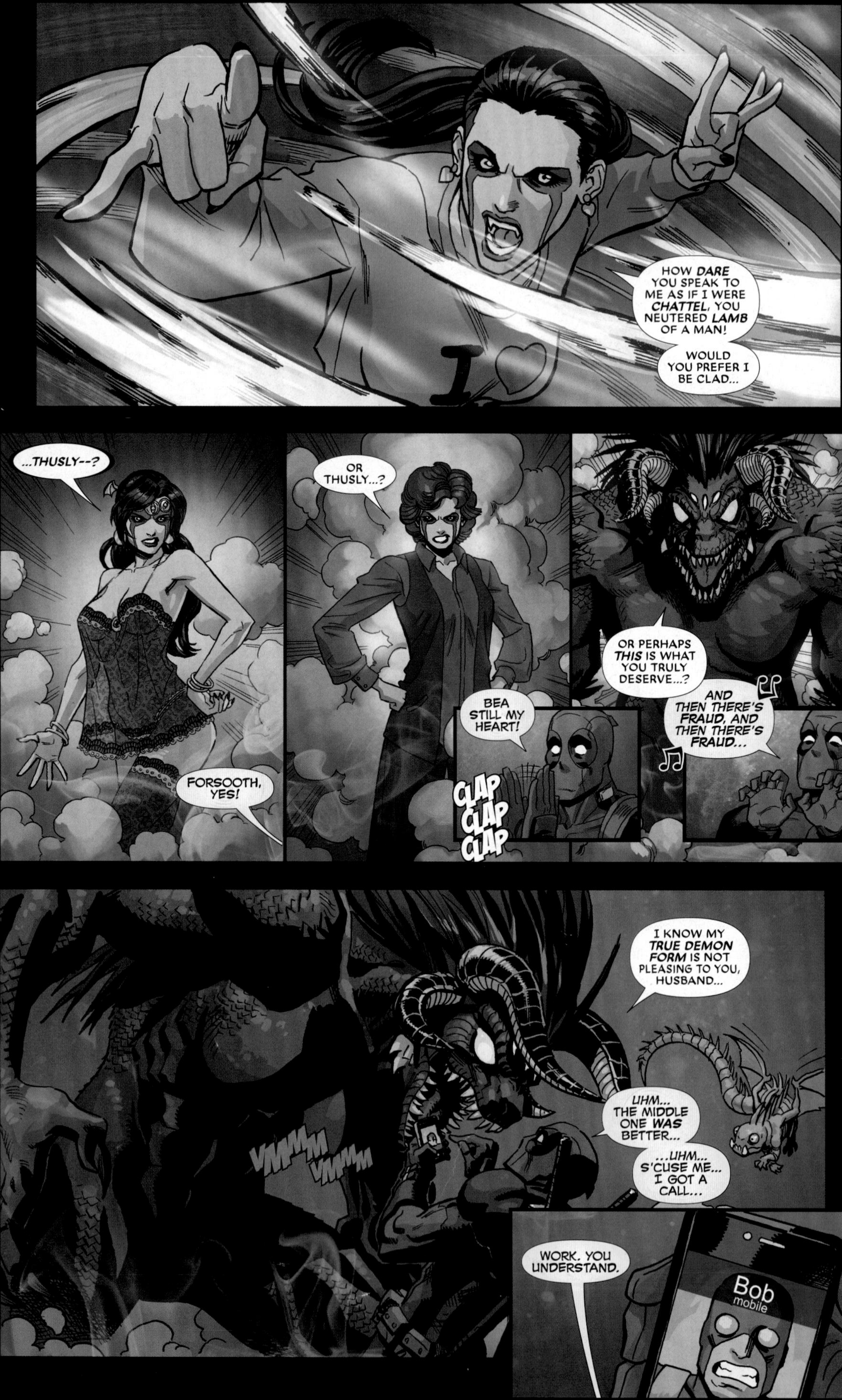
HOW DARE YOU SPEAK TO ME AS IF I WERE CHATTEL, YOU NEUTERED LAMB OF A MAN!
WOULD YOU PREFER I BE CLAD...
...THUSLY--?
FORSOOTH, YES!
OR THUSLY...?
BEA STILL MY HEART!
CLAP CLAP CLAP
OR PERHAPS THIS IS WHAT YOU TRULY DESERVE...?
AND THEN THERE'S FRAUD, AND THEN THERE'S FRAUD...
I KNOW MY TRUE DEMON FORM IS NOT PLEASING TO YOU, HUSBAND...
UHM... THE MIDDLE ONE WAS BETTER...
...UHM... S'CUSE ME... I GOT A CALL...
VMMMM VMMMM
WORK. YOU UNDERSTAND.
Bob
mobile

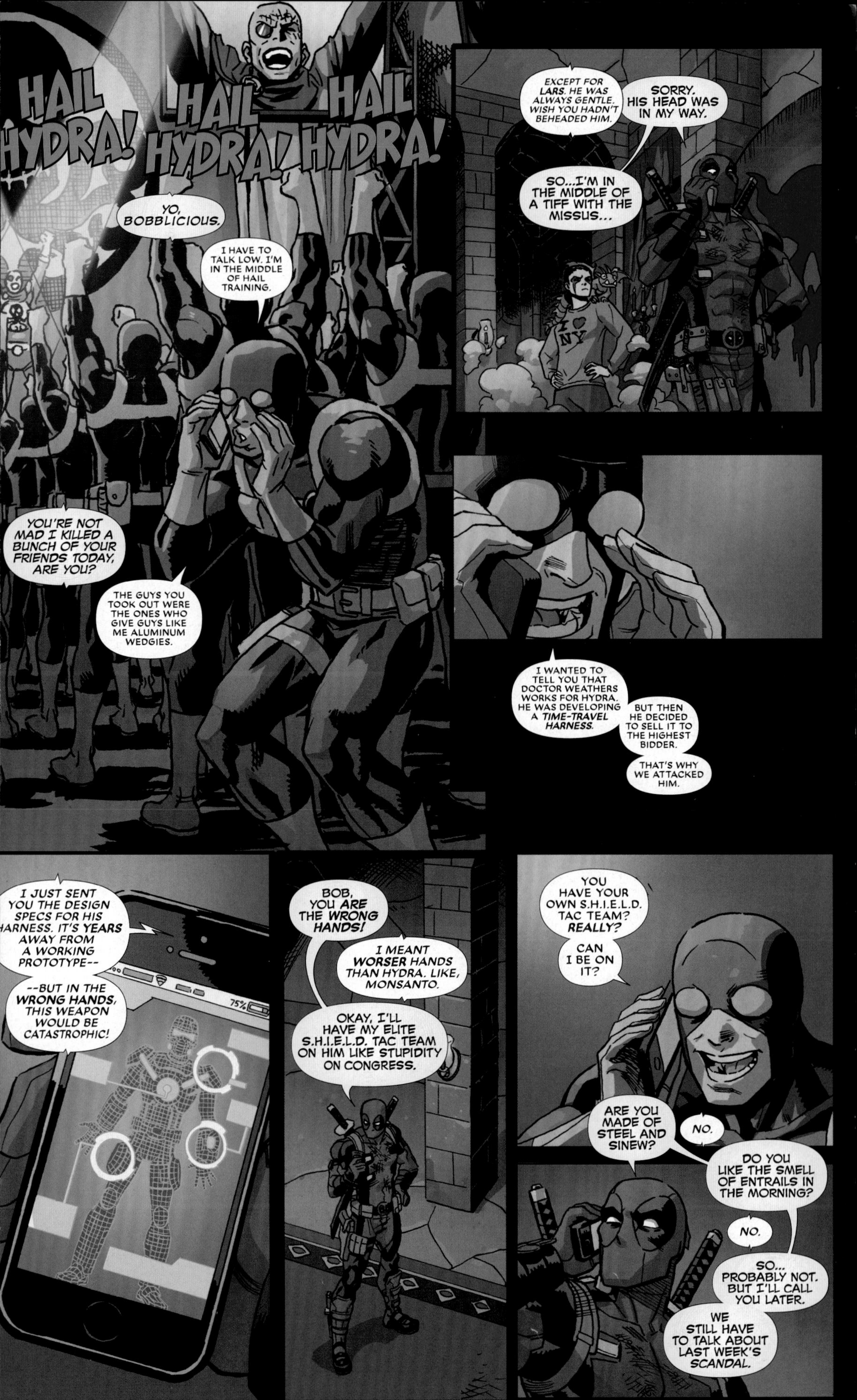
HAIL HYDRA! HAIL HYDRA! HAIL HYDRA!
YO, BOBBLICIOUS.
I HAVE TO TALK LOW. I'M IN THE MIDDLE OF HAIL TRAINING.
EXCEPT FOR LARS. HE WAS ALWAYS GENTLE. WISH YOU HADN'T BEHEADED HIM.
SORRY. HIS HEAD WAS IN MY WAY.
SO...I'M IN THE MIDDLE OF A TIFF WITH THE MISSUS...
YOU'RE NOT MAD I KILLED A BUNCH OF YOUR FRIENDS TODAY, ARE YOU?
THE GUYS YOU TOOK OUT WERE THE ONES WHO GIVE GUYS LIKE ME ALUMINUM WEDGIES.
I WANTED TO TELL YOU THAT DOCTOR WEATHERS WORKS FOR HYDRA. HE WAS DEVELOPING A TIME-TRAVEL HARNESS.
BUT THEN HE DECIDED TO SELL IT TO THE HIGHEST BIDDER.
THAT'S WHY WE ATTACKED HIM.
I JUST SENT YOU THE DESIGN SPECS FOR HIS HARNESS. IT'S YEARS AWAY FROM A WORKING PROTOTYPE--
--BUT IN THE WRONG HANDS, THIS WEAPON WOULD BE CATASTROPHIC!
75%
BOB, YOU ARE THE WRONG HANDS!
I MEANT WORSER HANDS THAN HYDRA. LIKE, MONSANTO.
OKAY, I'LL HAVE MY ELITE S.H.I.E.L.D. TAC TEAM ON HIM LIKE STUPIDITY ON CONGRESS.
YOU HAVE YOUR OWN S.H.I.E.L.D. TAC TEAM? REALLY?
CAN I BE ON IT?
ARE YOU MADE OF STEEL AND SINEW?
NO.
DO YOU LIKE THE SMELL OF ENTRAILS IN THE MORNING?
NO.
SO... PROBABLY NOT. BUT I'LL CALL YOU LATER.
WE STILL HAVE TO TALK ABOUT LAST WEEK'S SCANDAL.

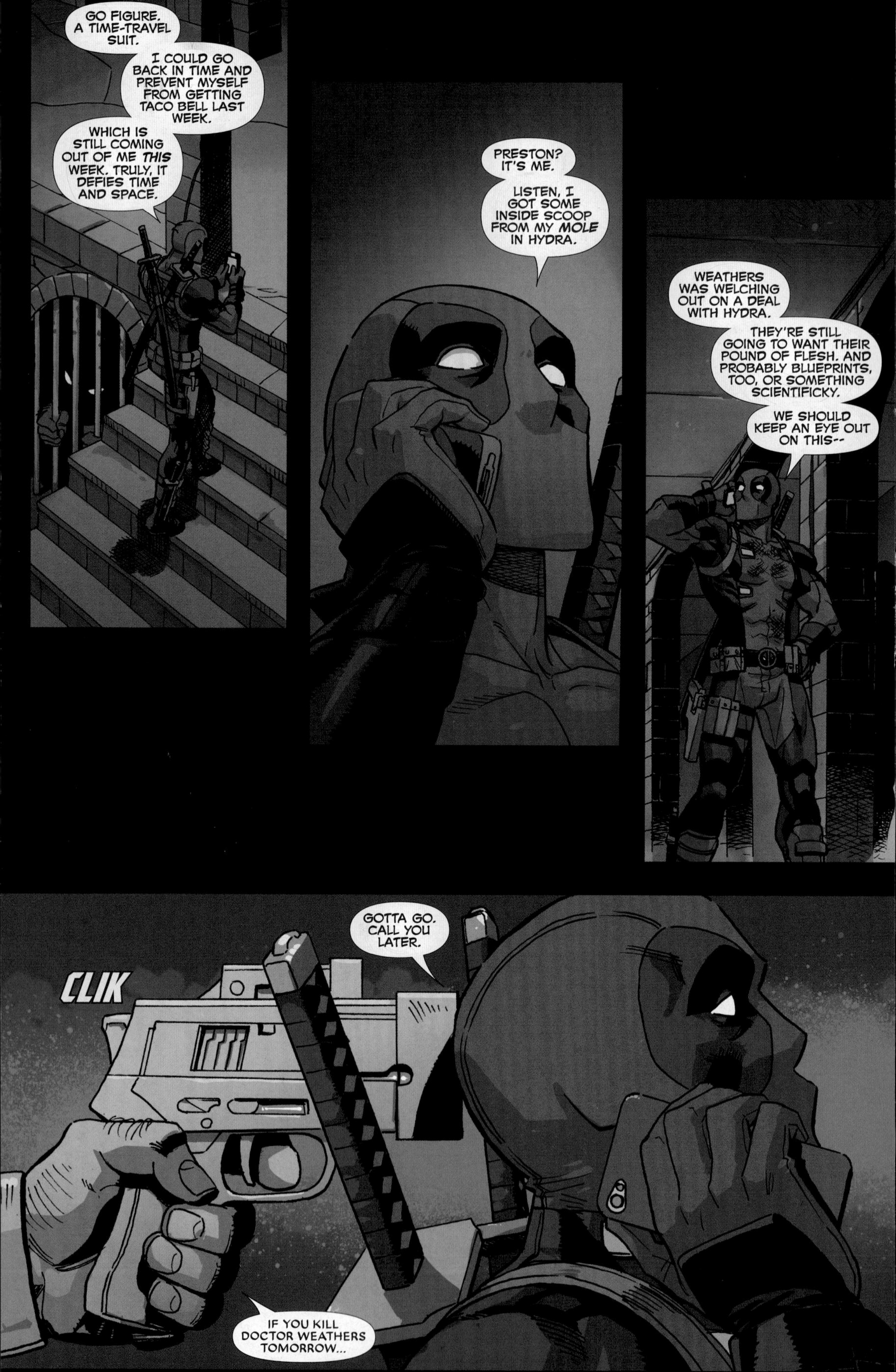
GO FIGURE. A TIME-TRAVEL SUIT.
I COULD GO BACK IN TIME AND PREVENT MYSELF FROM GETTING TACO BELL LAST WEEK.
WHICH IS STILL COMING OUT OF ME THIS WEEK. TRULY, IT DEFIES TIME AND SPACE.
PRESTON? IT'S ME.
LISTEN, I GOT SOME INSIDE SCOOP FROM MY MOLE IN HYDRA.
WEATHERS WAS WELCHING OUT ON A DEAL WITH HYDRA.
THEY'RE STILL GOING TO WANT THEIR POUND OF FLESH. AND PROBABLY BLUEPRINTS, TOO, OR SOMETHING SCIENTIFICKY.
WE SHOULD KEEP AN EYE OUT ON THIS--
GOTTA GO. CALL YOU LATER.
CLIK
IF YOU KILL DOCTOR WEATHERS TOMORROW...

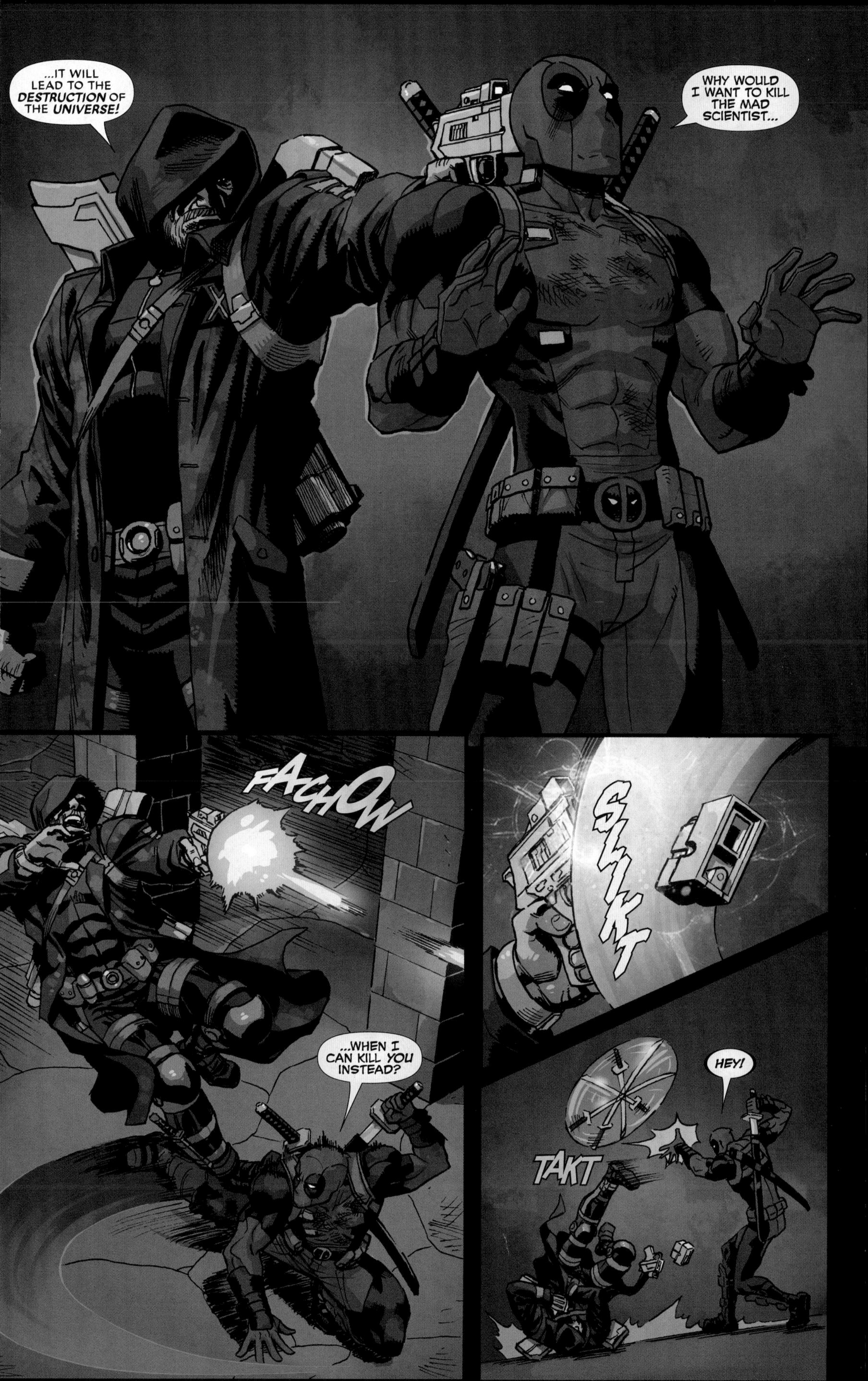
...IT WILL LEAD TO THE DESTRUCTION OF THE UNIVERSE!
WHY WOULD I WANT TO KILL THE MAD SCIENTIST...
FACHOW
...WHEN I CAN KILL YOU INSTEAD?
SLIKT
HEY!
TAKT

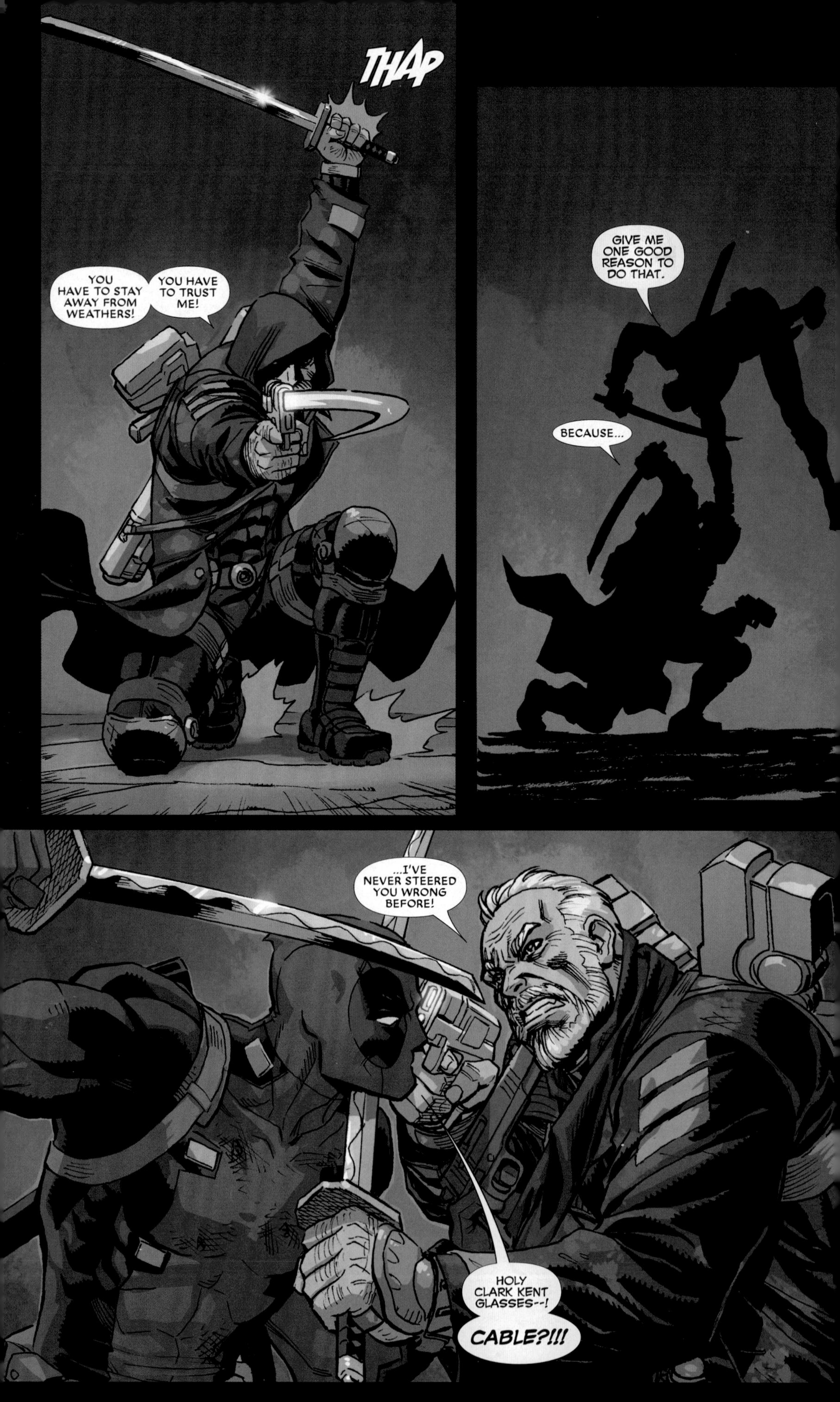
THAP
YOU HAVE TO STAY AWAY FROM WEATHERS!
YOU HAVE TO TRUST ME!
GIVE ME ONE GOOD REASON TO DO THAT.
BECAUSE...
...I'VE NEVER STEERED YOU WRONG BEFORE!
HOLY CLARK KENT GLASSES--!
CABLE?!!!

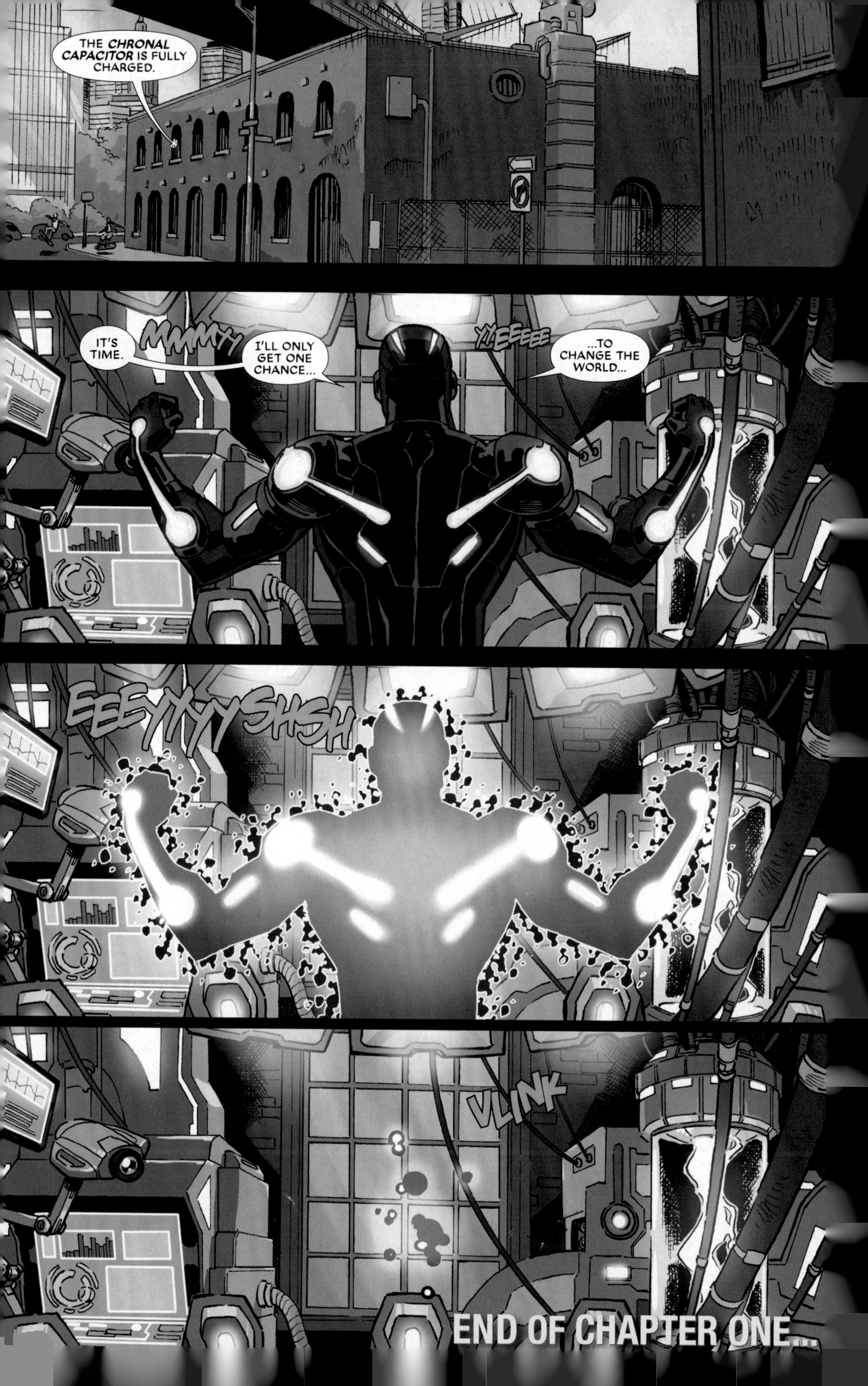
THE CHRONAL CAPACITOR IS FULLY CHARGED.
MMMHH
IT'S TIME.
I'LL ONLY GET ONE CHANCE...
YYEEEEE
...TO CHANGE THE WORLD...
EEEYYYYSHSH
VLINK
END OF CHAPTER ONE...

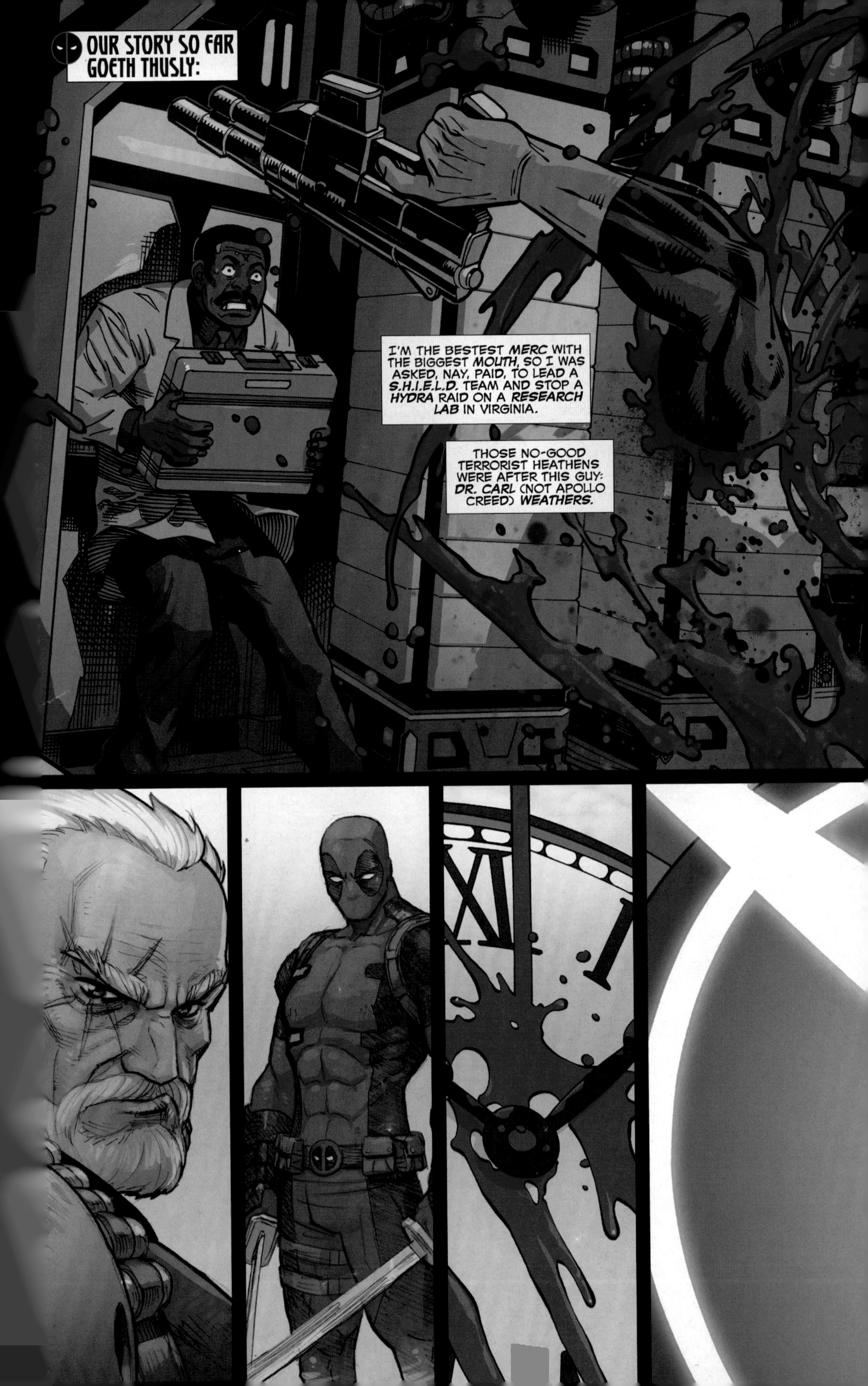
OUR STORY SO FAR GOETH THUSLY:
I'M THE BESTEST MERC WITH THE BIGGEST MOUTH, SO I WAS ASKED, NAY, PAID, TO LEAD A S.H.I.E.L.D. TEAM AND STOP A HYDRA RAID ON A RESEARCH LAB IN VIRGINIA.
THOSE NO-GOOD TERRORIST HEATHENS WERE AFTER THIS GUY: DR. CARL (NOT APOLLO CREED) WEATHERS.

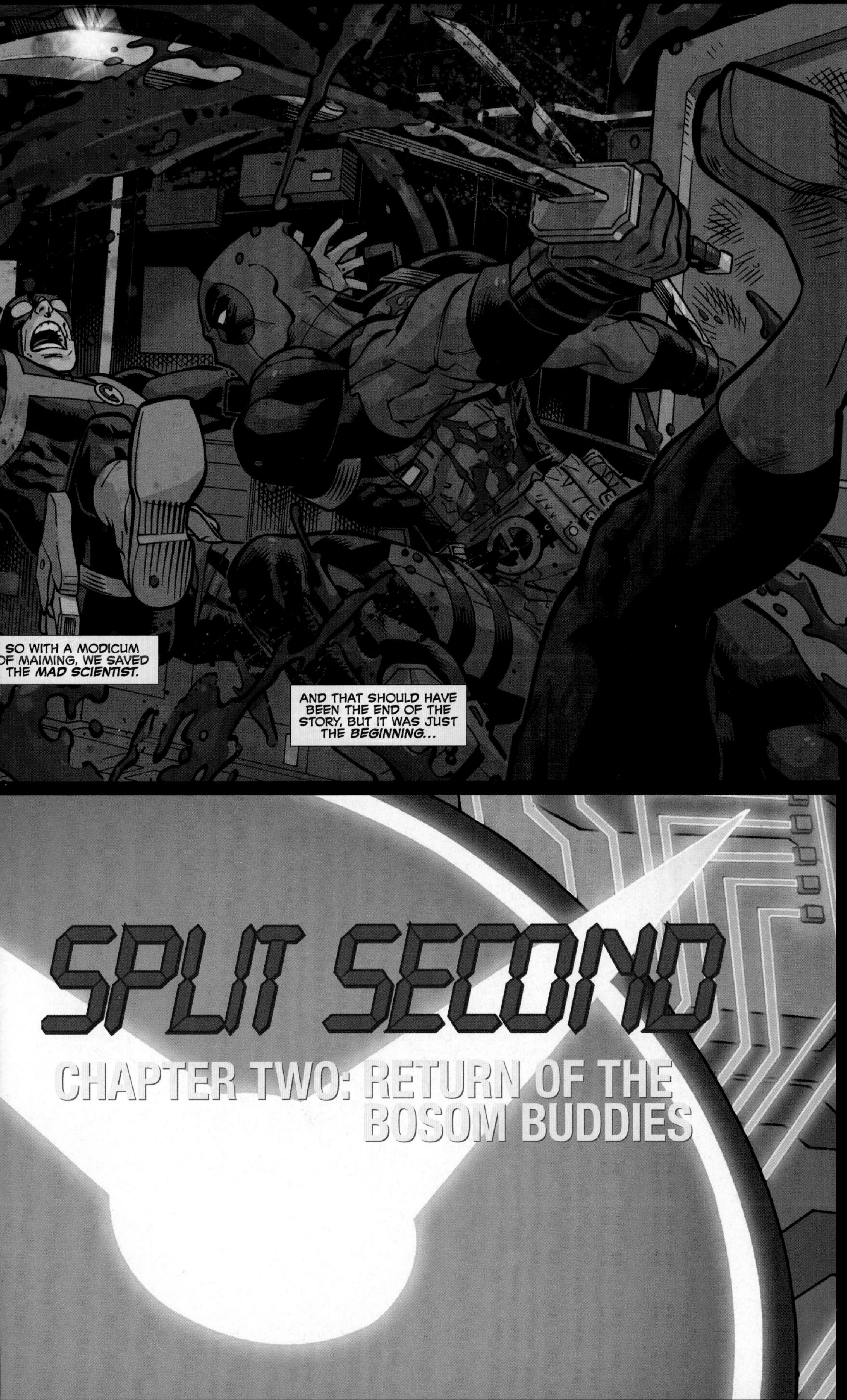
SO WITH A MODICUM OF MAIMING, WE SAVED THE MAD SCIENTIST.
AND THAT SHOULD HAVE BEEN THE END OF THE STORY, BUT IT WAS JUST THE BEGINNING...
SPLIT SECOND
CHAPTER TWO: RETURN OF THE BOSOM BUDDIES

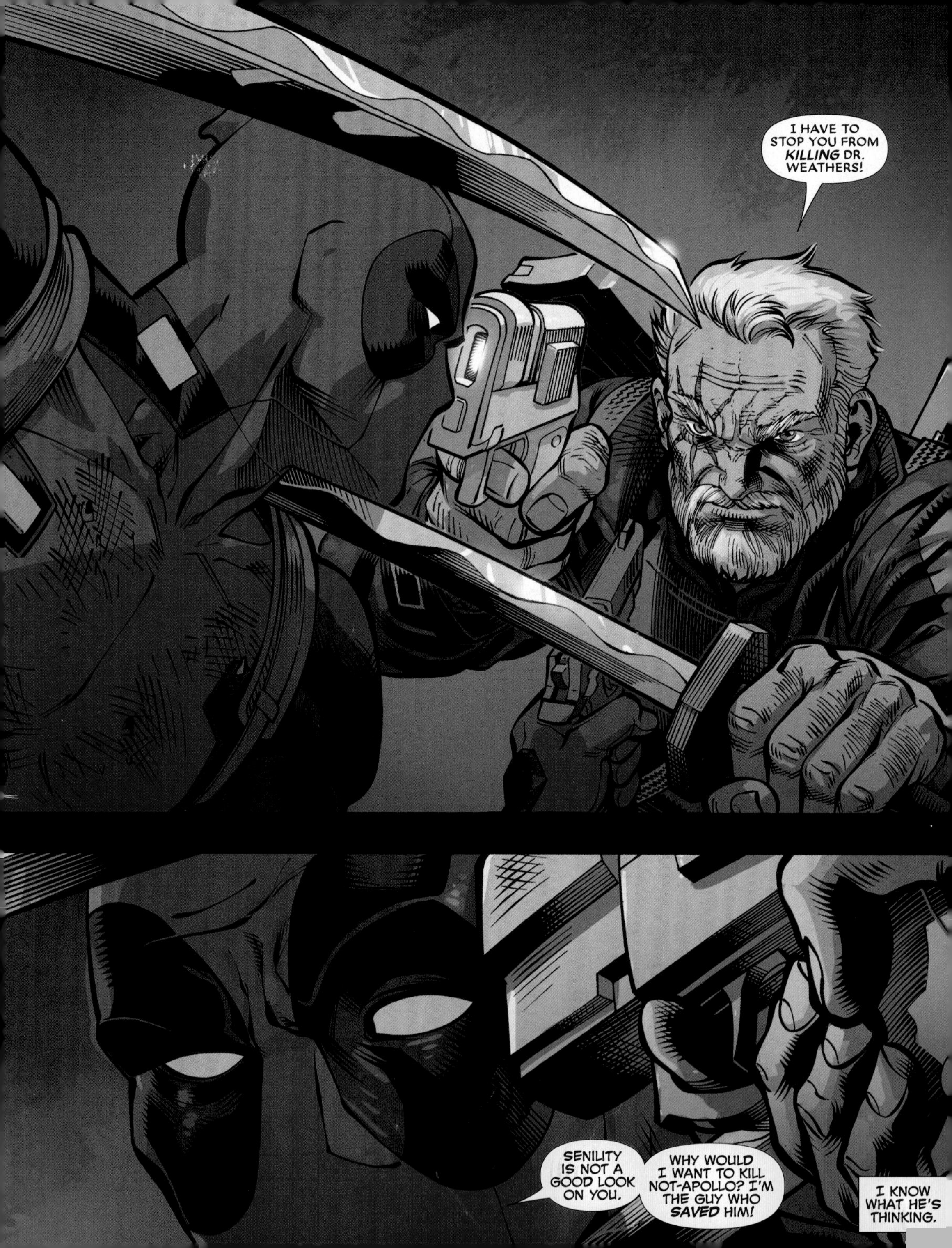
I HAVE TO STOP YOU FROM *KILLING* DR. WEATHERS!
SENILITY IS NOT A GOOD LOOK ON YOU.
WHY WOULD I WANT TO KILL NOT-APOLLO? I'M THE GUY WHO *SAVED* HIM!
I KNOW WHAT HE'S THINKING.

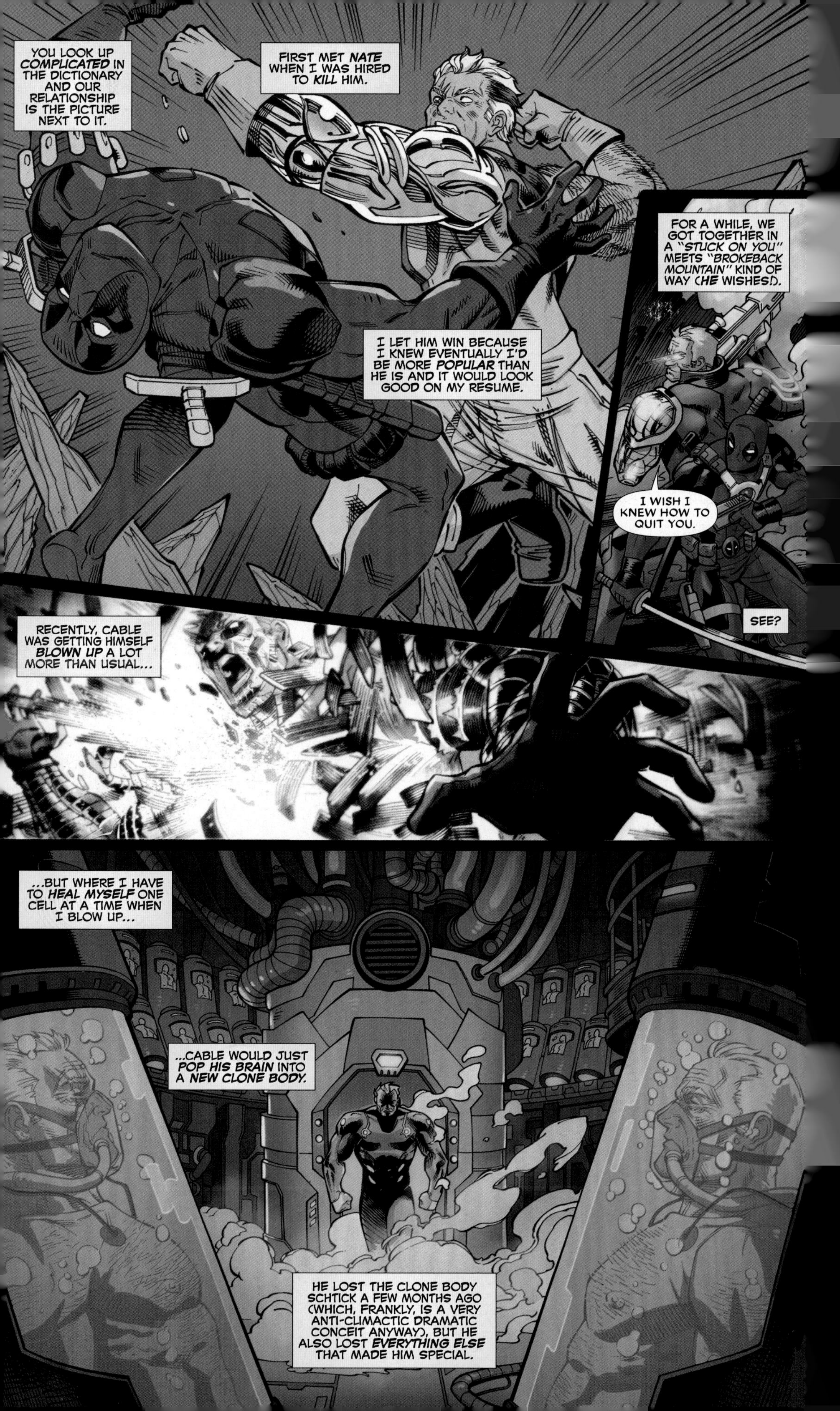

YOU LOOK UP COMPLICATED IN THE DICTIONARY AND OUR RELATIONSHIP IS THE PICTURE NEXT TO IT.
FIRST MET NATE WHEN I WAS HIRED TO KILL HIM.
I LET HIM WIN BECAUSE I KNEW EVENTUALLY I'D BE MORE POPULAR THAN HE IS AND IT WOULD LOOK GOOD ON MY RESUME.
FOR A WHILE, WE GOT TOGETHER IN A "STUCK ON YOU" MEETS "BROKEBACK MOUNTAIN" KIND OF WAY (HE WISHES!).
I WISH I KNEW HOW TO QUIT YOU.
SEE?
RECENTLY, CABLE WAS GETTING HIMSELF BLOWN UP A LOT MORE THAN USUAL...
...BUT WHERE I HAVE TO HEAL MYSELF ONE CELL AT A TIME WHEN I BLOW UP...
...CABLE WOULD JUST POP HIS BRAIN INTO A NEW CLONE BODY.
HE LOST THE CLONE BODY SCHTICK A FEW MONTHS AGO (WHICH, FRANKLY, IS A VERY ANTI-CLIMACTIC DRAMATIC CONCEIT ANYWAY), BUT HE ALSO LOST EVERYTHING ELSE THAT MADE HIM SPECIAL.

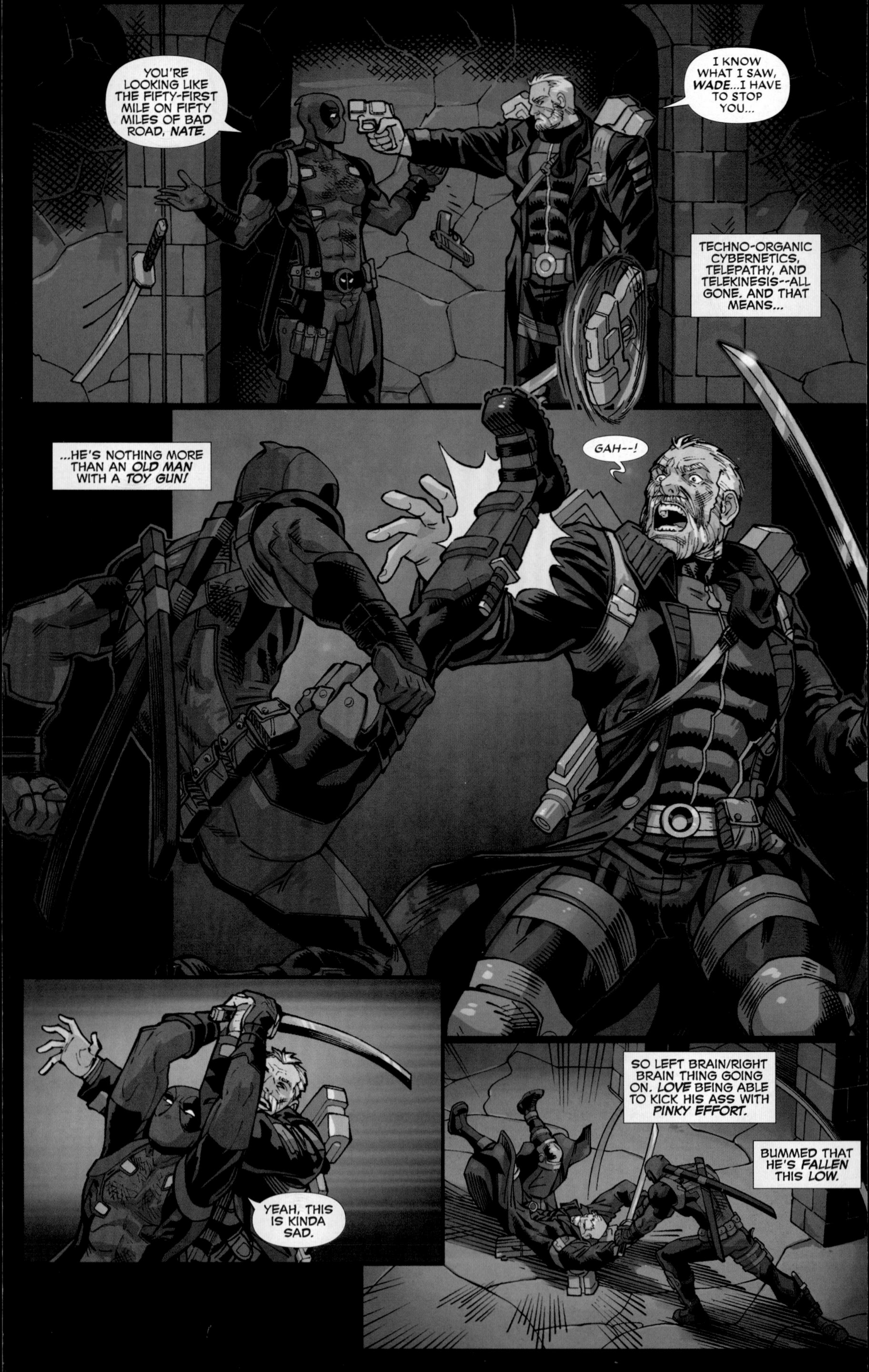
YOU'RE LOOKING LIKE THE FIFTY-FIRST MILE ON FIFTY MILES OF BAD ROAD, NATE.
I KNOW WHAT I SAW, WADE...I HAVE TO STOP YOU...
TECHNO-ORGANIC CYBERNETICS, TELEPATHY, AND TELEKINESIS--ALL GONE. AND THAT MEANS...
...HE'S NOTHING MORE THAN AN OLD MAN WITH A TOY GUN!
GAH--!
YEAH, THIS IS KINDA SAD.
SO LEFT BRAIN/RIGHT BRAIN THING GOING ON. LOVE BEING ABLE TO KICK HIS ASS WITH PINKY EFFORT.
BUMMED THAT HE'S FALLEN THIS LOW.

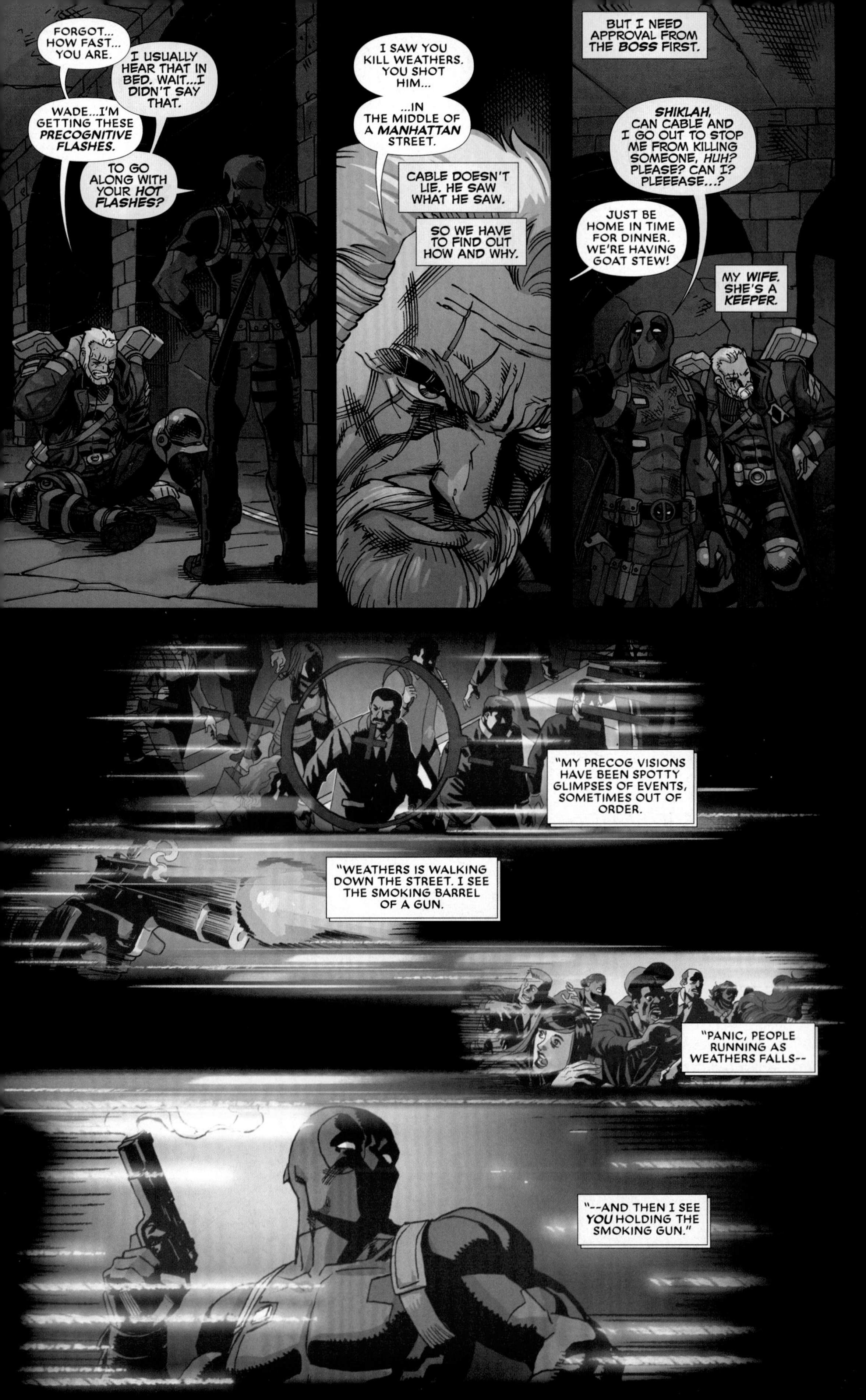
FORGOT... HOW FAST... YOU ARE.
I USUALLY HEAR THAT IN BED. WAIT...I DIDN'T SAY THAT.
WADE...I'M GETTING THESE PRECOGNITIVE FLASHES.
TO GO ALONG WITH YOUR HOT FLASHES?
I SAW YOU KILL WEATHERS. YOU SHOT HIM...
...IN THE MIDDLE OF A MANHATTAN STREET.
CABLE DOESN'T LIE. HE SAW WHAT HE SAW.
SO WE HAVE TO FIND OUT HOW AND WHY.
BUT I NEED APPROVAL FROM THE BOSS FIRST.
SHIKLAH, CAN CABLE AND I GO OUT TO STOP ME FROM KILLING SOMEONE, HUH? PLEASE? CAN I? PLEEEASE...?
JUST BE HOME IN TIME FOR DINNER. WE'RE HAVING GOAT STEW!
MY WIFE. SHE'S A KEEPER.
"MY PRECOG VISIONS HAVE BEEN SPOTTY GLIMPSES OF EVENTS, SOMETIMES OUT OF ORDER.
"WEATHERS IS WALKING DOWN THE STREET. I SEE THE SMOKING BARREL OF A GUN.
"PANIC, PEOPLE RUNNING AS WEATHERS FALLS--
"--AND THEN I SEE YOU HOLDING THE SMOKING GUN."

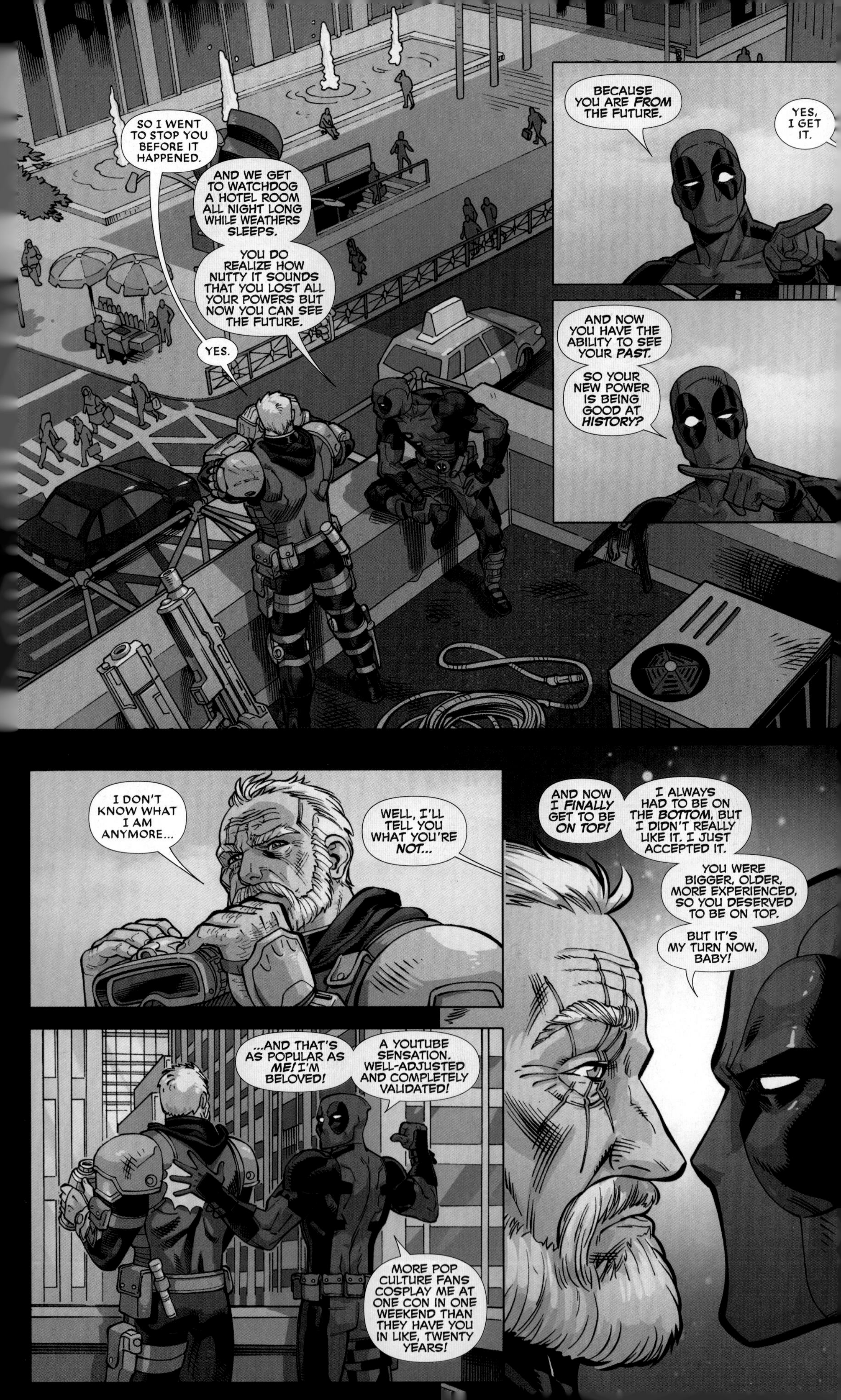
SO I WENT TO STOP YOU BEFORE IT HAPPENED.
AND WE GET TO WATCHDOG A HOTEL ROOM ALL NIGHT LONG WHILE WEATHERS SLEEPS.
YOU DO REALIZE HOW NUTTY IT SOUNDS THAT YOU LOST ALL YOUR POWERS BUT NOW YOU CAN SEE THE FUTURE.
YES.
BECAUSE YOU ARE FROM THE FUTURE.
YES, I GET IT.
AND NOW YOU HAVE THE ABILITY TO SEE YOUR PAST.
SO YOUR NEW POWER IS BEING GOOD AT HISTORY?
I DON'T KNOW WHAT I AM ANYMORE...
WELL, I'LL TELL YOU WHAT YOU'RE NOT...
...AND THAT'S AS POPULAR AS ME! I'M BELOVED!
A YOUTUBE SENSATION. WELL-ADJUSTED AND COMPLETELY VALIDATED!
MORE POP CULTURE FANS COSPLAY ME AT ONE CON IN ONE WEEKEND THAN THEY HAVE YOU IN LIKE, TWENTY YEARS!
AND NOW I FINALLY GET TO BE ON TOP!
I ALWAYS HAD TO BE ON THE BOTTOM, BUT I DIDN'T REALLY LIKE IT. I JUST ACCEPTED IT.
YOU WERE BIGGER, OLDER, MORE EXPERIENCED, SO YOU DESERVED TO BE ON TOP.
BUT IT'S MY TURN NOW, BABY!

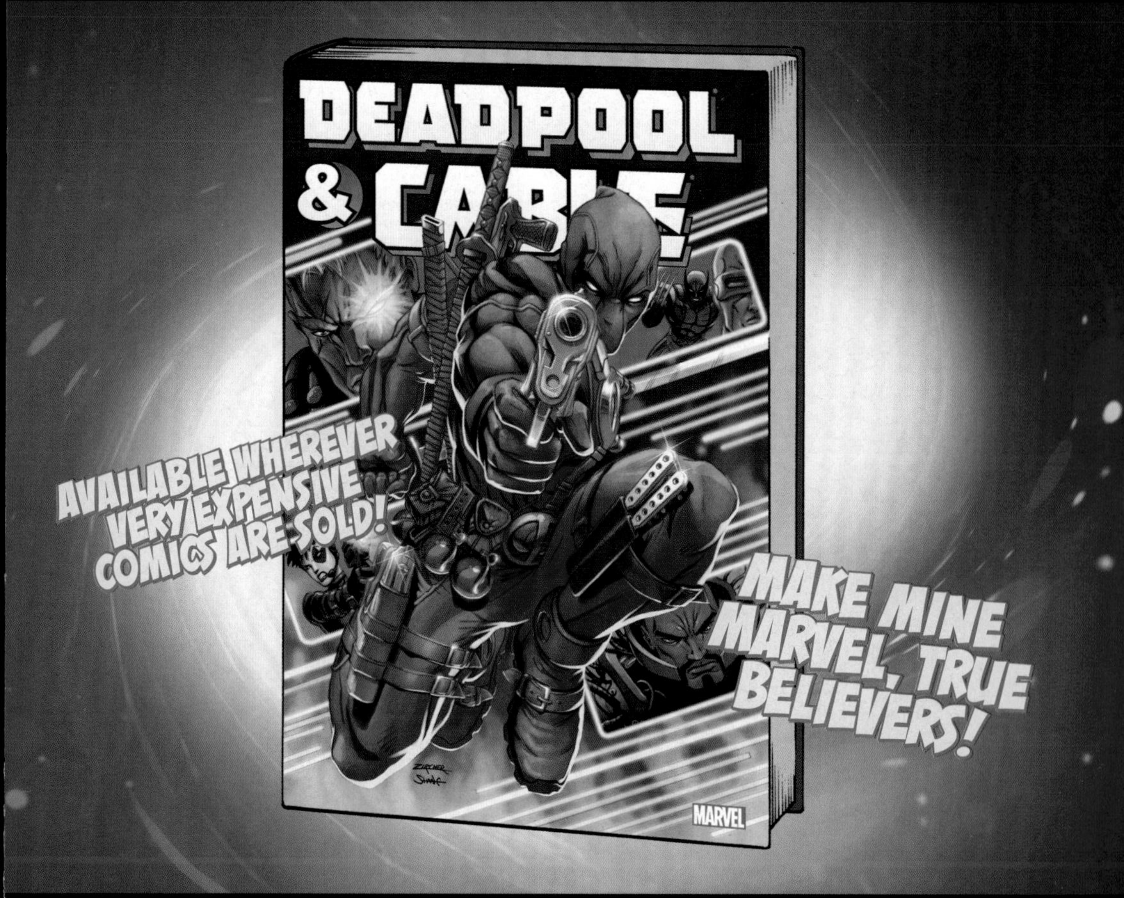
DEADPOOL & CABLE
AVAILABLE WHEREVER VERY EXPENSIVE COMICS ARE SOLD!
MAKE MINE MARVEL, TRUE BELIEVERS!
MARVEL

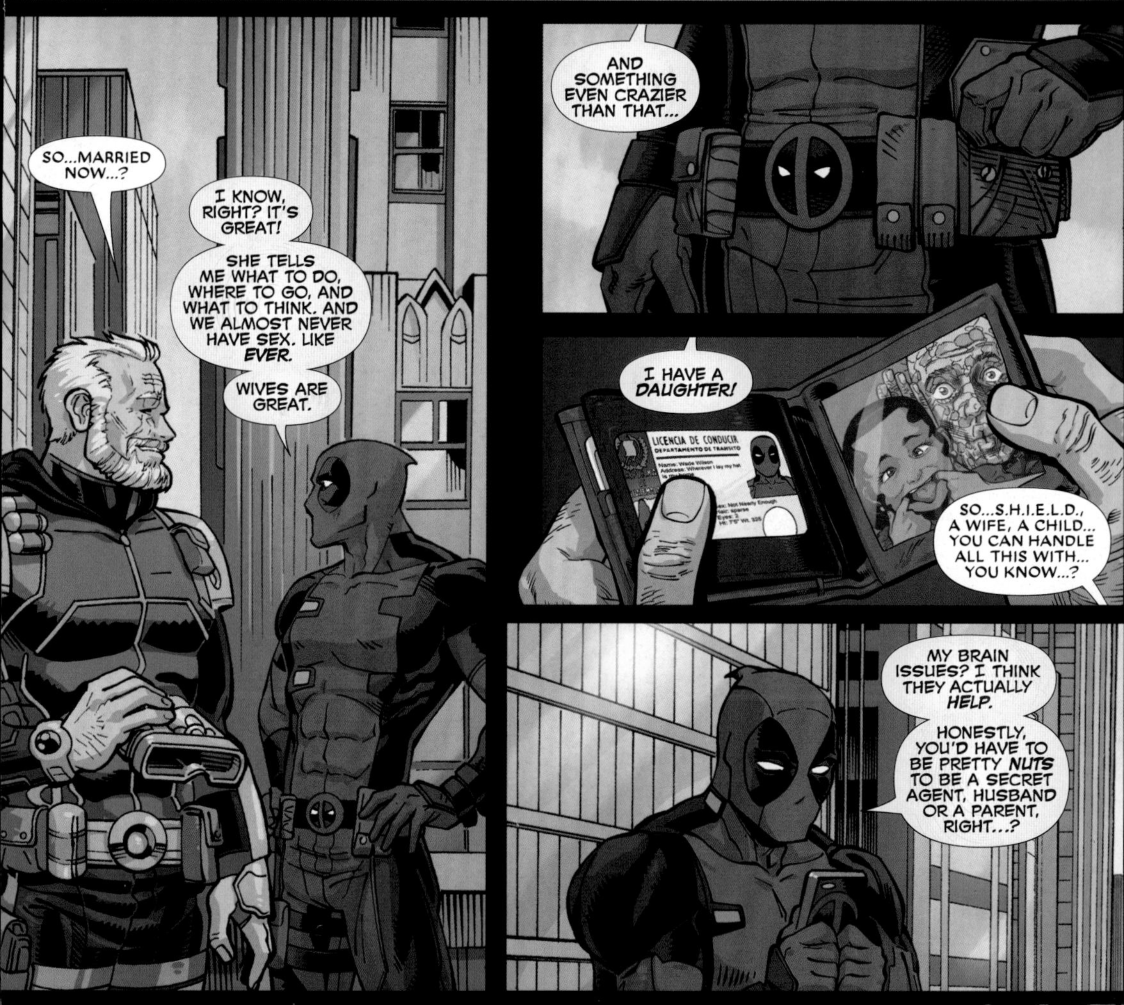
SO...MARRIED NOW...?
I KNOW, RIGHT? IT'S GREAT!
SHE TELLS ME WHAT TO DO, WHERE TO GO, AND WHAT TO THINK. AND WE ALMOST NEVER HAVE SEX. LIKE *EVER.*
WIVES ARE GREAT.
AND SOMETHING EVEN CRAZIER THAN THAT...
I HAVE A *DAUGHTER!*
LICENCIA DE CONDUCIR
DEPARTAMENTO DE TRANSITO
SO...S.H.I.E.L.D., A WIFE, A CHILD... YOU CAN HANDLE ALL THIS WITH... YOU KNOW...?
MY BRAIN ISSUES? I THINK THEY ACTUALLY *HELP.*
HONESTLY, YOU'D HAVE TO BE PRETTY *NUTS* TO BE A SECRET AGENT, HUSBAND OR A PARENT, RIGHT...?

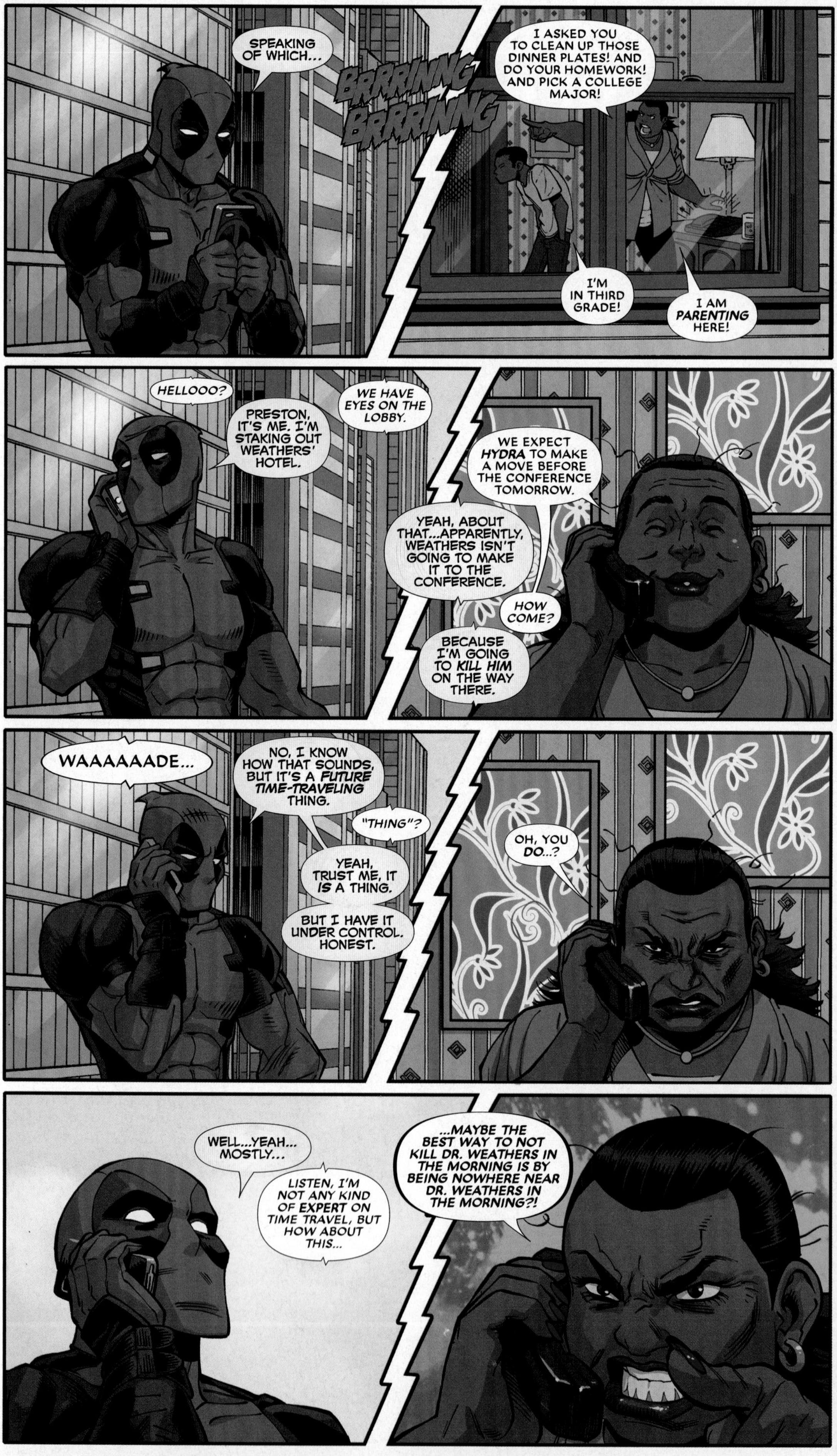

SPEAKING OF WHICH...
BRRRINNG BRRRINNG
I ASKED YOU TO CLEAN UP THOSE DINNER PLATES! AND DO YOUR HOMEWORK! AND PICK A COLLEGE MAJOR!
I'M IN THIRD GRADE!
I AM PARENTING HERE!
HELLOOO?
PRESTON, IT'S ME. I'M STAKING OUT WEATHERS' HOTEL.
WE HAVE EYES ON THE LOBBY.
WE EXPECT HYDRA TO MAKE A MOVE BEFORE THE CONFERENCE TOMORROW.
YEAH, ABOUT THAT...APPARENTLY, WEATHERS ISN'T GOING TO MAKE IT TO THE CONFERENCE.
HOW COME?
BECAUSE I'M GOING TO KILL HIM ON THE WAY THERE.
WAAAAAADE...
NO, I KNOW HOW THAT SOUNDS, BUT IT'S A FUTURE TIME-TRAVELING THING.
"THING"?
YEAH, TRUST ME, IT IS A THING.
BUT I HAVE IT UNDER CONTROL. HONEST.
OH, YOU DO...?
WELL...YEAH... MOSTLY...
LISTEN, I'M NOT ANY KIND OF EXPERT ON TIME TRAVEL, BUT HOW ABOUT THIS...
...MAYBE THE BEST WAY TO NOT KILL DR. WEATHERS IN THE MORNING IS BY BEING NOWHERE NEAR DR. WEATHERS IN THE MORNING?!

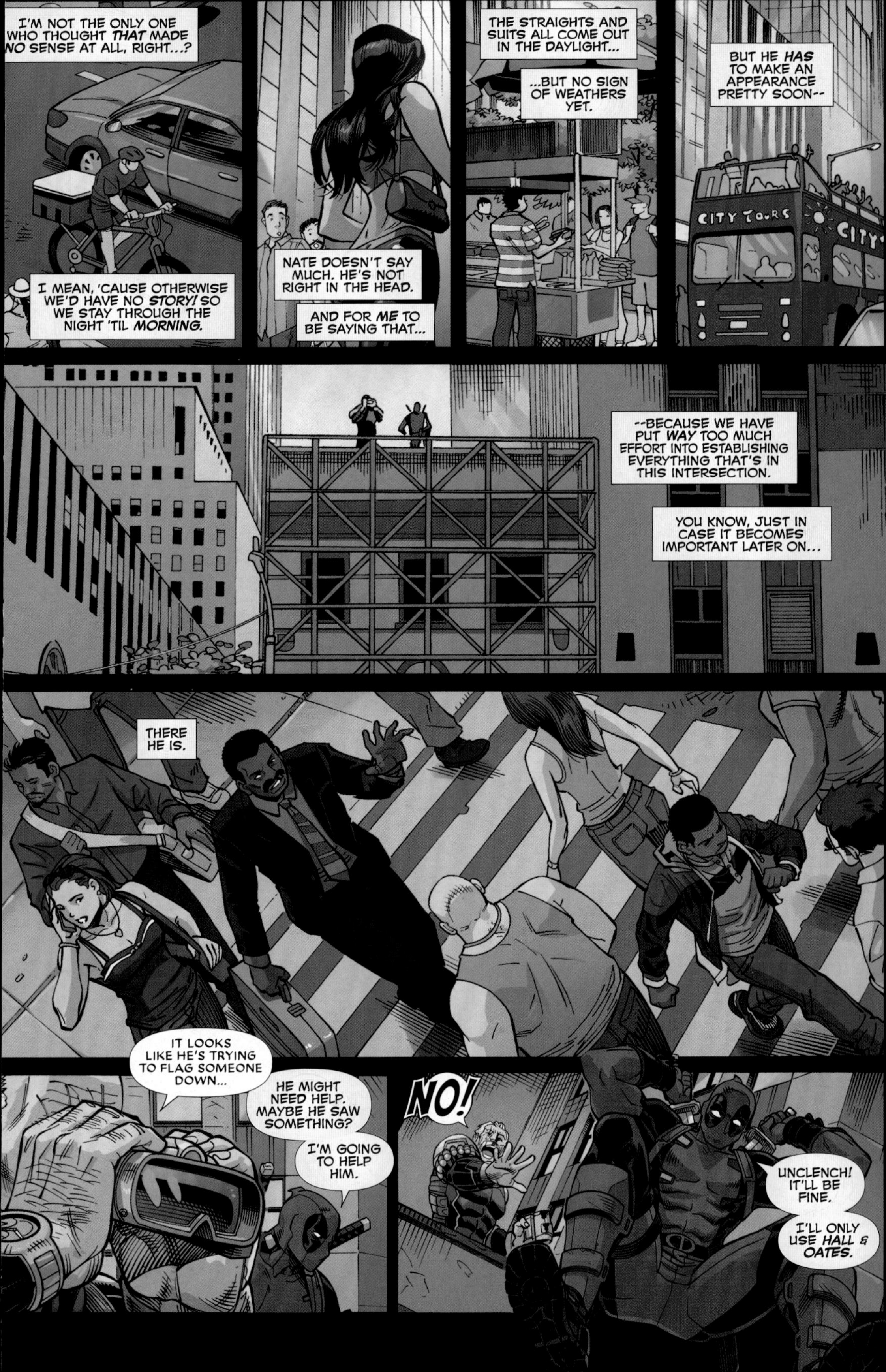

I'M NOT THE ONLY ONE WHO THOUGHT *THAT* MADE NO SENSE AT ALL, RIGHT...?
I MEAN, 'CAUSE OTHERWISE WE'D HAVE NO *STORY!* SO WE STAY THROUGH THE NIGHT 'TIL *MORNING.*
NATE DOESN'T SAY MUCH. HE'S NOT RIGHT IN THE HEAD.
AND FOR *ME* TO BE SAYING THAT...
THE STRAIGHTS AND SUITS ALL COME OUT IN THE DAYLIGHT...
...BUT NO SIGN OF WEATHERS YET.
BUT HE *HAS* TO MAKE AN APPEARANCE PRETTY SOON--
CITY TOURS
CITY
--BECAUSE WE HAVE PUT *WAY* TOO MUCH EFFORT INTO ESTABLISHING EVERYTHING THAT'S IN THIS INTERSECTION.
YOU KNOW, JUST IN CASE IT BECOMES IMPORTANT LATER ON...
THERE HE IS.
IT LOOKS LIKE HE'S TRYING TO FLAG SOMEONE DOWN...
HE MIGHT NEED HELP. MAYBE HE SAW SOMETHING?
I'M GOING TO HELP HIM.
NO!
UNCLENCH! IT'LL BE FINE.
I'LL ONLY USE *HALL & OATES.*

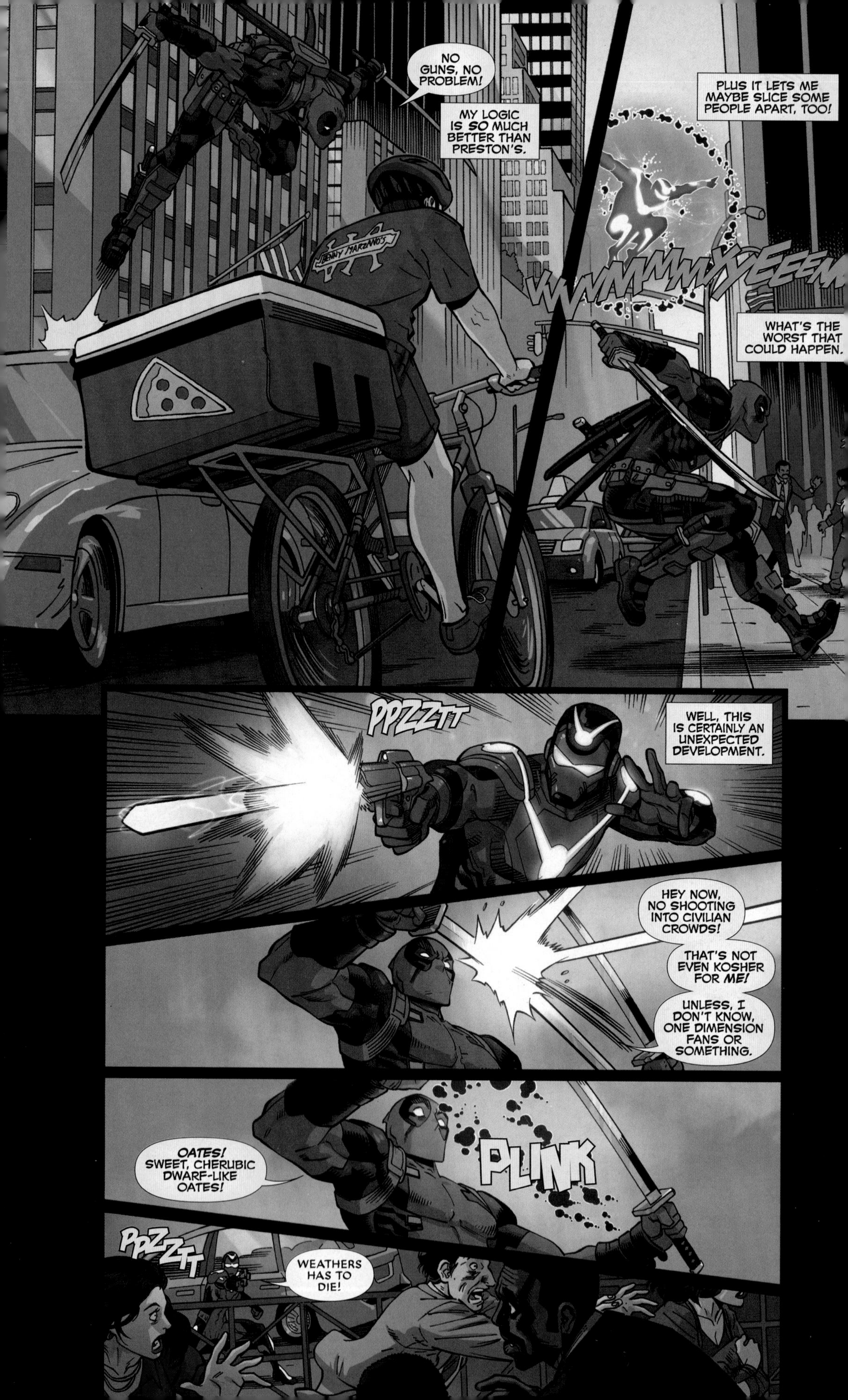

NO GUNS, NO PROBLEM!
MY LOGIC IS SO MUCH BETTER THAN PRESTON'S.
BENNY MARZANO'S
PLUS IT LETS ME MAYBE SLICE SOME PEOPLE APART, TOO!
WWMMMMYEEEM
WHAT'S THE WORST THAT COULD HAPPEN.
PPZZTT
WELL, THIS IS CERTAINLY AN UNEXPECTED DEVELOPMENT.
HEY NOW, NO SHOOTING INTO CIVILIAN CROWDS!
THAT'S NOT EVEN KOSHER FOR ME!
UNLESS, I DON'T KNOW, ONE DIMENSION FANS OR SOMETHING.
OATES! SWEET, CHERUBIC DWARF-LIKE OATES!
PLINK
PPZZTT
WEATHERS HAS TO DIE!

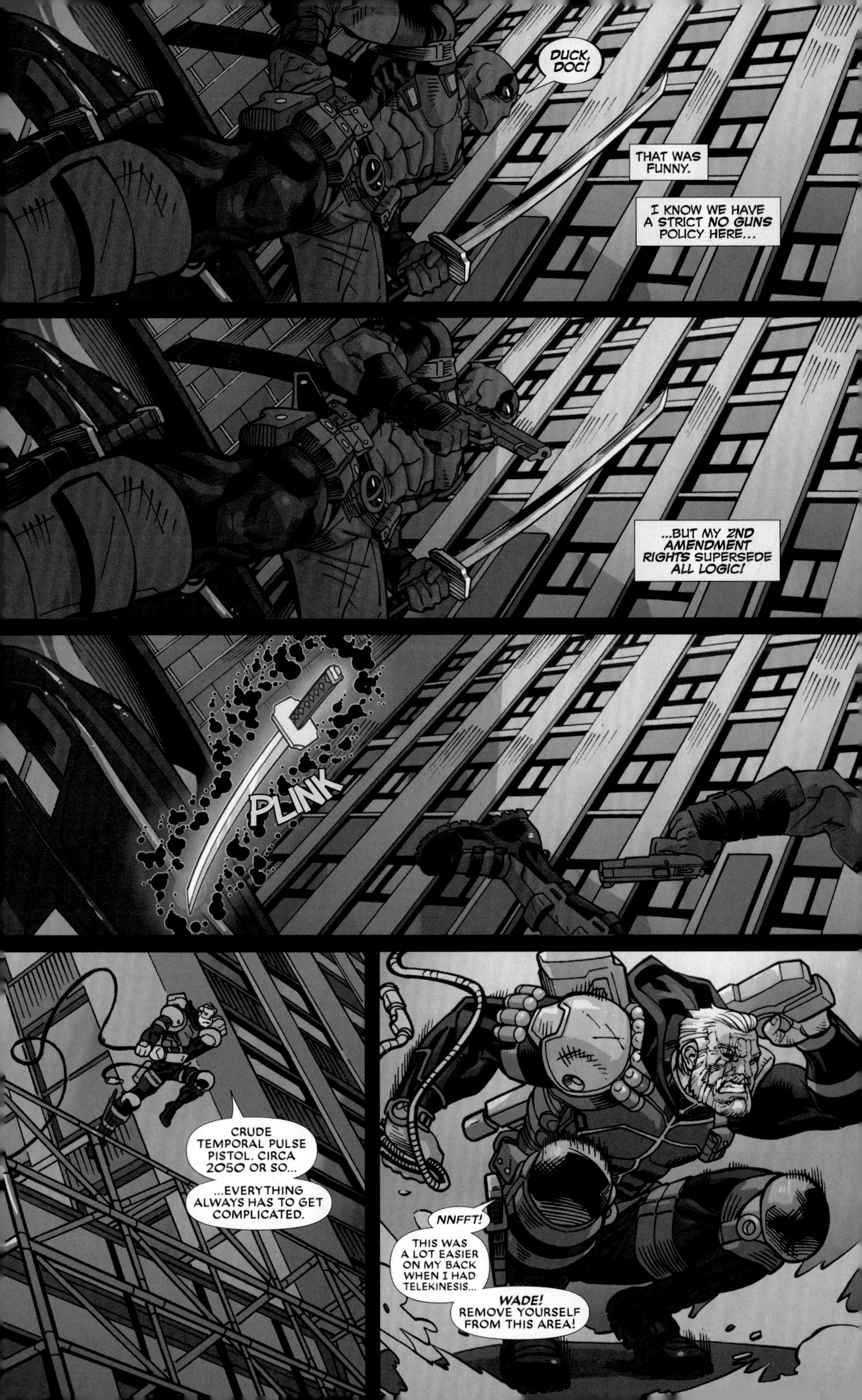
DUCK, DOC!
THAT WAS FUNNY.
I KNOW WE HAVE A STRICT NO GUNS POLICY HERE...
...BUT MY 2ND AMENDMENT RIGHTS SUPERSEDE ALL LOGIC!
PLINK
CRUDE TEMPORAL PULSE PISTOL. CIRCA 2050 OR SO...
...EVERYTHING ALWAYS HAS TO GET COMPLICATED.
NNFFT!
THIS WAS A LOT EASIER ON MY BACK WHEN I HAD TELEKINESIS...
WADE! REMOVE YOURSELF FROM THIS AREA!

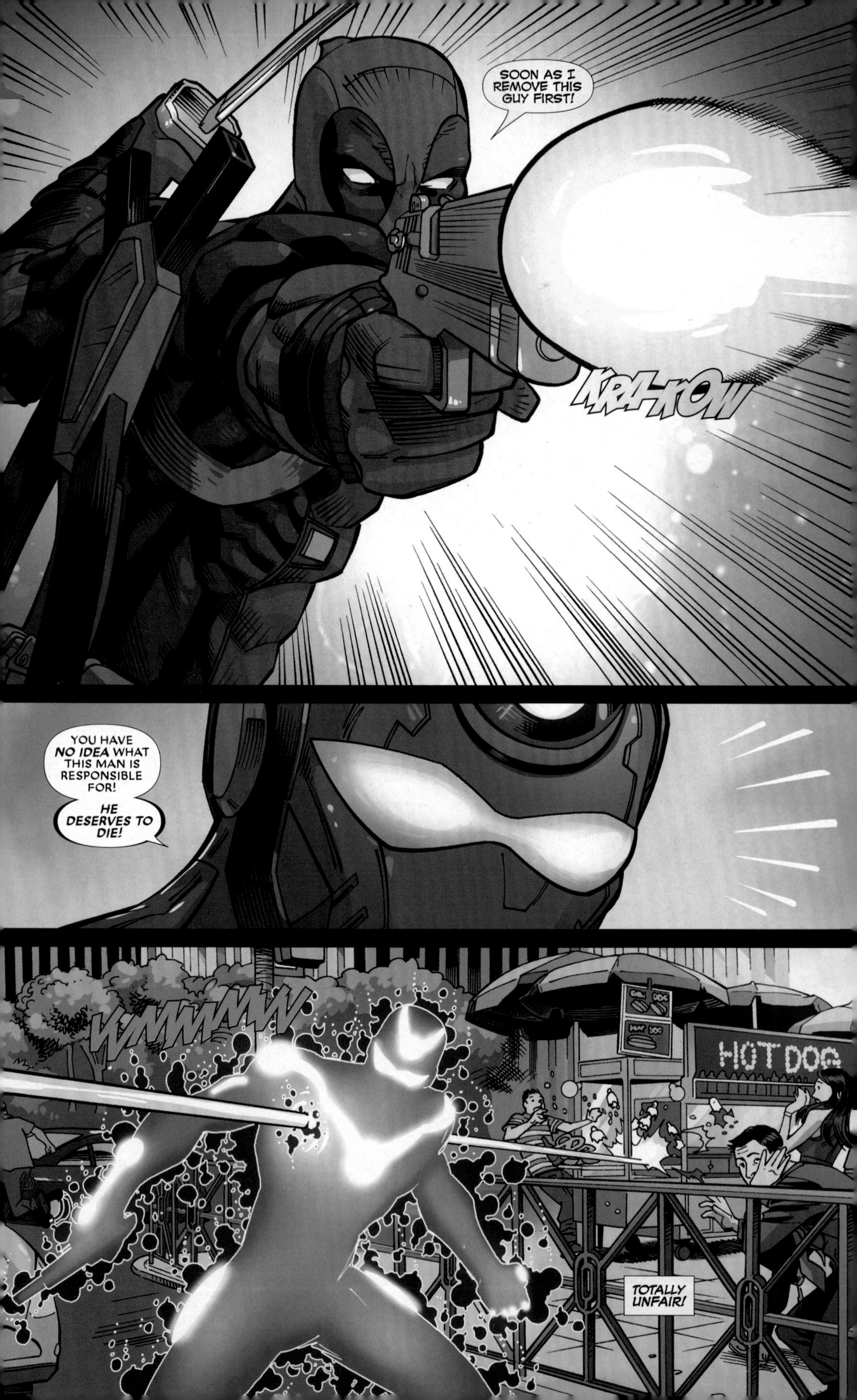
SOON AS I REMOVE THIS GUY FIRST!
KRA-KOW
YOU HAVE NO IDEA WHAT THIS MAN IS RESPONSIBLE FOR!
HE DESERVES TO DIE!
WMMMMMM
HOT DOG
TOTALLY UNFAIR!

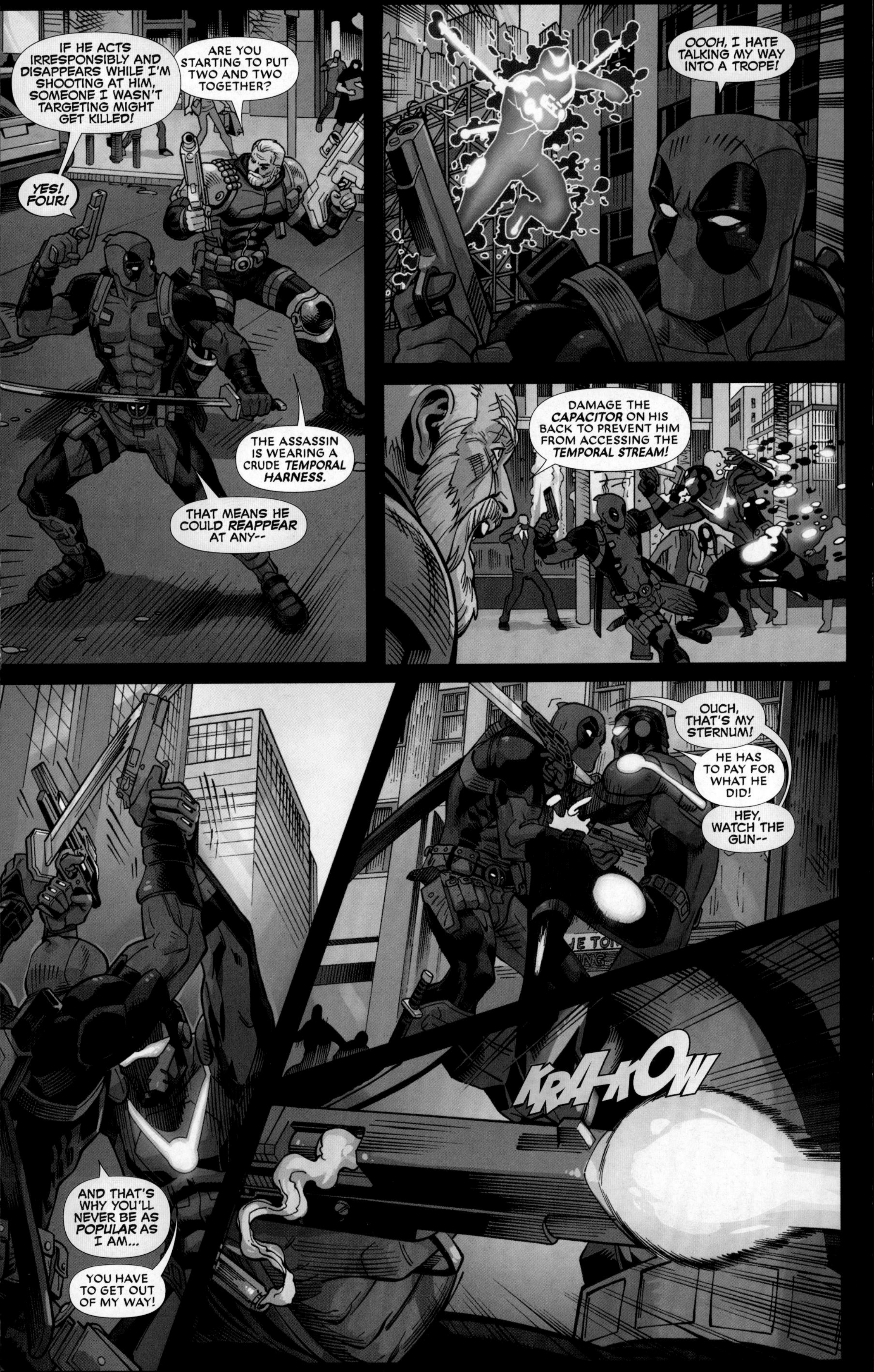
IF HE ACTS IRRESPONSIBLY AND DISAPPEARS WHILE I'M SHOOTING AT HIM, SOMEONE I WASN'T TARGETING MIGHT GET KILLED!
ARE YOU STARTING TO PUT TWO AND TWO TOGETHER?
YES! FOUR!
THE ASSASSIN IS WEARING A CRUDE TEMPORAL HARNESS.
THAT MEANS HE COULD REAPPEAR AT ANY--
OOOH, I HATE TALKING MY WAY INTO A TROPE!
DAMAGE THE CAPACITOR ON HIS BACK TO PREVENT HIM FROM ACCESSING THE TEMPORAL STREAM!
OUCH, THAT'S MY STERNUM!
HE HAS TO PAY FOR WHAT HE DID!
HEY, WATCH THE GUN--
KRAKOW
AND THAT'S WHY YOU'LL NEVER BE AS POPULAR AS I AM...
YOU HAVE TO GET OUT OF MY WAY!

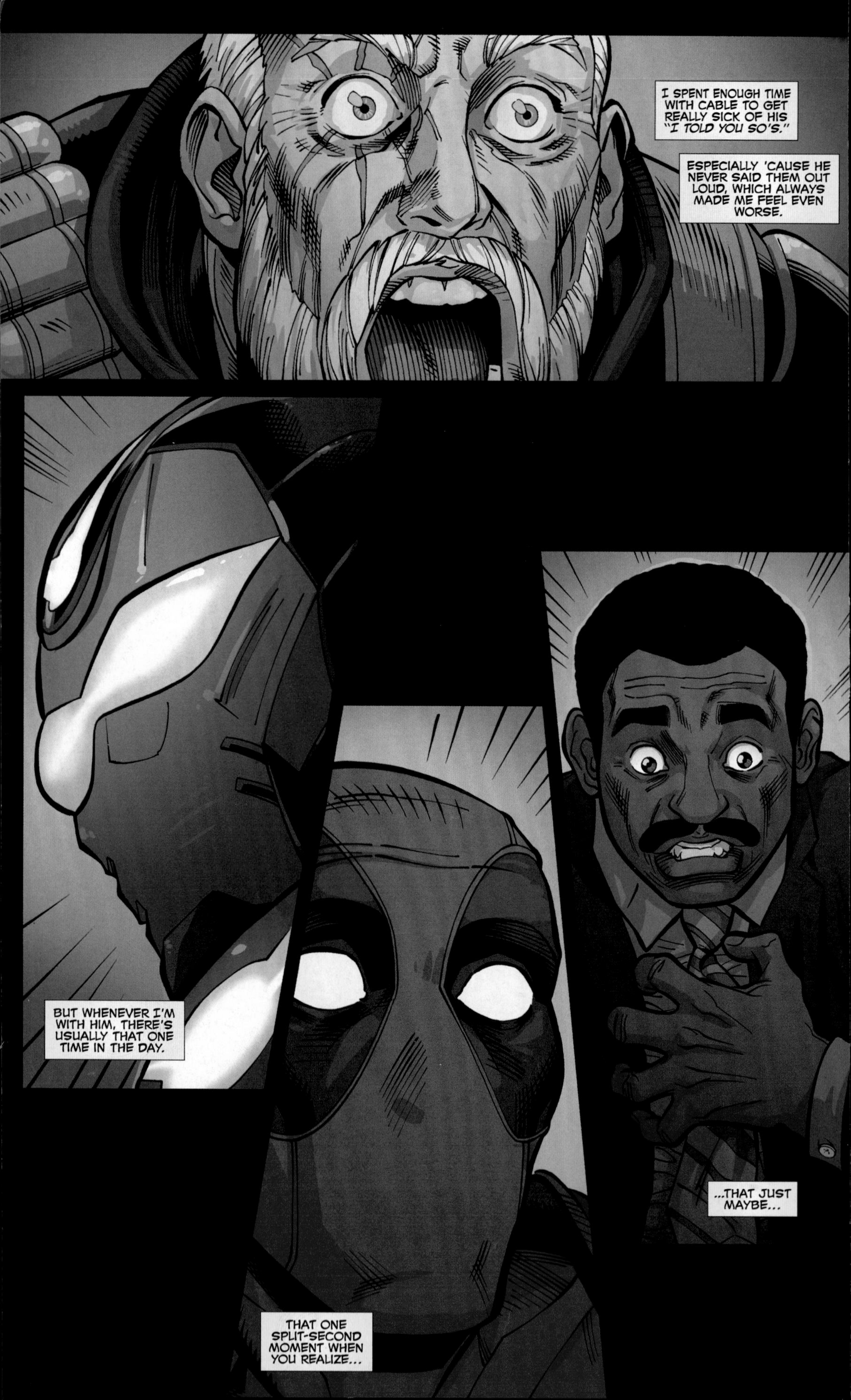
I SPENT ENOUGH TIME WITH CABLE TO GET REALLY SICK OF HIS *"I TOLD YOU SO'S."*
ESPECIALLY 'CAUSE HE NEVER SAID THEM OUT LOUD, WHICH ALWAYS MADE ME FEEL EVEN WORSE.
BUT WHENEVER I'M WITH HIM, THERE'S USUALLY THAT ONE TIME IN THE DAY.
THAT ONE SPLIT-SECOND MOMENT WHEN YOU REALIZE...
...THAT JUST MAYBE...

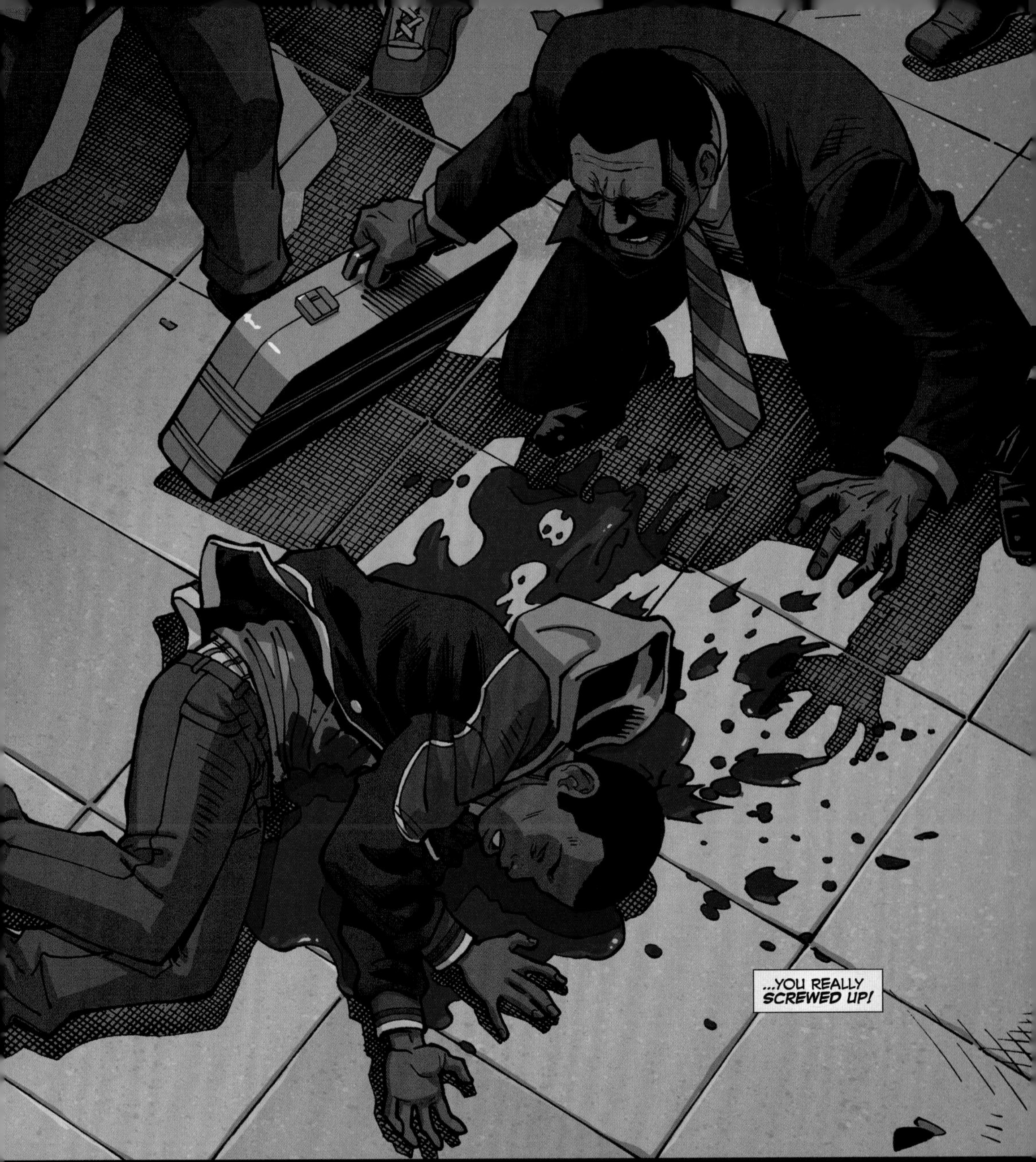
...YOU REALLY SCREWED UP!

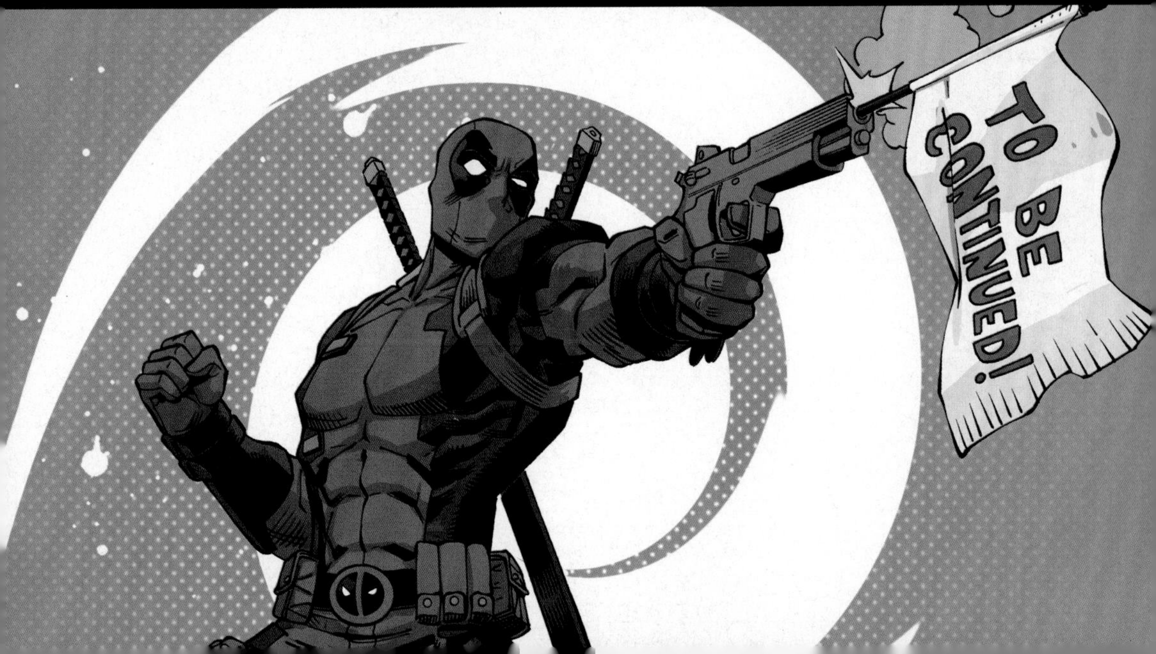
TO BE CONTINUED!

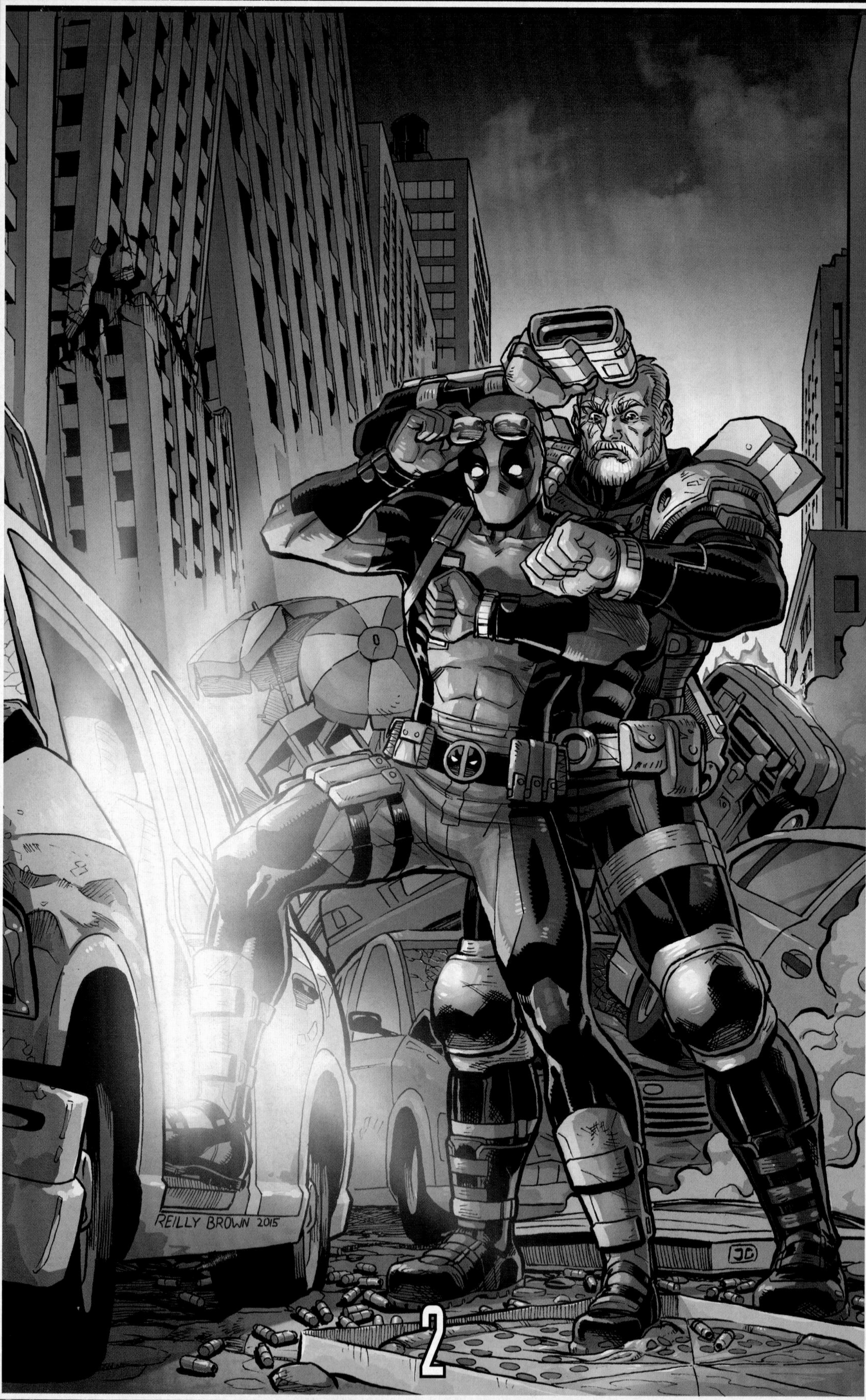
REILLY BROWN 2015
JC
2

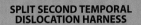

SPLIT SECOND TEMPORAL DISLOCATION HARNESS

DEADPOOL & CABLE

EXCERPTED FROM THE JOURNAL OF DR. CARL WEATHERS.

ANNOTATED NOVEMBER 14, 2041.

OCULAR REGULATOR

WHAT HAD BEEN AN EXPERIMENT BECAME AN OBSESSION.

INVERSION FIELD
CXF27 X 3.3.21.00
STABILIZER
44.55.44.002

CHAPTER THREE: SANTAYANA WAS RIGHT

ONCE, LONG AGO, I'D PLANNED TO SELL THE TIME HARNESS TO THE HIGHEST BIDDER.

BUT INSTEAD, I HAVE TRIED TO PERFECT IT AS A WAY TO CHANGE THE PAST AND SAVE HIS LIFE.

IT DOESN'T WORK! TO THE DETRIMENT OF MY FAMILY AND MY HEALTH.

I HAVE BECOME AHAB-- AND TIME TRAVEL, MY WHITE WHALE.

SPLIT SEC

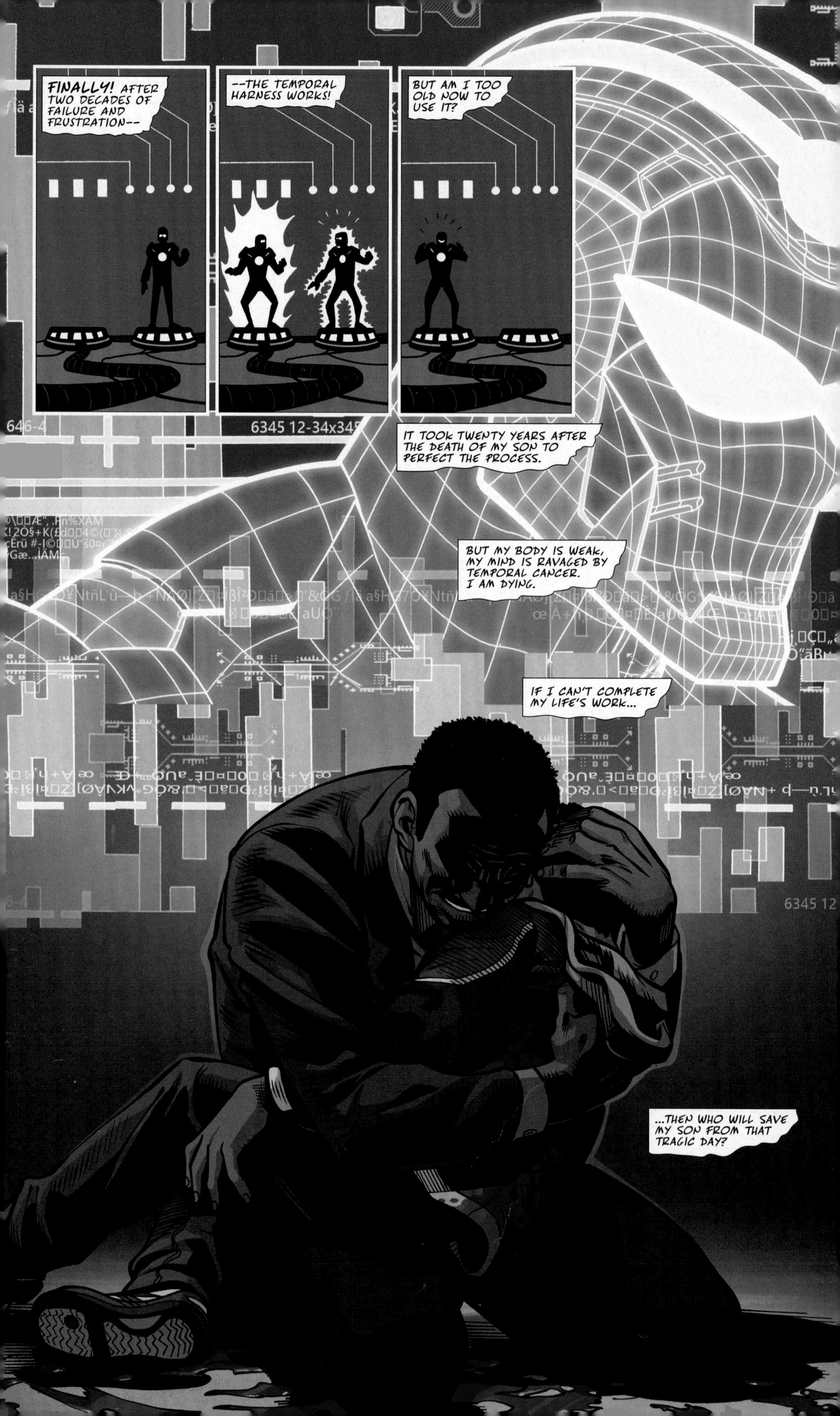

FINALLY! AFTER TWO DECADES OF FAILURE AND FRUSTRATION--
--THE TEMPORAL HARNESS WORKS!
BUT AM I TOO OLD NOW TO USE IT?
IT TOOK TWENTY YEARS AFTER THE DEATH OF MY SON TO PERFECT THE PROCESS.
BUT MY BODY IS WEAK, MY MIND IS RAVAGED BY TEMPORAL CANCER. I AM DYING.
IF I CAN'T COMPLETE MY LIFE'S WORK...
...THEN WHO WILL SAVE MY SON FROM THAT TRAGIC DAY?

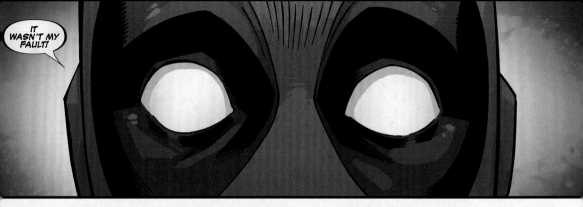

IT WASN'T MY FAULT!

WAS IT? I MEAN, I DID DO IT, BUT I DIDN'T MEAN TO!

YES, IT WAS MY GUN, BUT I DIDN'T FIRE IT!

WELL, OKAY, TECHNICALLY, I DID PULL THE TRIGGER, BUT I DIDN'T REALLY PULL IT, HE DID!

IT WASN'T SUPPOSED TO HAPPEN THIS WAY...

STOP HIM!

HE'S WEARING A PRIMITIVE TIME-TRAVEL HARNESS THAT WILL--

LET HIM TRAVEL THROUGH TIME? I MEAN, JUST TAKING A WILD GUESS.

PPZZTT

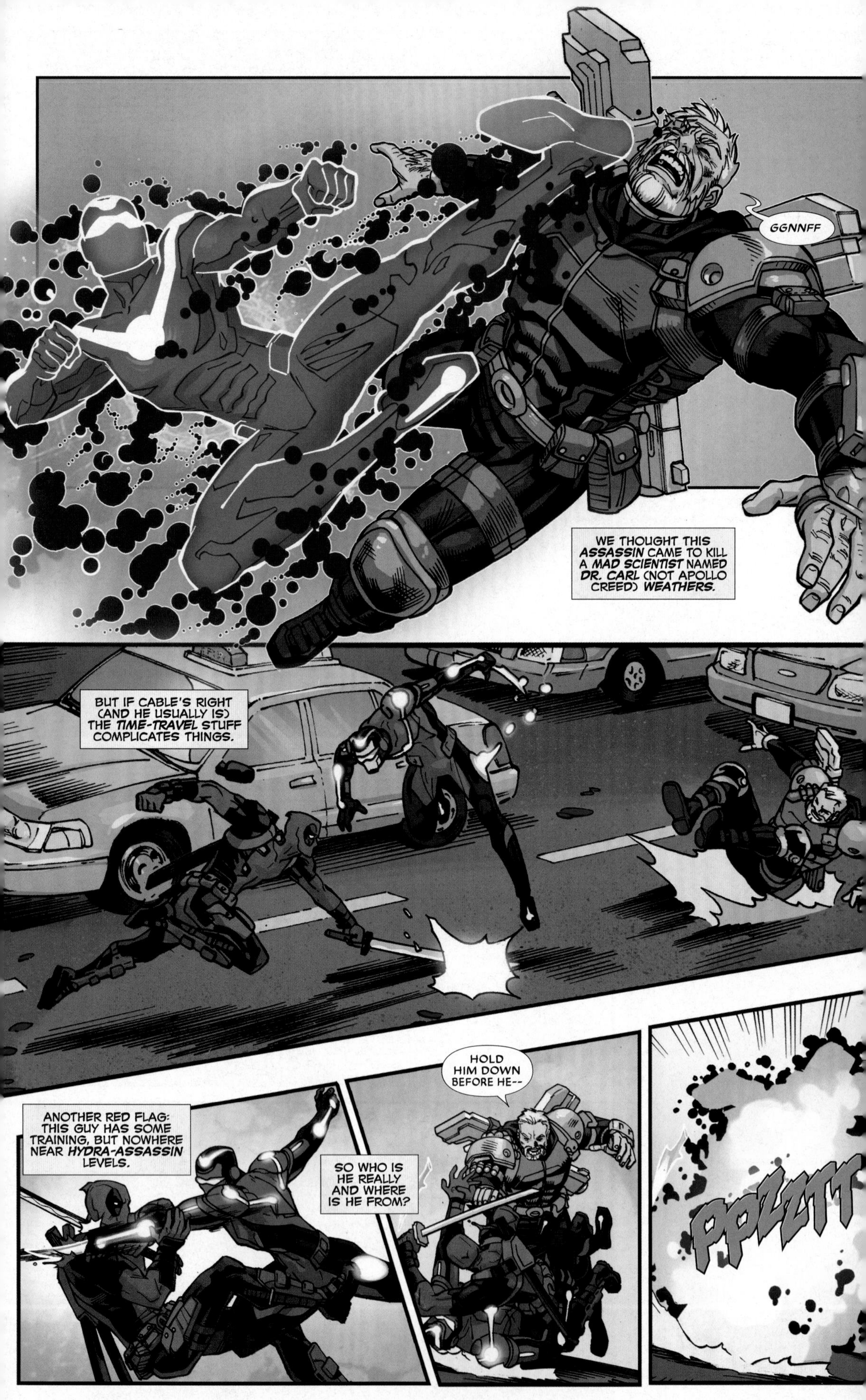
GGNNFF
WE THOUGHT THIS ASSASSIN CAME TO KILL A MAD SCIENTIST NAMED DR. CARL (NOT APOLLO CREED) WEATHERS.
BUT IF CABLE'S RIGHT (AND HE USUALLY IS) THE TIME-TRAVEL STUFF COMPLICATES THINGS.
ANOTHER RED FLAG: THIS GUY HAS SOME TRAINING, BUT NOWHERE NEAR HYDRA-ASSASSIN LEVELS.
HOLD HIM DOWN BEFORE HE--
SO WHO IS HE REALLY AND WHERE IS HE FROM?
PPZZTT

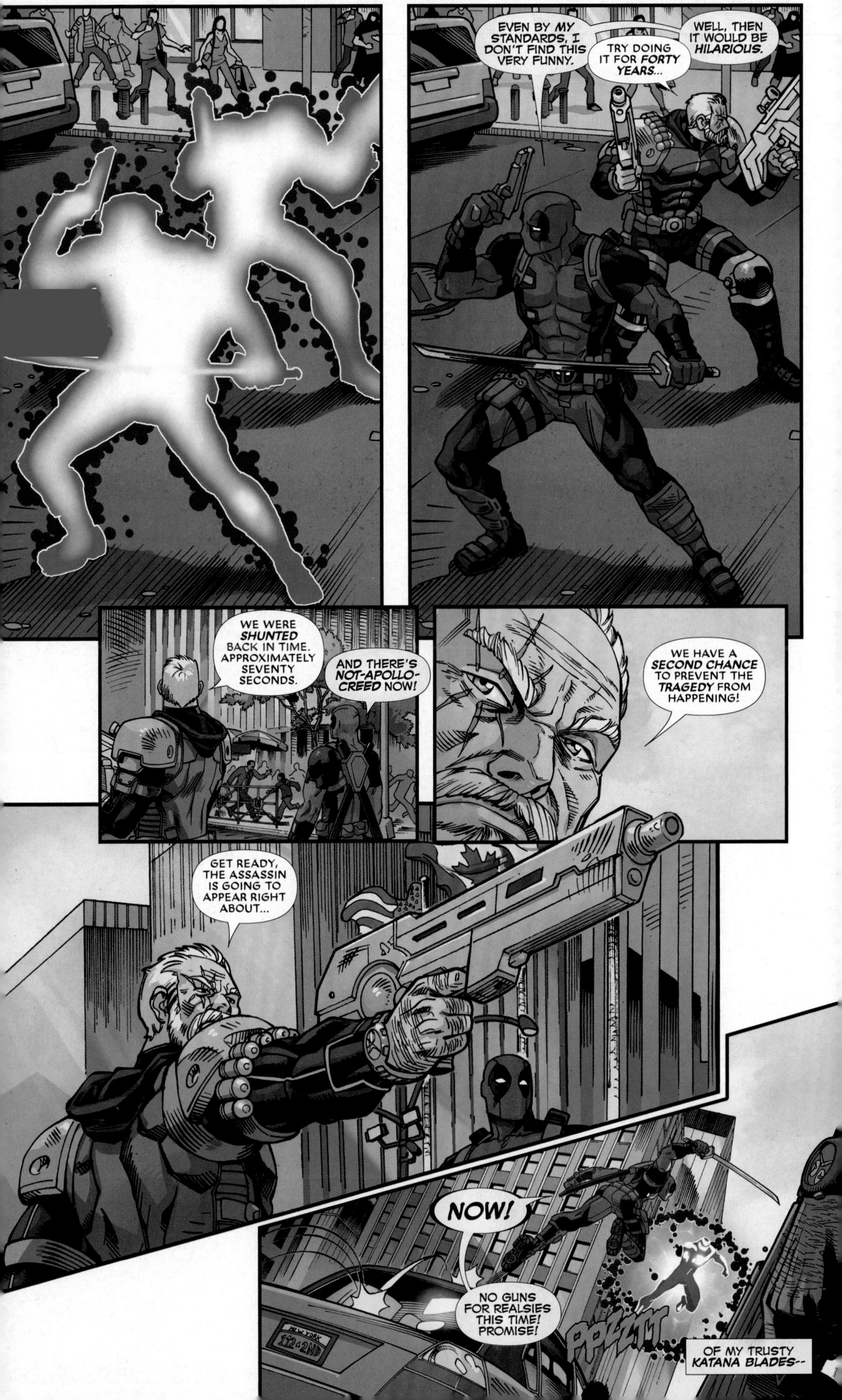
EVEN BY MY STANDARDS, I DON'T FIND THIS VERY FUNNY.
TRY DOING IT FOR FORTY YEARS...
WELL, THEN IT WOULD BE HILARIOUS.
WE WERE SHUNTED BACK IN TIME. APPROXIMATELY SEVENTY SECONDS.
AND THERE'S NOT-APOLLO-CREED NOW!
WE HAVE A SECOND CHANCE TO PREVENT THE TRAGEDY FROM HAPPENING!
GET READY, THE ASSASSIN IS GOING TO APPEAR RIGHT ABOUT...
NOW!
NO GUNS FOR REALSIES THIS TIME! PROMISE!
PPZZTT
OF MY TRUSTY KATANA BLADES--

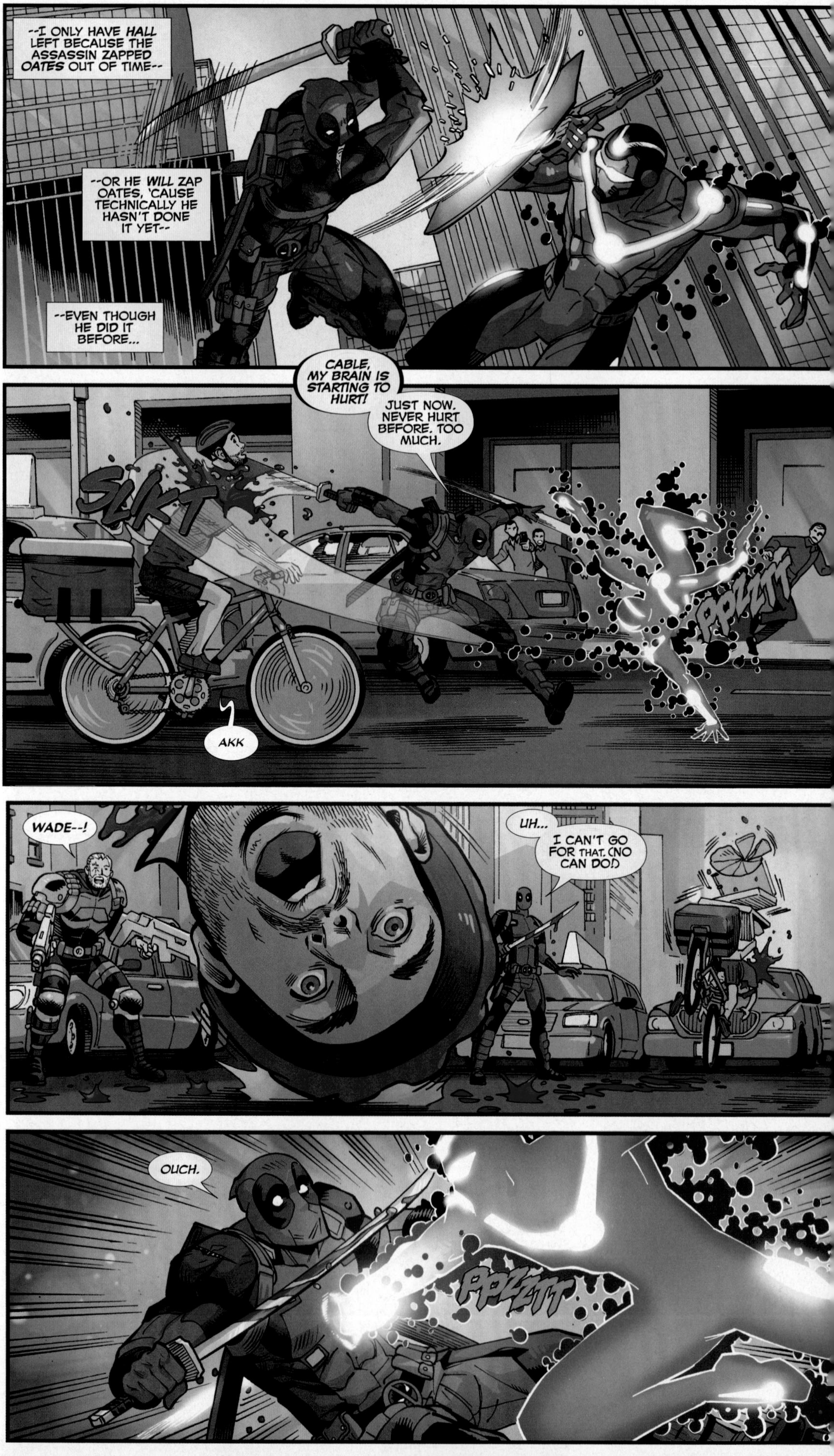
--I ONLY HAVE HALL LEFT BECAUSE THE ASSASSIN ZAPPED OATES OUT OF TIME--
--OR HE WILL ZAP OATES, 'CAUSE TECHNICALLY HE HASN'T DONE IT YET--
--EVEN THOUGH HE DID IT BEFORE...
CABLE, MY BRAIN IS STARTING TO HURT!
JUST NOW. NEVER HURT BEFORE. TOO MUCH.
SLIKT
PPZZTT
AKK
WADE--!
UH... I CAN'T GO FOR THAT. (NO CAN DO.)
OUCH.
PPZZTT

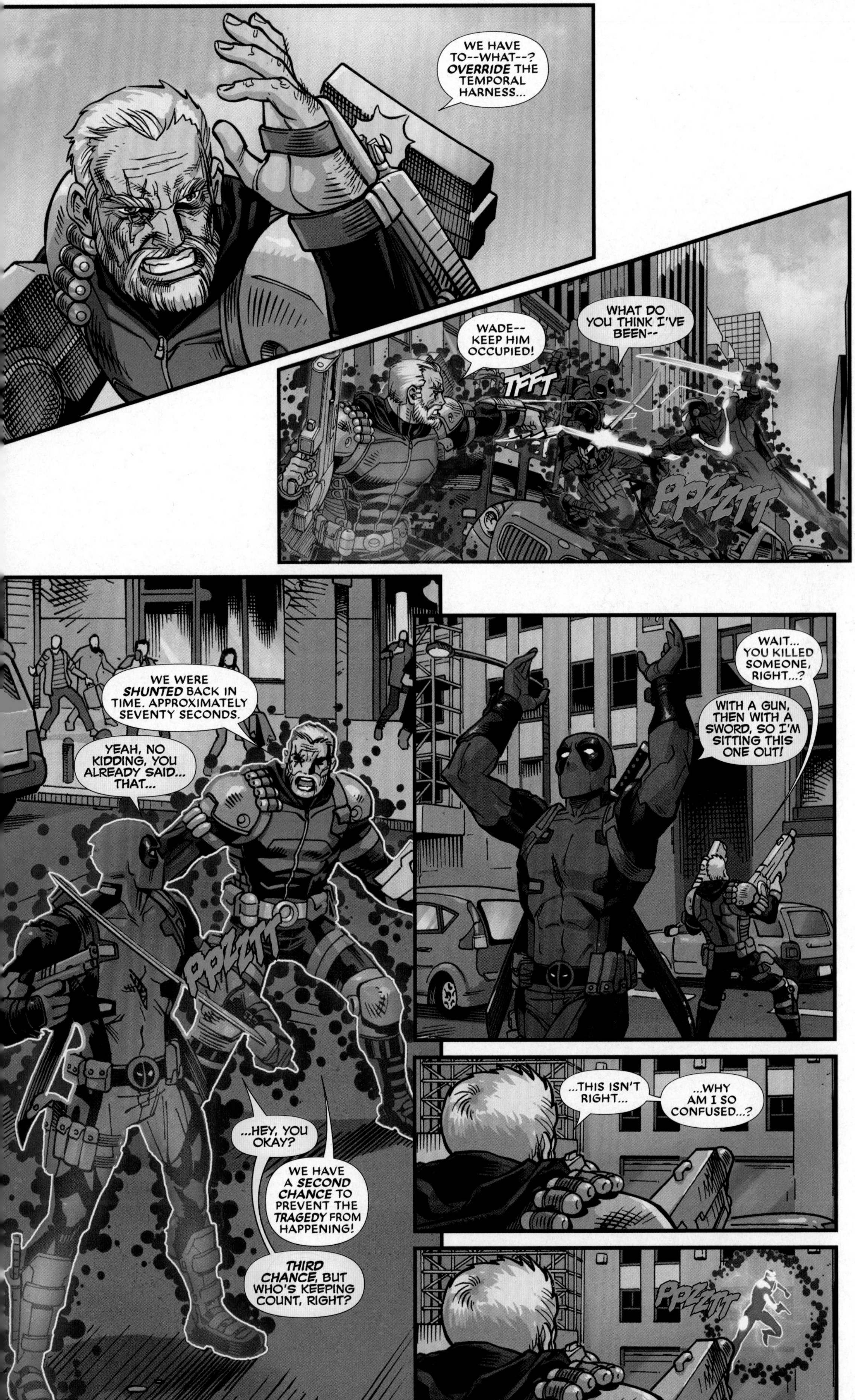
WE HAVE TO--WHAT--? OVERRIDE THE TEMPORAL HARNESS...
WADE-- KEEP HIM OCCUPIED!
WHAT DO YOU THINK I'VE BEEN--
TFFT
PPZZTT
WE WERE SHUNTED BACK IN TIME. APPROXIMATELY SEVENTY SECONDS.
YEAH, NO KIDDING, YOU ALREADY SAID... THAT...
PPZZTT
...HEY, YOU OKAY?
WE HAVE A SECOND CHANCE TO PREVENT THE TRAGEDY FROM HAPPENING!
THIRD CHANCE, BUT WHO'S KEEPING COUNT, RIGHT?
WAIT... YOU KILLED SOMEONE, RIGHT...?
WITH A GUN, THEN WITH A SWORD, SO I'M SITTING THIS ONE OUT!
...THIS ISN'T RIGHT...
...WHY AM I SO CONFUSED...?
PPZZTT

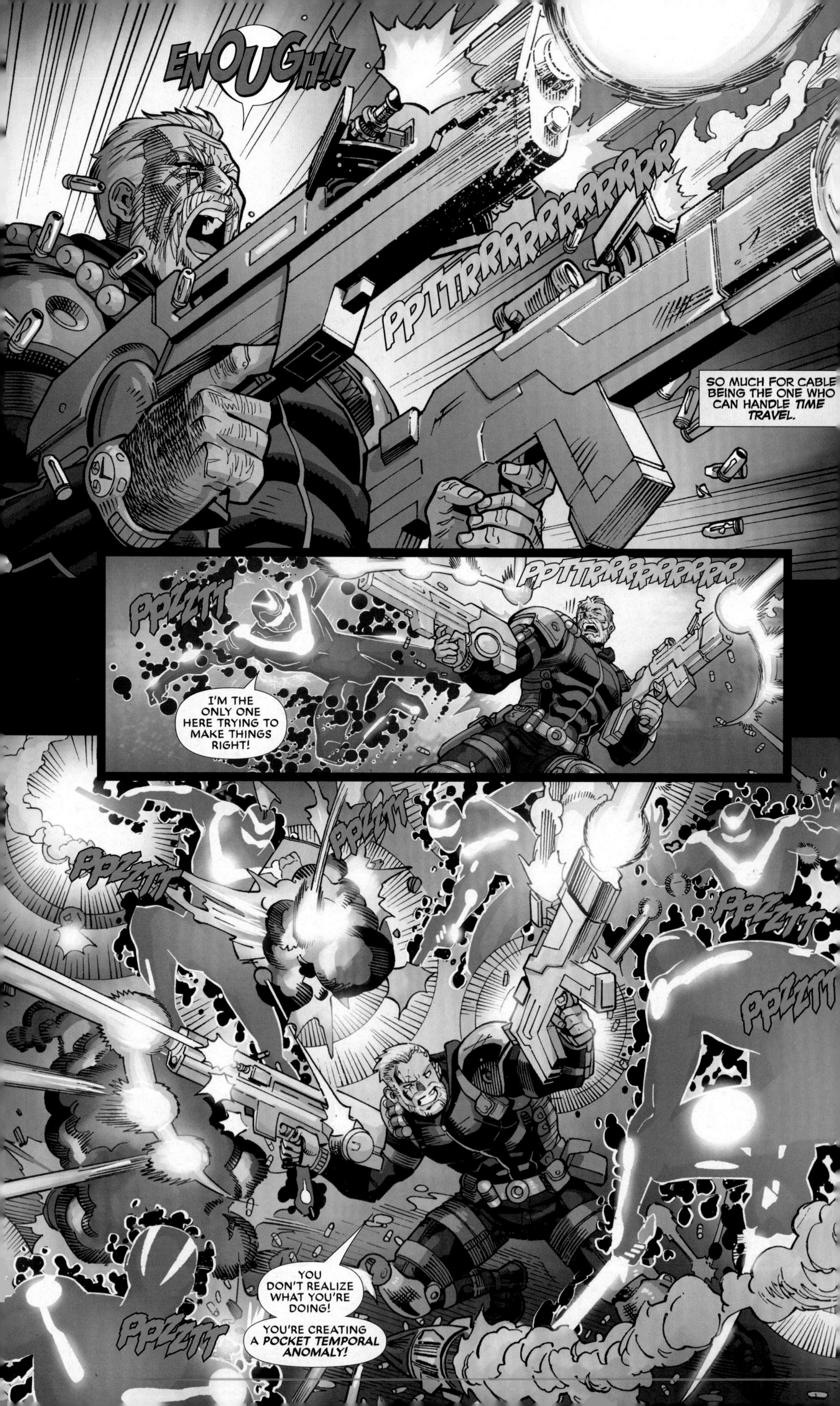
ENOUGH!!!
PPTTTRRRRRRRRRRRRRRRR
SO MUCH FOR CABLE BEING THE ONE WHO CAN HANDLE *TIME TRAVEL.*
PPZZTT
PPTTTRRRRRRRRRRR
I'M THE ONLY ONE HERE TRYING TO MAKE THINGS RIGHT!
PPZZTT
PPZZTT
PPZZTT
PPZZTT
YOU DON'T REALIZE WHAT YOU'RE DOING!
YOU'RE CREATING A *POCKET TEMPORAL ANOMALY!*
PPZZTT

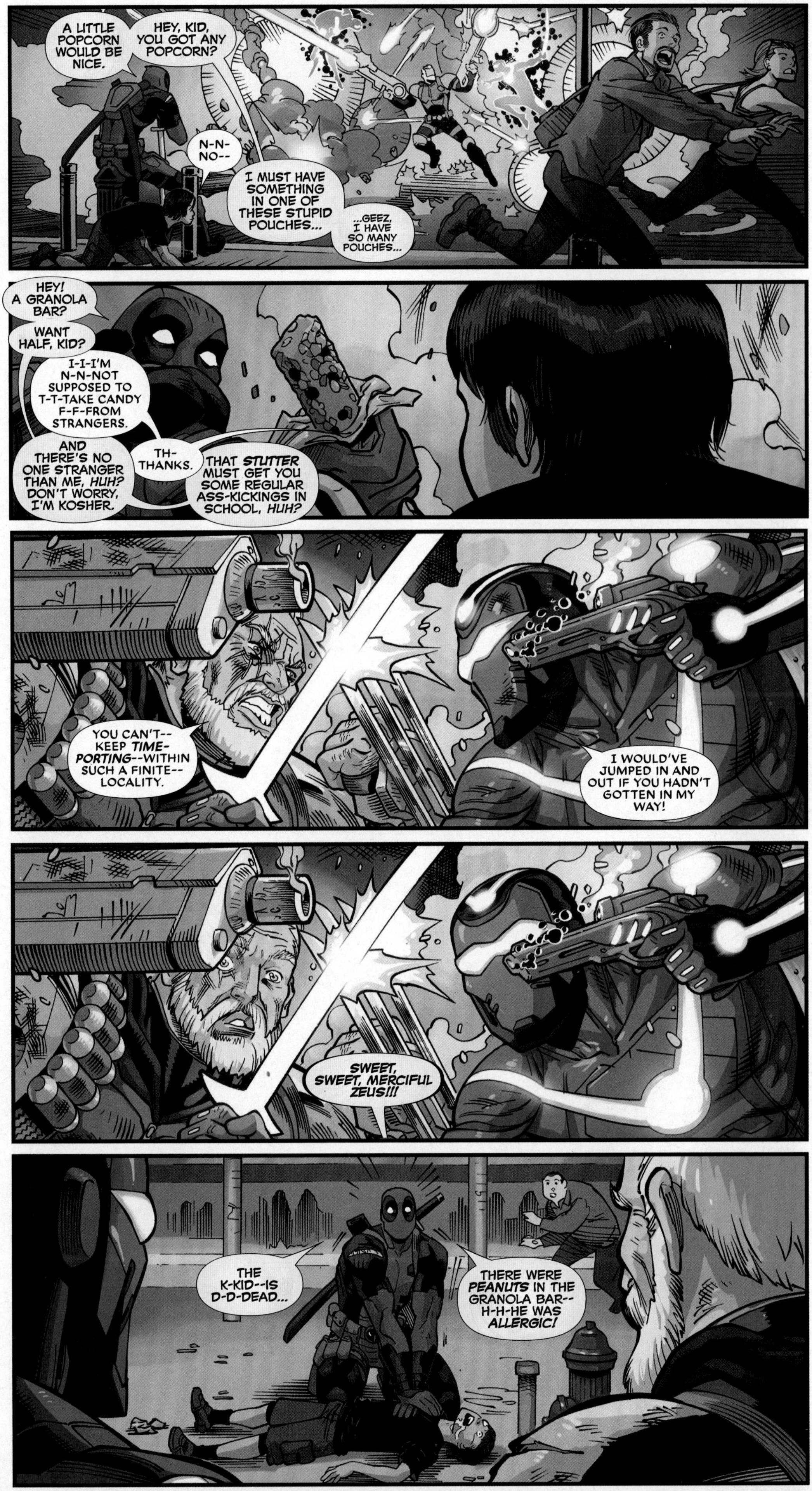
A LITTLE POPCORN WOULD BE NICE.
HEY, KID, YOU GOT ANY POPCORN?
N-N-NO--
I MUST HAVE SOMETHING IN ONE OF THESE STUPID POUCHES...
...GEEZ, I HAVE SO MANY POUCHES...
HEY! A GRANOLA BAR?
WANT HALF, KID?
I-I-I'M N-N-NOT SUPPOSED TO T-T-TAKE CANDY F-F-FROM STRANGERS.
AND THERE'S NO ONE STRANGER THAN ME, HUH? DON'T WORRY, I'M KOSHER.
TH-THANKS.
THAT STUTTER MUST GET YOU SOME REGULAR ASS-KICKINGS IN SCHOOL, HUH?
YOU CAN'T--KEEP TIME-PORTING--WITHIN SUCH A FINITE--LOCALITY.
I WOULD'VE JUMPED IN AND OUT IF YOU HADN'T GOTTEN IN MY WAY!
SWEET, SWEET, MERCIFUL ZEUS!!!
THE K-KID--IS D-D-DEAD...
THERE WERE PEANUTS IN THE GRANOLA BAR--H-H-HE WAS ALLERGIC!

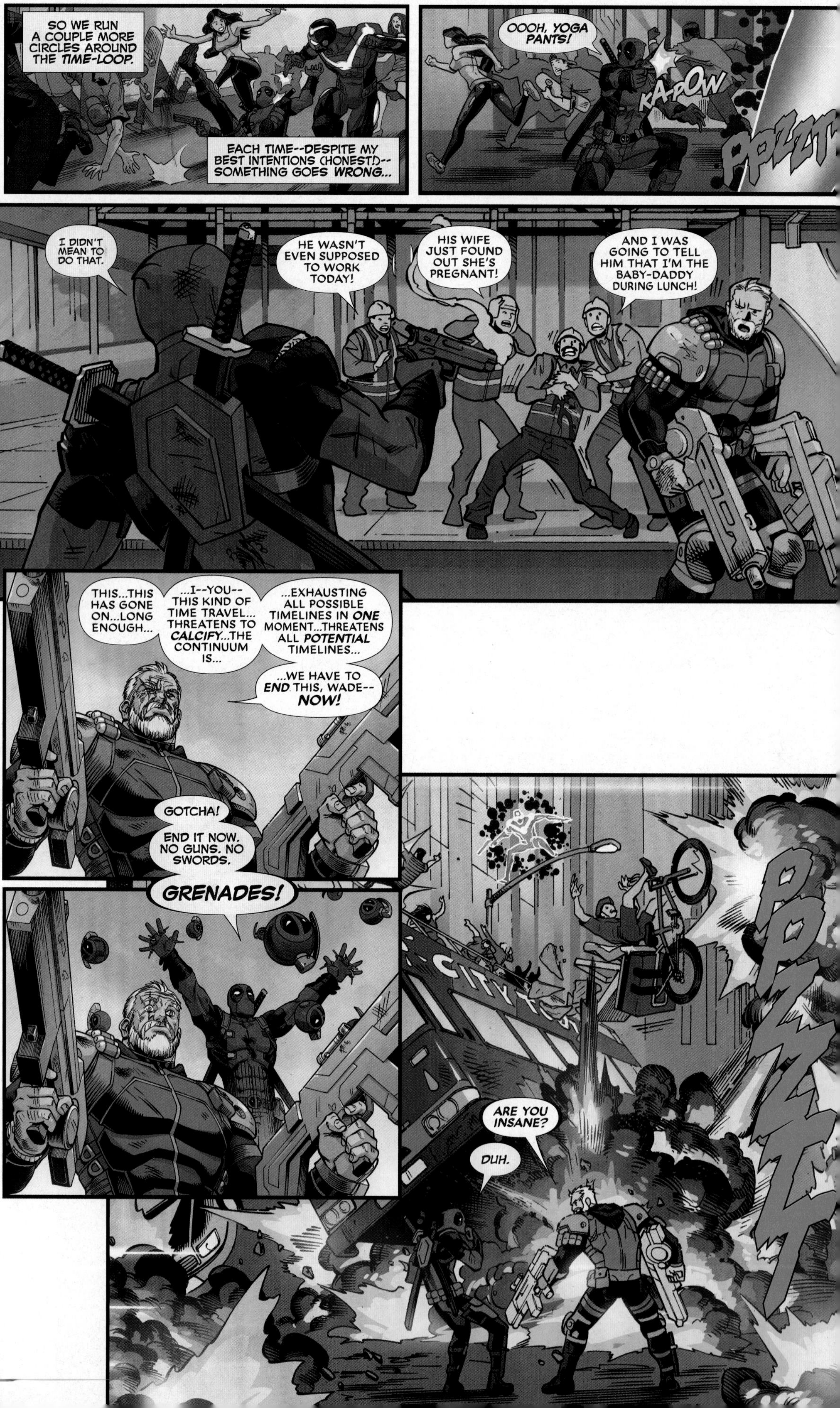

SO WE RUN A COUPLE MORE CIRCLES AROUND THE TIME-LOOP.
EACH TIME--DESPITE MY BEST INTENTIONS (HONEST!)--SOMETHING GOES WRONG...
OOOH, YOGA PANTS!
KA-POW
PPZZT
I DIDN'T MEAN TO DO THAT.
HE WASN'T EVEN SUPPOSED TO WORK TODAY!
HIS WIFE JUST FOUND OUT SHE'S PREGNANT!
AND I WAS GOING TO TELL HIM THAT I'M THE BABY-DADDY DURING LUNCH!
THIS...THIS HAS GONE ON...LONG ENOUGH...
...I--YOU--THIS KIND OF TIME TRAVEL...THREATENS TO CALCIFY...THE CONTINUUM IS...
...EXHAUSTING ALL POSSIBLE TIMELINES IN ONE MOMENT...THREATENS ALL POTENTIAL TIMELINES...
...WE HAVE TO END THIS, WADE--NOW!
GOTCHA!
END IT NOW. NO GUNS. NO SWORDS.
GRENADES!
CITY
ARE YOU INSANE?
DUH.

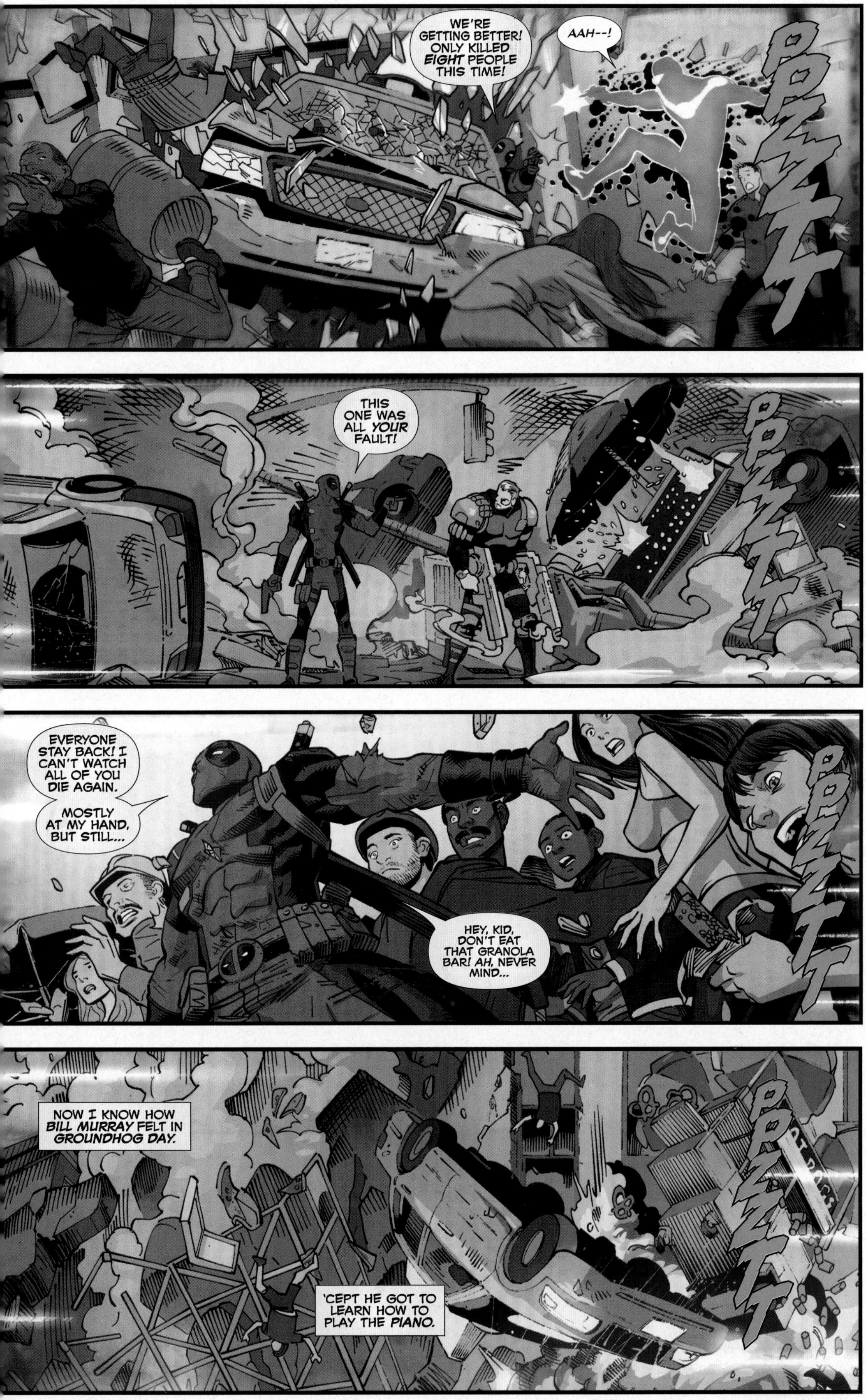
WE'RE GETTING BETTER! ONLY KILLED EIGHT PEOPLE THIS TIME!
AAH--!
THIS ONE WAS ALL YOUR FAULT!
EVERYONE STAY BACK! I CAN'T WATCH ALL OF YOU DIE AGAIN.
MOSTLY AT MY HAND, BUT STILL...
HEY, KID, DON'T EAT THAT GRANOLA BAR! AH, NEVER MIND...
NOW I KNOW HOW BILL MURRAY FELT IN GROUNDHOG DAY.
'CEPT HE GOT TO LEARN HOW TO PLAY THE PIANO.

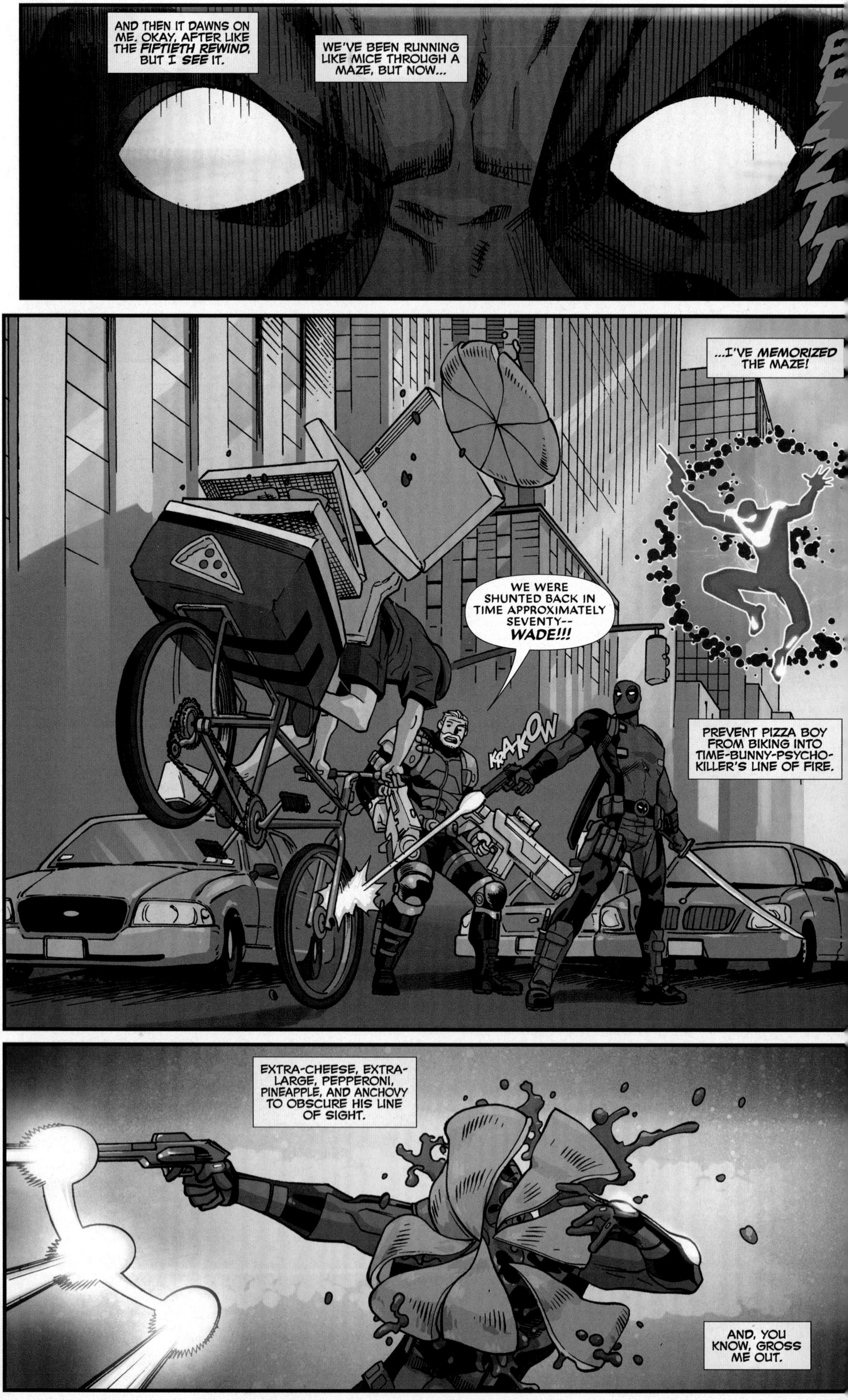
AND THEN IT DAWNS ON ME. OKAY, AFTER LIKE THE *FIFTIETH REWIND*, BUT I *SEE* IT.
WE'VE BEEN RUNNING LIKE MICE THROUGH A MAZE, BUT NOW...
...I'VE *MEMORIZED* THE MAZE!
WE WERE SHUNTED BACK IN TIME APPROXIMATELY SEVENTY-- **WADE!!!**
KRAKOW
PREVENT PIZZA BOY FROM BIKING INTO TIME-BUNNY-PSYCHO-KILLER'S LINE OF FIRE.
EXTRA-CHEESE, EXTRA-LARGE, PEPPERONI, PINEAPPLE, AND ANCHOVY TO OBSCURE HIS LINE OF SIGHT.
AND, YOU KNOW, GROSS ME OUT.

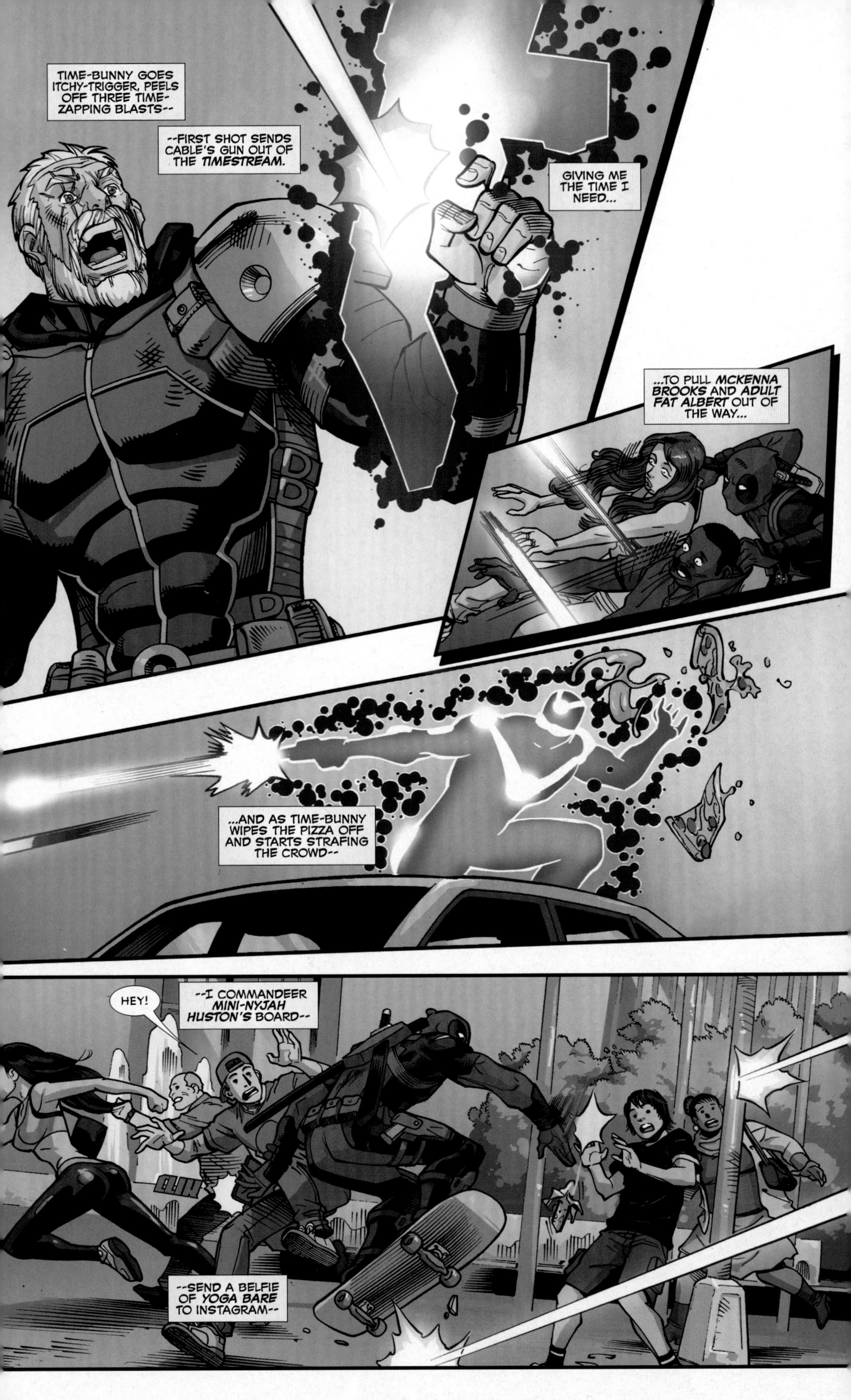

TIME-BUNNY GOES ITCHY-TRIGGER, PEELS OFF THREE TIME-ZAPPING BLASTS--
--FIRST SHOT SENDS CABLE'S GUN OUT OF THE TIMESTREAM.
GIVING ME THE TIME I NEED...
...TO PULL MCKENNA BROOKS AND ADULT FAT ALBERT OUT OF THE WAY...
...AND AS TIME-BUNNY WIPES THE PIZZA OFF AND STARTS STRAFING THE CROWD--
HEY!
--I COMMANDEER MINI-NYJAH HUSTON'S BOARD--
--SEND A BELFIE OF YOGA BARE TO INSTAGRAM--

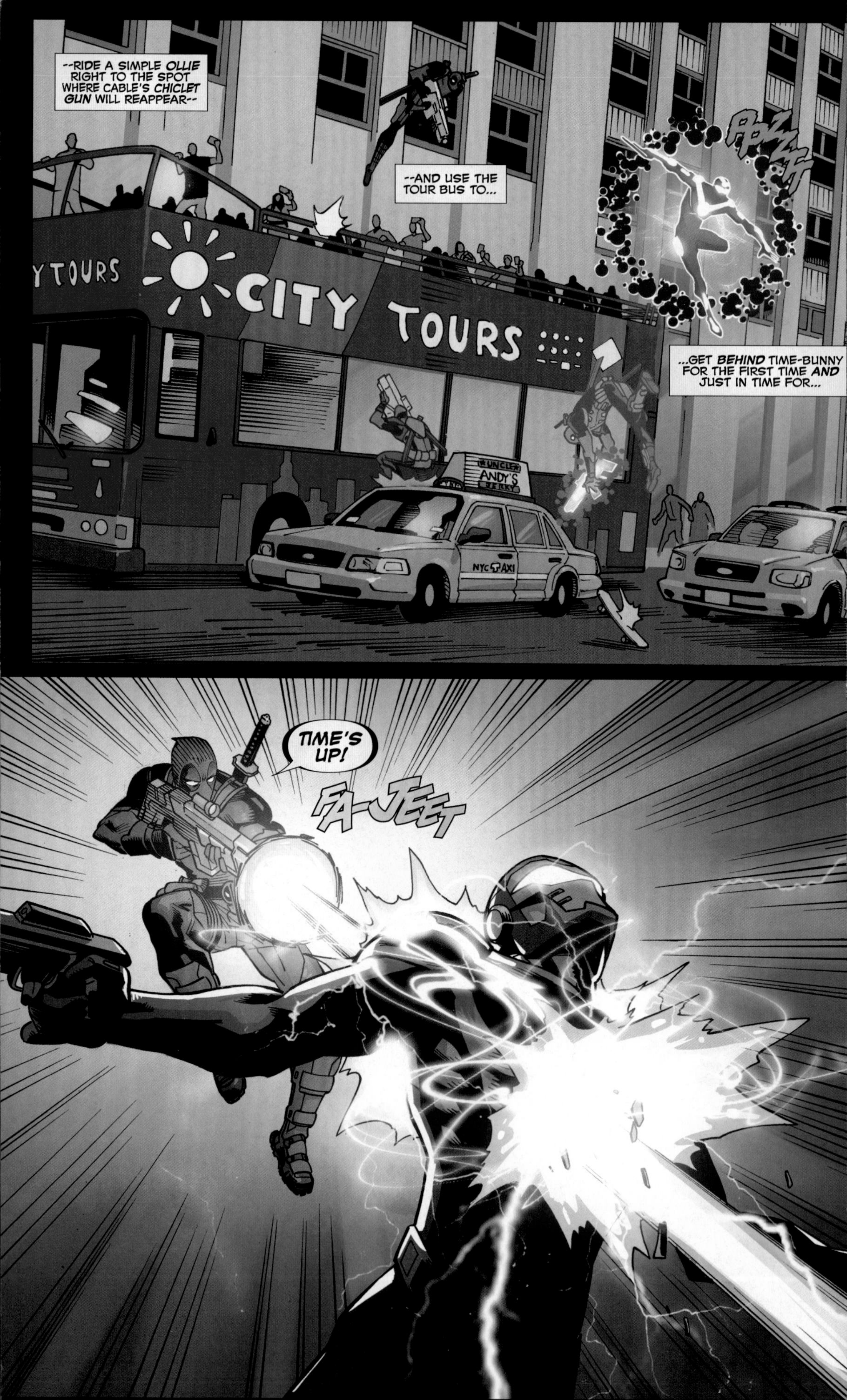
--RIDE A SIMPLE OLLIE RIGHT TO THE SPOT WHERE CABLE'S CHICLET GUN WILL REAPPEAR--
--AND USE THE TOUR BUS TO...
...GET BEHIND TIME-BUNNY FOR THE FIRST TIME AND JUST IN TIME FOR...
CITY TOURS
YTOURS
UNCLE ANDY'S
NYC TAXI
TIME'S UP!
FA-JEET

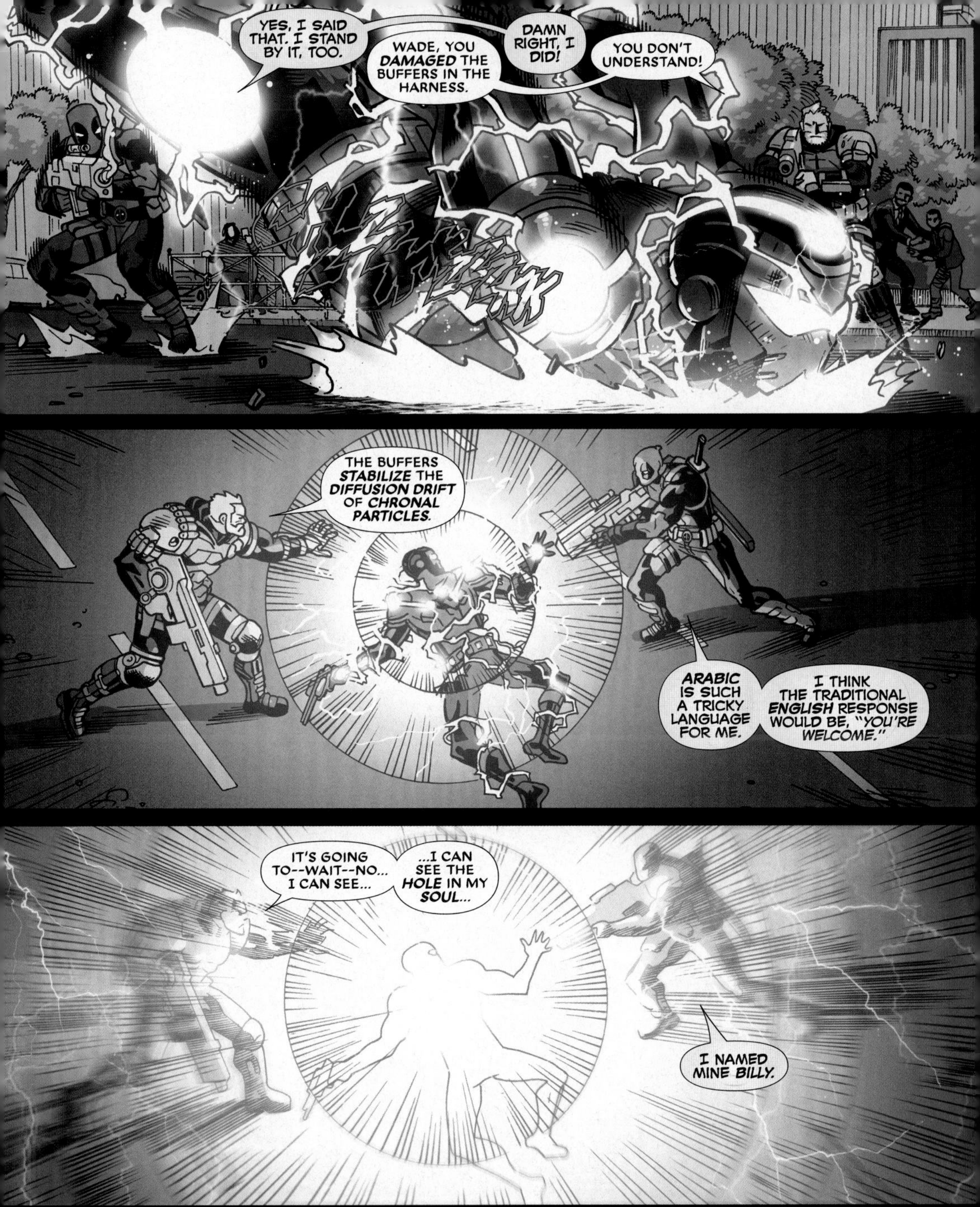
YES, I SAID THAT. I STAND BY IT, TOO.
WADE, YOU DAMAGED THE BUFFERS IN THE HARNESS.
DAMN RIGHT, I DID!
YOU DON'T UNDERSTAND!
THE BUFFERS STABILIZE THE DIFFUSION DRIFT OF CHRONAL PARTICLES.
ARABIC IS SUCH A TRICKY LANGUAGE FOR ME.
I THINK THE TRADITIONAL ENGLISH RESPONSE WOULD BE, "YOU'RE WELCOME."
IT'S GOING TO--WAIT--NO... I CAN SEE...
...I CAN SEE THE HOLE IN MY SOUL...
I NAMED MINE BILLY.

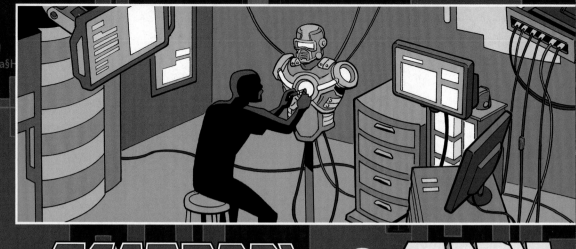

DEADPOOL & CABLE

DAILY BUGLE

Time Hole Bites Big Apple

AVENGERS VANISH IN TEMPORAL ANOMALY

SPLIT SECOND

CHAPTER FOUR:
THE FUTURE ISN'T
WHAT IT USED TO BE!

CARL
WEATHERS
R.I.P.

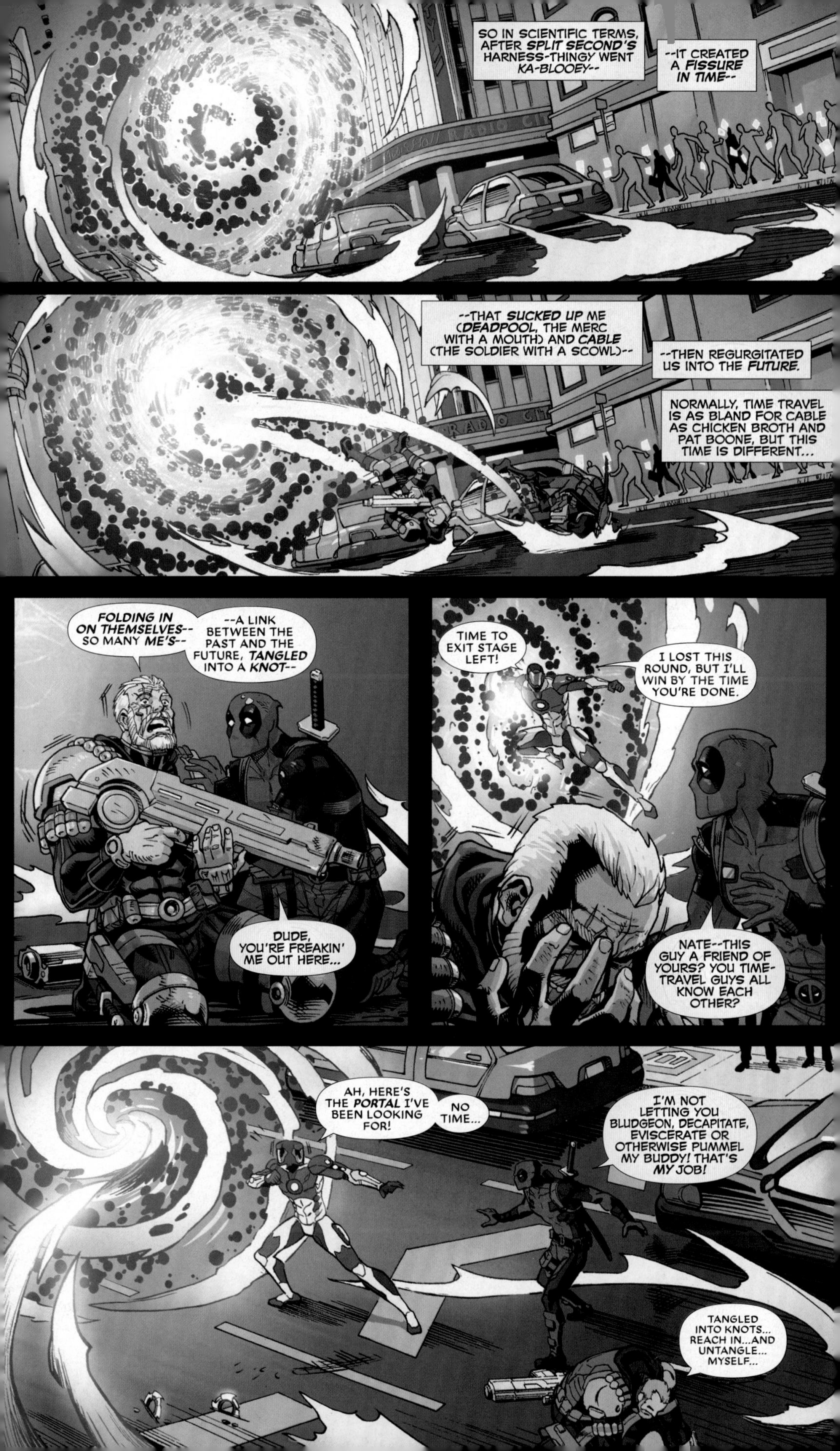
SO IN SCIENTIFIC TERMS, AFTER SPLIT SECOND'S HARNESS-THINGY WENT KA-BLOOEY--
--IT CREATED A FISSURE IN TIME--
--THAT SUCKED UP ME (DEADPOOL, THE MERC WITH A MOUTH) AND CABLE (THE SOLDIER WITH A SCOWL)--
--THEN REGURGITATED US INTO THE FUTURE.
NORMALLY, TIME TRAVEL IS AS BLAND FOR CABLE AS CHICKEN BROTH AND PAT BOONE, BUT THIS TIME IS DIFFERENT...
FOLDING IN ON THEMSELVES-- SO MANY ME'S--
--A LINK BETWEEN THE PAST AND THE FUTURE, TANGLED INTO A KNOT--
DUDE, YOU'RE FREAKIN' ME OUT HERE...
TIME TO EXIT STAGE LEFT!
I LOST THIS ROUND, BUT I'LL WIN BY THE TIME YOU'RE DONE.
NATE--THIS GUY A FRIEND OF YOURS? YOU TIME-TRAVEL GUYS ALL KNOW EACH OTHER?
AH, HERE'S THE PORTAL I'VE BEEN LOOKING FOR!
NO TIME...
I'M NOT LETTING YOU BLUDGEON, DECAPITATE, EVISCERATE OR OTHERWISE PUMMEL MY BUDDY! THAT'S MY JOB!
TANGLED INTO KNOTS... REACH IN...AND UNTANGLE... MYSELF...

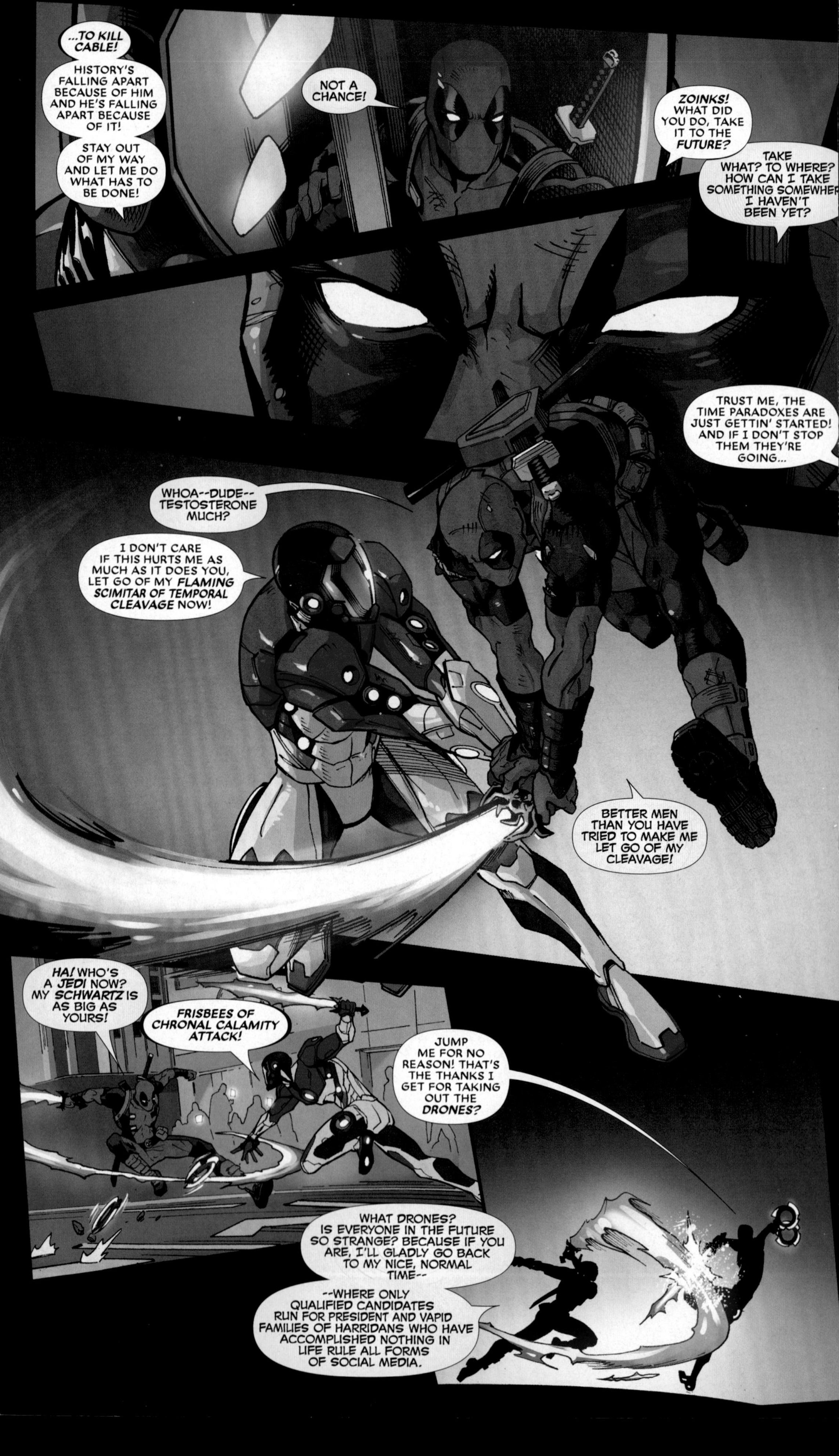
...TO KILL CABLE!
HISTORY'S FALLING APART BECAUSE OF HIM AND HE'S FALLING APART BECAUSE OF IT!
STAY OUT OF MY WAY AND LET ME DO WHAT HAS TO BE DONE!
NOT A CHANCE!
ZOINKS! WHAT DID YOU DO, TAKE IT TO THE FUTURE?
TAKE WHAT? TO WHERE? HOW CAN I TAKE SOMETHING SOMEWHER I HAVEN'T BEEN YET?
TRUST ME, THE TIME PARADOXES ARE JUST GETTIN' STARTED! AND IF I DON'T STOP THEM THEY'RE GOING...
WHOA--DUDE--TESTOSTERONE MUCH?
I DON'T CARE IF THIS HURTS ME AS MUCH AS IT DOES YOU, LET GO OF MY FLAMING SCIMITAR OF TEMPORAL CLEAVAGE NOW!
BETTER MEN THAN YOU HAVE TRIED TO MAKE ME LET GO OF MY CLEAVAGE!
HA! WHO'S A JEDI NOW? MY SCHWARTZ IS AS BIG AS YOURS!
FRISBEES OF CHRONAL CALAMITY ATTACK!
JUMP ME FOR NO REASON! THAT'S THE THANKS I GET FOR TAKING OUT THE DRONES?
WHAT DRONES? IS EVERYONE IN THE FUTURE SO STRANGE? BECAUSE IF YOU ARE, I'LL GLADLY GO BACK TO MY NICE, NORMAL TIME--
--WHERE ONLY QUALIFIED CANDIDATES RUN FOR PRESIDENT AND VAPID FAMILIES OF HARRIDANS WHO HAVE ACCOMPLISHED NOTHING IN LIFE RULE ALL FORMS OF SOCIAL MEDIA.

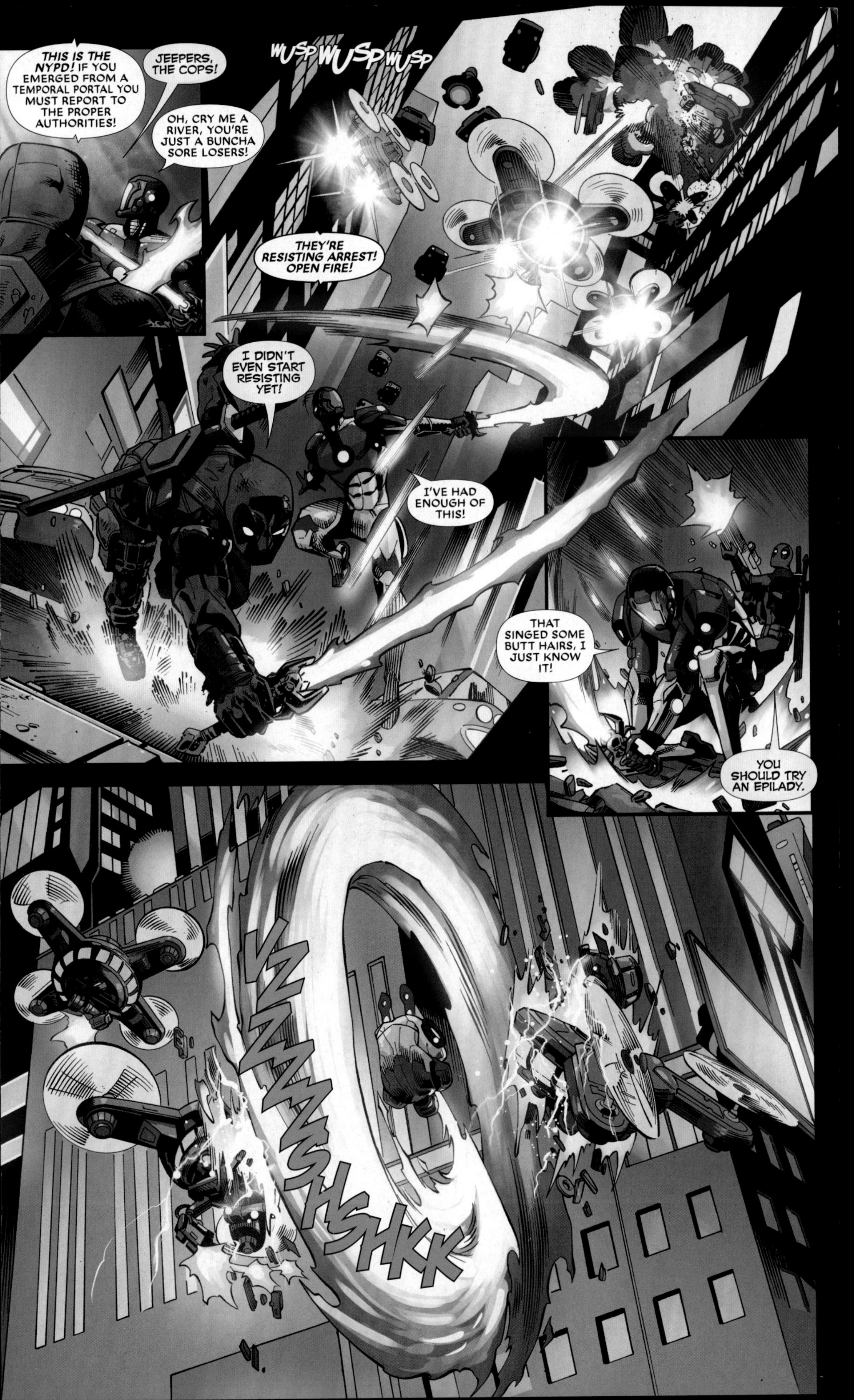
THIS IS THE NYPD! IF YOU EMERGED FROM A TEMPORAL PORTAL YOU MUST REPORT TO THE PROPER AUTHORITIES!
JEEPERS, THE COPS!
OH, CRY ME A RIVER, YOU'RE JUST A BUNCHA SORE LOSERS!
WUSP WUSP WUSP
THEY'RE RESISTING ARREST! OPEN FIRE!
I DIDN'T EVEN START RESISTING YET!
I'VE HAD ENOUGH OF THIS!
THAT SINGED SOME BUTT HAIRS, I JUST KNOW IT!
YOU SHOULD TRY AN EPILADY.
VZZZWWWSHSHKK

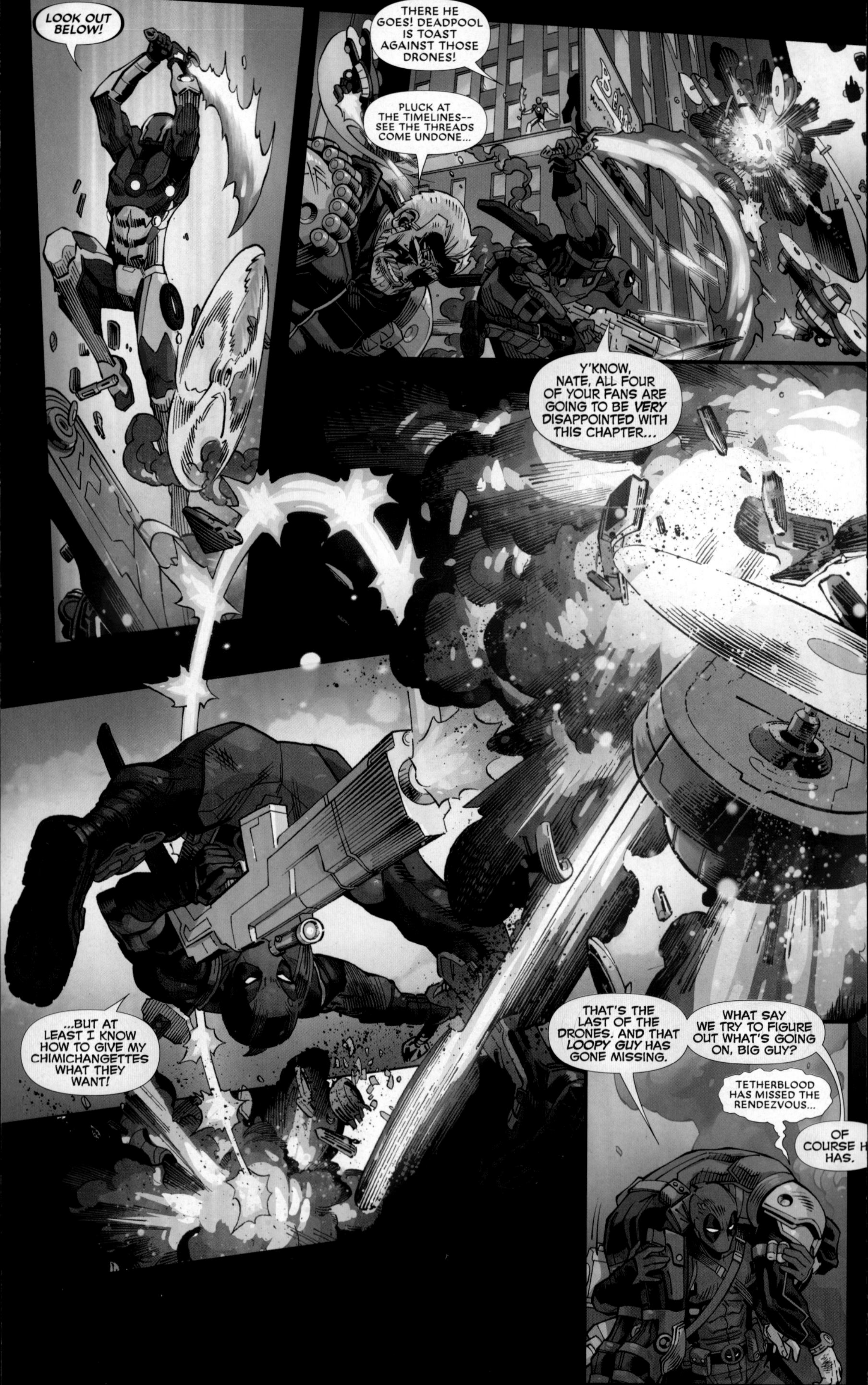
LOOK OUT BELOW!
THERE HE GOES! DEADPOOL IS TOAST AGAINST THOSE DRONES!
PLUCK AT THE TIMELINES-- SEE THE THREADS COME UNDONE...
Y'KNOW, NATE, ALL FOUR OF YOUR FANS ARE GOING TO BE VERY DISAPPOINTED WITH THIS CHAPTER...
...BUT AT LEAST I KNOW HOW TO GIVE MY CHIMICHANGETTES WHAT THEY WANT!
THAT'S THE LAST OF THE DRONES, AND THAT LOOPY GUY HAS GONE MISSING.
WHAT SAY WE TRY TO FIGURE OUT WHAT'S GOING ON, BIG GUY?
TETHERBLOOD HAS MISSED THE RENDEZVOUS...
OF COURSE H HAS.

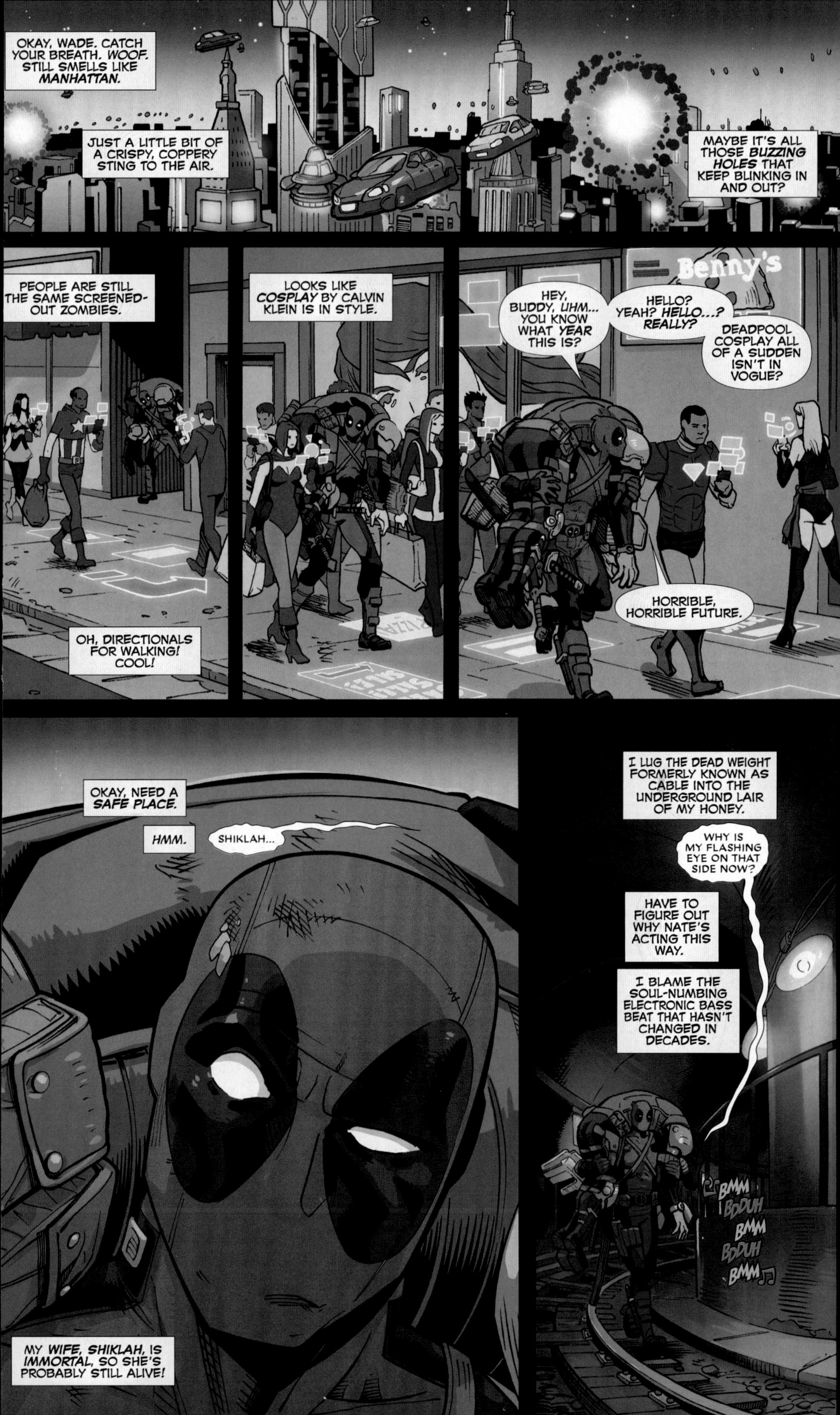

OKAY, WADE. CATCH YOUR BREATH. WOOF. STILL SMELLS LIKE MANHATTAN.
JUST A LITTLE BIT OF A CRISPY, COPPERY STING TO THE AIR.
MAYBE IT'S ALL THOSE BUZZING HOLES THAT KEEP BLINKING IN AND OUT?
PEOPLE ARE STILL THE SAME SCREENED-OUT ZOMBIES.
OH, DIRECTIONALS FOR WALKING! COOL!
LOOKS LIKE COSPLAY BY CALVIN KLEIN IS IN STYLE.
Benny's
HEY, BUDDY, UHM... YOU KNOW WHAT YEAR THIS IS?
HELLO? YEAH? HELLO...? REALLY?
DEADPOOL COSPLAY ALL OF A SUDDEN ISN'T IN VOGUE?
HORRIBLE, HORRIBLE FUTURE.
OKAY, NEED A SAFE PLACE.
HMM.
SHIKLAH...
MY WIFE, SHIKLAH, IS IMMORTAL, SO SHE'S PROBABLY STILL ALIVE!
I LUG THE DEAD WEIGHT FORMERLY KNOWN AS CABLE INTO THE UNDERGROUND LAIR OF MY HONEY.
WHY IS MY FLASHING EYE ON THAT SIDE NOW?
HAVE TO FIGURE OUT WHY NATE'S ACTING THIS WAY.
I BLAME THE SOUL-NUMBING ELECTRONIC BASS BEAT THAT HASN'T CHANGED IN DECADES.
BMM BDDUH BMM BDDUH BMM

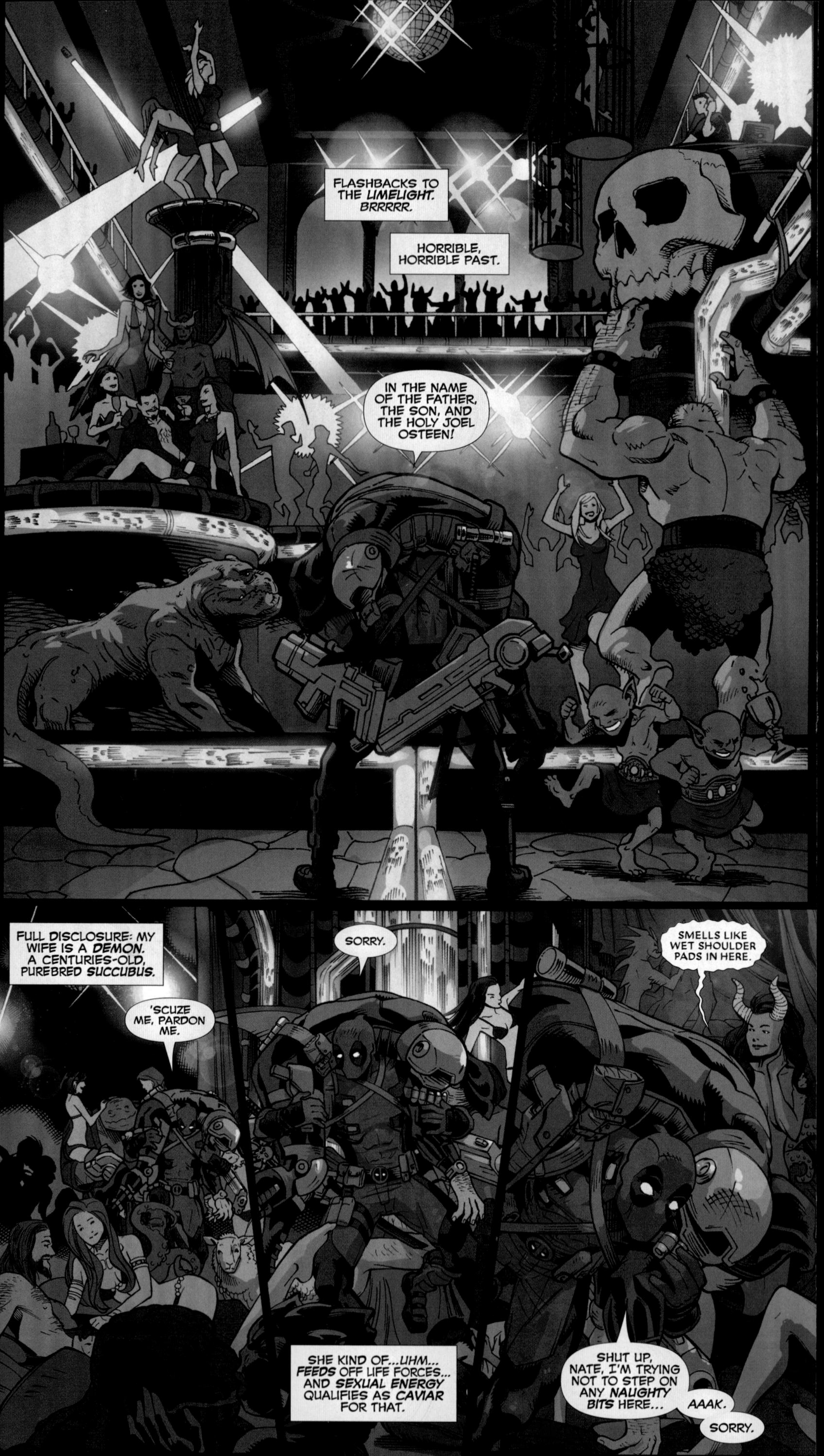
FLASHBACKS TO THE *LIMELIGHT.* *BRRRRR.*
HORRIBLE, HORRIBLE PAST.
IN THE NAME OF THE FATHER, THE SON, AND THE HOLY JOEL OSTEEN!
FULL DISCLOSURE: MY WIFE IS A ***DEMON.*** A CENTURIES-OLD, PUREBRED ***SUCCUBUS.***
'SCUZE ME, PARDON ME.
SORRY.
SMELLS LIKE WET SHOULDER PADS IN HERE.
SHE KIND OF...UHM... ***FEEDS*** OFF LIFE FORCES... AND ***SEXUAL ENERGY*** QUALIFIES AS ***CAVIAR*** FOR THAT.
SHUT UP, NATE, I'M TRYING NOT TO STEP ON ANY ***NAUGHTY BITS*** HERE...
AAAK.
SORRY.

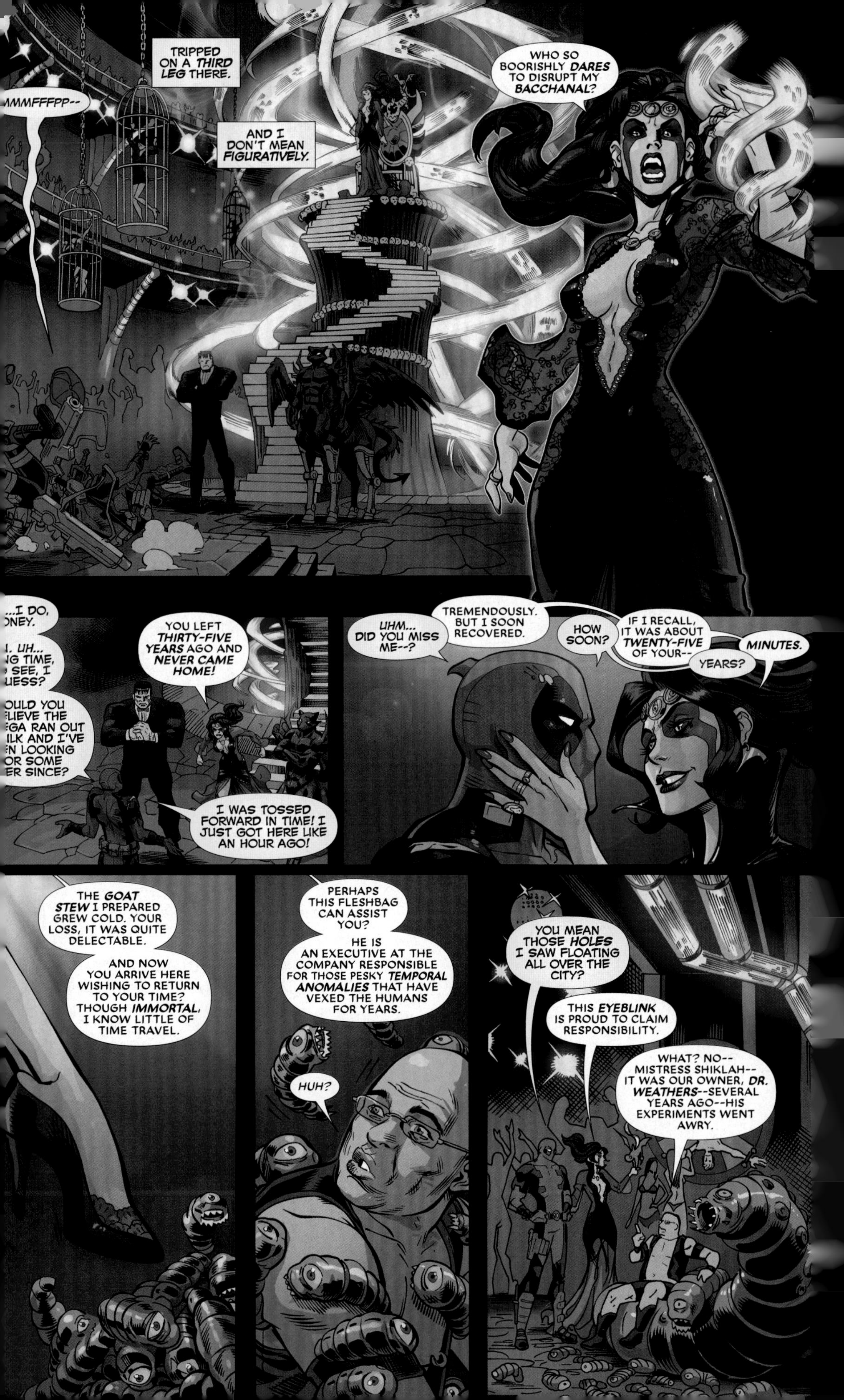

TRIPPED ON A THIRD LEG THERE.
MMMFFFPP--
AND I DON'T MEAN FIGURATIVELY.
WHO SO BOORISHLY DARES TO DISRUPT MY BACCHANAL?
...I DO, ONEY.
. UH... IG TIME, SEE, I UESS?
OULD YOU ELIEVE THE EGA RAN OUT ILK AND I'VE EN LOOKING OR SOME ER SINCE?
YOU LEFT THIRTY-FIVE YEARS AGO AND NEVER CAME HOME!
I WAS TOSSED FORWARD IN TIME! I JUST GOT HERE LIKE AN HOUR AGO!
UHM... DID YOU MISS ME--?
TREMENDOUSLY. BUT I SOON RECOVERED.
HOW SOON?
IF I RECALL, IT WAS ABOUT TWENTY-FIVE OF YOUR--
YEARS?
MINUTES.
THE GOAT STEW I PREPARED GREW COLD. YOUR LOSS, IT WAS QUITE DELECTABLE.
AND NOW YOU ARRIVE HERE WISHING TO RETURN TO YOUR TIME? THOUGH IMMORTAL, I KNOW LITTLE OF TIME TRAVEL.
PERHAPS THIS FLESHBAG CAN ASSIST YOU?
HE IS AN EXECUTIVE AT THE COMPANY RESPONSIBLE FOR THOSE PESKY TEMPORAL ANOMALIES THAT HAVE VEXED THE HUMANS FOR YEARS.
HUH?
YOU MEAN THOSE HOLES I SAW FLOATING ALL OVER THE CITY?
THIS EYEBLINK IS PROUD TO CLAIM RESPONSIBILITY.
WHAT? NO-- MISTRESS SHIKLAH-- IT WAS OUR OWNER, DR. WEATHERS--SEVERAL YEARS AGO--HIS EXPERIMENTS WENT AWRY.

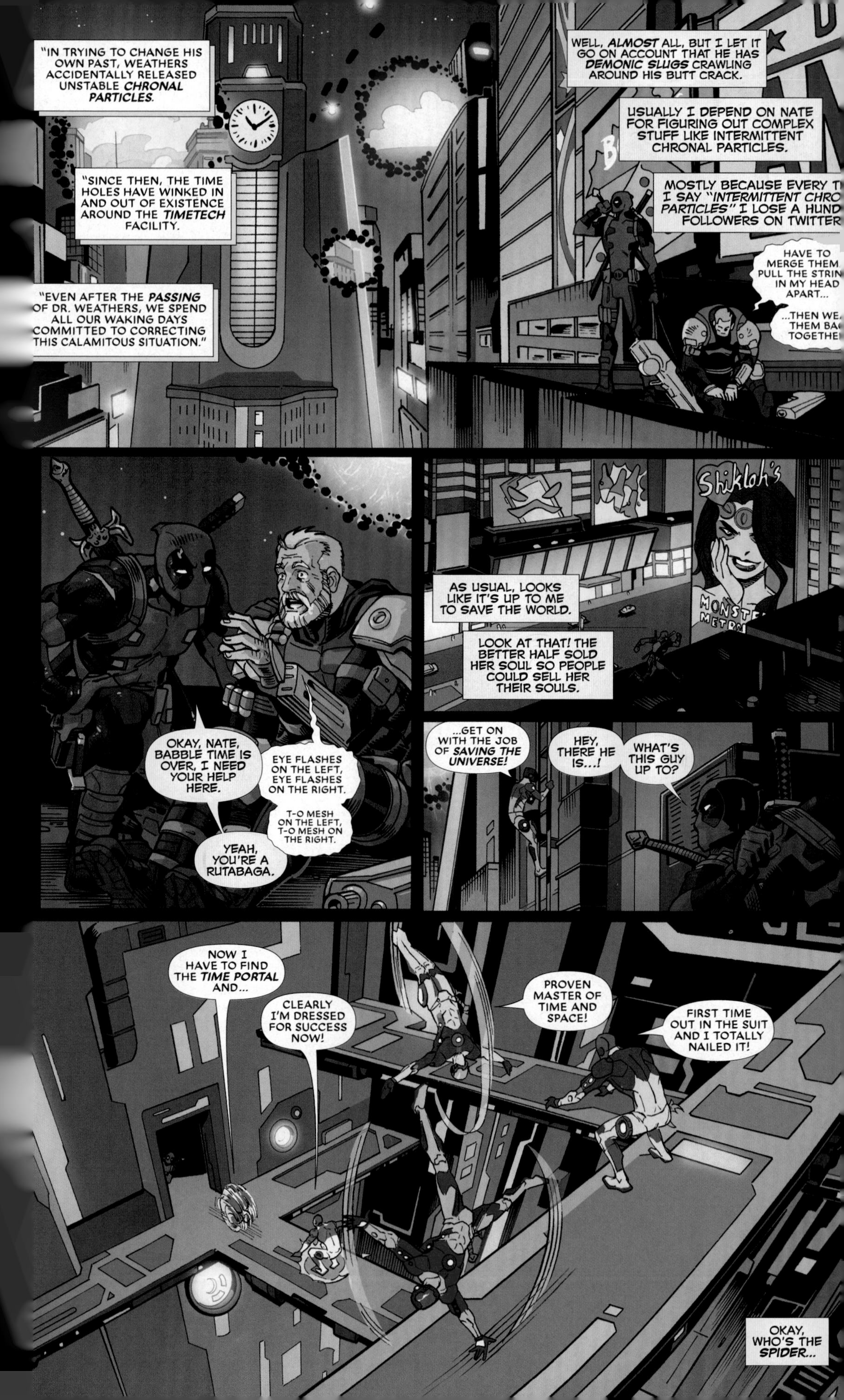
"IN TRYING TO CHANGE HIS OWN PAST, WEATHERS ACCIDENTALLY RELEASED UNSTABLE CHRONAL PARTICLES.
"SINCE THEN, THE TIME HOLES HAVE WINKED IN AND OUT OF EXISTENCE AROUND THE TIMETECH FACILITY.
"EVEN AFTER THE PASSING OF DR. WEATHERS, WE SPEND ALL OUR WAKING DAYS COMMITTED TO CORRECTING THIS CALAMITOUS SITUATION."
WELL, ALMOST ALL, BUT I LET IT GO ON ACCOUNT THAT HE HAS DEMONIC SLUGS CRAWLING AROUND HIS BUTT CRACK.
USUALLY I DEPEND ON NATE FOR FIGURING OUT COMPLEX STUFF LIKE INTERMITTENT CHRONAL PARTICLES.
MOSTLY BECAUSE EVERY T
I SAY "INTERMITTENT CHRO
PARTICLES" I LOSE A HUND
FOLLOWERS ON TWITTER
HAVE TO MERGE THEM PULL THE STRIN IN MY HEAD APART...
...THEN WE THEM BA TOGETHE
OKAY, NATE, BABBLE TIME IS OVER, I NEED YOUR HELP HERE.
EYE FLASHES ON THE LEFT, EYE FLASHES ON THE RIGHT.
T-O MESH ON THE LEFT, T-O MESH ON THE RIGHT.
YEAH, YOU'RE A RUTABAGA.
Shikloh's
AS USUAL, LOOKS LIKE IT'S UP TO ME TO SAVE THE WORLD.
LOOK AT THAT! THE BETTER HALF SOLD HER SOUL SO PEOPLE COULD SELL HER THEIR SOULS.
...GET ON WITH THE JOB OF SAVING THE UNIVERSE!
HEY, THERE HE IS...!
WHAT'S THIS GUY UP TO?
NOW I HAVE TO FIND THE TIME PORTAL AND...
CLEARLY I'M DRESSED FOR SUCCESS NOW!
PROVEN MASTER OF TIME AND SPACE!
FIRST TIME OUT IN THE SUIT AND I TOTALLY NAILED IT!
OKAY, WHO'S THE SPIDER...

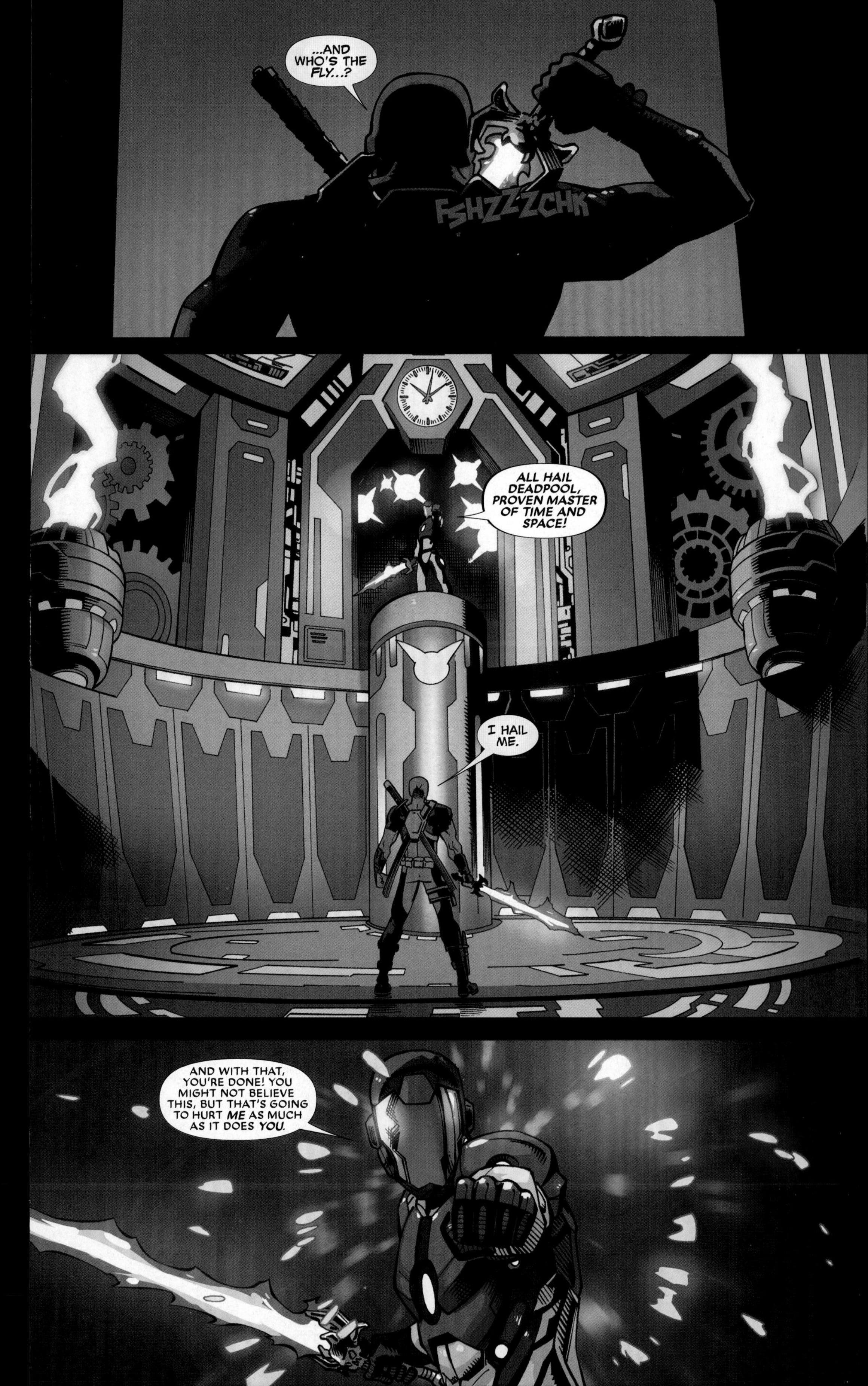
...AND WHO'S THE *FLY*...?
FSHZZZCHK
ALL HAIL DEADPOOL, PROVEN MASTER OF TIME AND SPACE!
I HAIL ME.
AND WITH THAT, YOU'RE DONE! YOU MIGHT NOT BELIEVE THIS, BUT THAT'S GOING TO HURT *ME* AS MUCH AS IT DOES *YOU*.

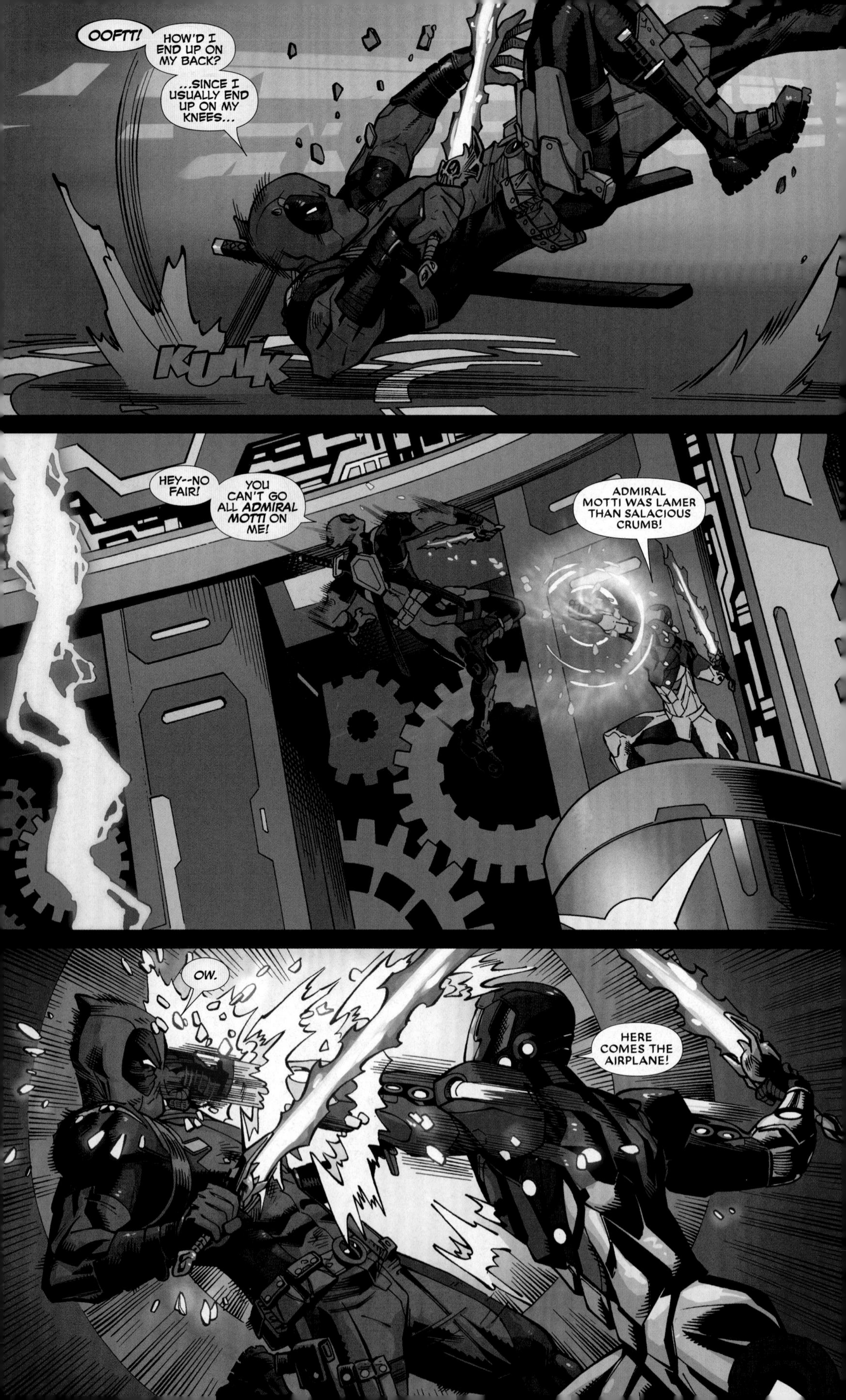
OOFTT!
HOW'D I END UP ON MY BACK?
...SINCE I USUALLY END UP ON MY KNEES...
KLUNK
HEY--NO FAIR!
YOU CAN'T GO ALL ADMIRAL MOTTI ON ME!
ADMIRAL MOTTI WAS LAMER THAN SALACIOUS CRUMB!
OW.
HERE COMES THE AIRPLANE!

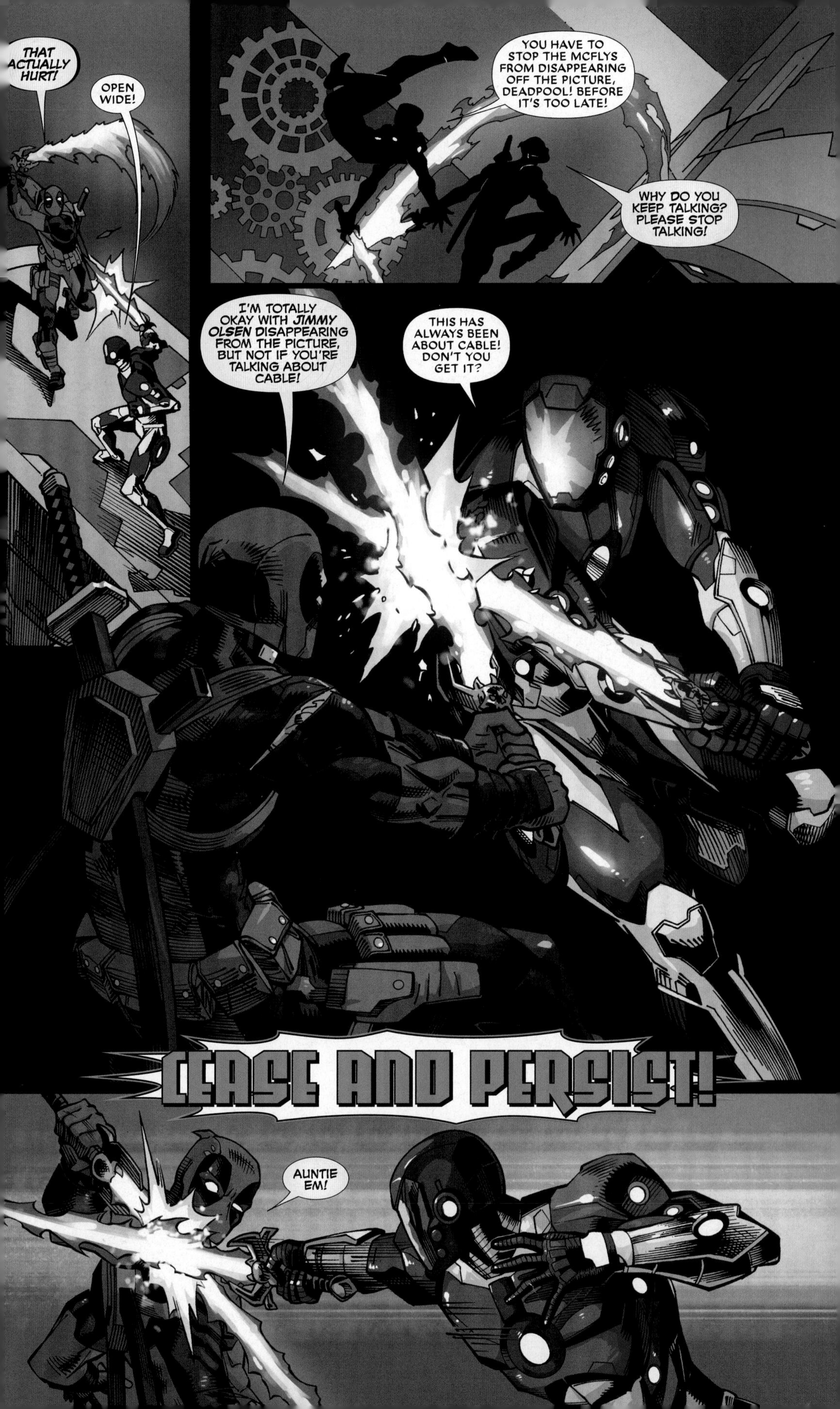

THAT ACTUALLY HURT!
OPEN WIDE!
YOU HAVE TO STOP THE MCFLYS FROM DISAPPEARING OFF THE PICTURE, DEADPOOL! BEFORE IT'S TOO LATE!
WHY DO YOU KEEP TALKING? PLEASE STOP TALKING!
I'M TOTALLY OKAY WITH JIMMY OLSEN DISAPPEARING FROM THE PICTURE, BUT NOT IF YOU'RE TALKING ABOUT CABLE!
THIS HAS ALWAYS BEEN ABOUT CABLE! DON'T YOU GET IT?
CEASE AND PERSIST!
AUNTIE EM!

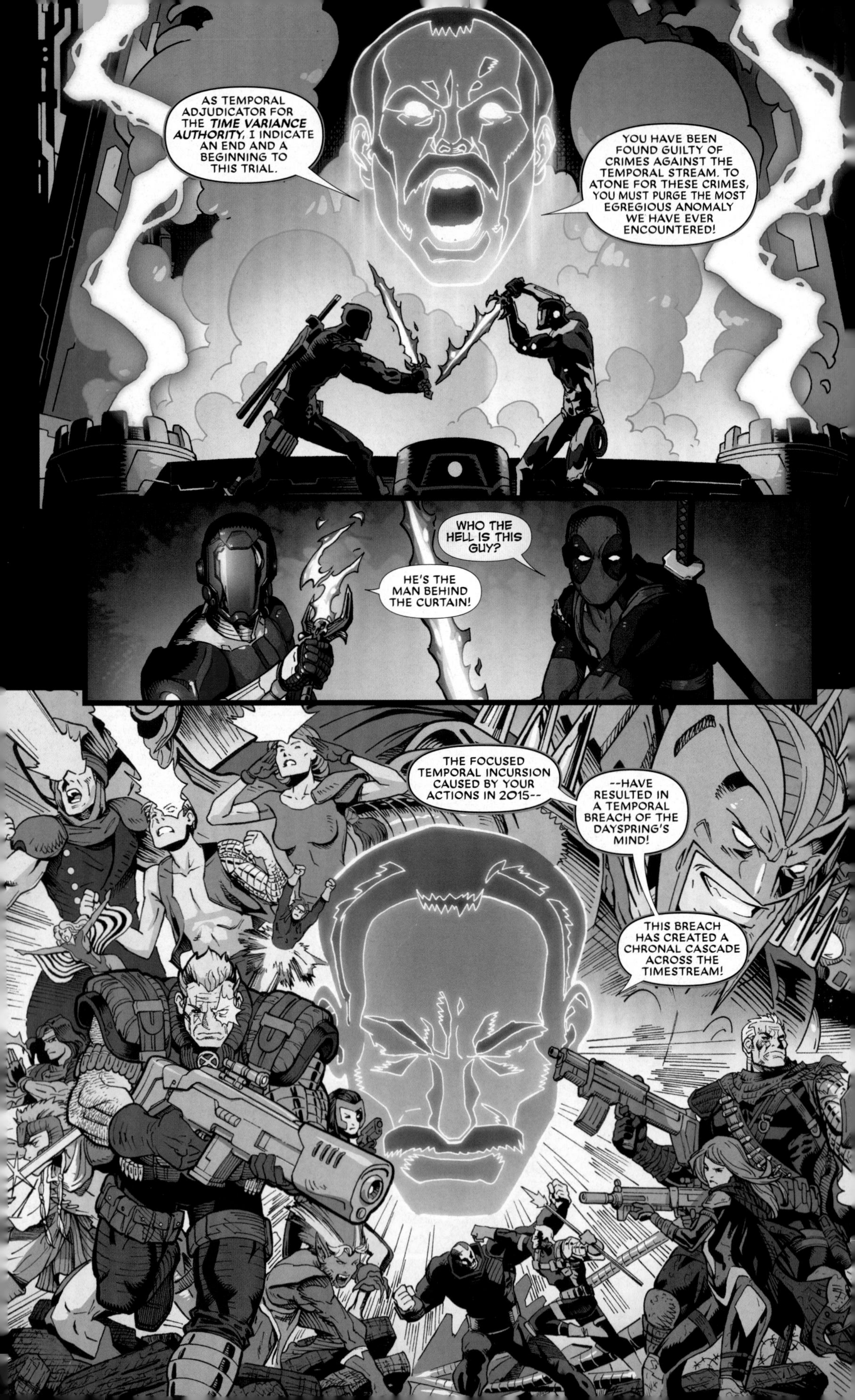
AS TEMPORAL ADJUDICATOR FOR THE *TIME VARIANCE AUTHORITY*, I INDICATE AN END AND A BEGINNING TO THIS TRIAL.
YOU HAVE BEEN FOUND GUILTY OF CRIMES AGAINST THE TEMPORAL STREAM. TO ATONE FOR THESE CRIMES, YOU MUST PURGE THE MOST EGREGIOUS ANOMALY WE HAVE EVER ENCOUNTERED!
WHO THE HELL IS THIS GUY?
HE'S THE MAN BEHIND THE CURTAIN!
THE FOCUSED TEMPORAL INCURSION CAUSED BY YOUR ACTIONS IN 2015--
--HAVE RESULTED IN A TEMPORAL BREACH OF THE DAYSPRING'S MIND!
THIS BREACH HAS CREATED A CHRONAL CASCADE ACROSS THE TIMESTREAM!

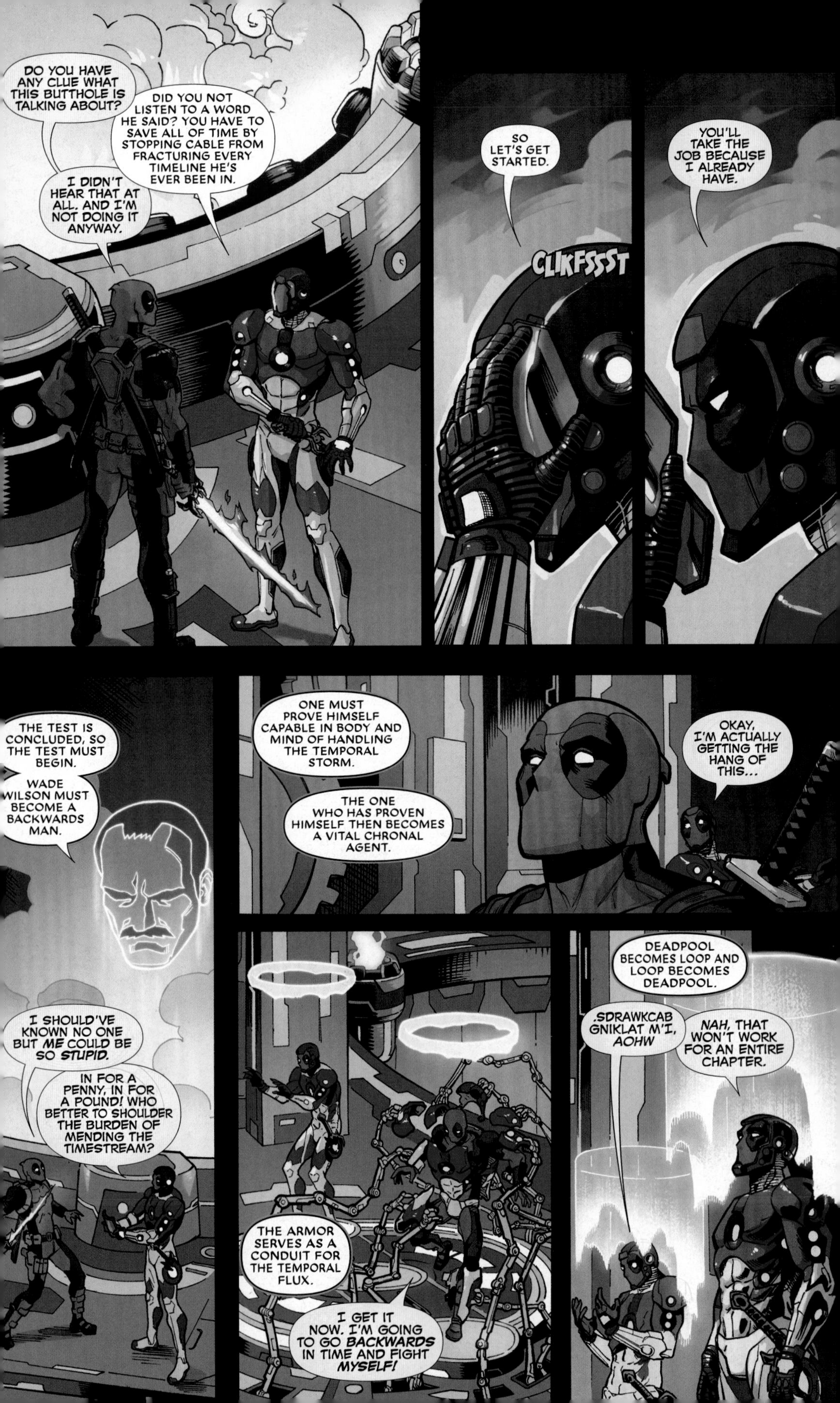
DO YOU HAVE ANY CLUE WHAT THIS BUTTHOLE IS TALKING ABOUT?
DID YOU NOT LISTEN TO A WORD HE SAID? YOU HAVE TO SAVE ALL OF TIME BY STOPPING CABLE FROM FRACTURING EVERY TIMELINE HE'S EVER BEEN IN.
I DIDN'T HEAR THAT AT ALL. AND I'M NOT DOING IT ANYWAY.
SO LET'S GET STARTED.
CLIKFSSST
YOU'LL TAKE THE JOB BECAUSE I ALREADY HAVE.
THE TEST IS CONCLUDED, SO THE TEST MUST BEGIN.
WADE WILSON MUST BECOME A BACKWARDS MAN.
ONE MUST PROVE HIMSELF CAPABLE IN BODY AND MIND OF HANDLING THE TEMPORAL STORM.
THE ONE WHO HAS PROVEN HIMSELF THEN BECOMES A VITAL CHRONAL AGENT.
OKAY, I'M ACTUALLY GETTING THE HANG OF THIS...
I SHOULD'VE KNOWN NO ONE BUT *ME* COULD BE SO *STUPID.*
IN FOR A PENNY, IN FOR A POUND! WHO BETTER TO SHOULDER THE BURDEN OF MENDING THE TIMESTREAM?
THE ARMOR SERVES AS A CONDUIT FOR THE TEMPORAL FLUX.
I GET IT NOW. I'M GOING TO GO *BACKWARDS* IN TIME AND FIGHT *MYSELF!*
DEADPOOL BECOMES LOOP AND LOOP BECOMES DEADPOOL.
.SDRAWKCAB GNIKLAT M'I, *AOHW*
NAH, THAT WON'T WORK FOR AN ENTIRE CHAPTER.

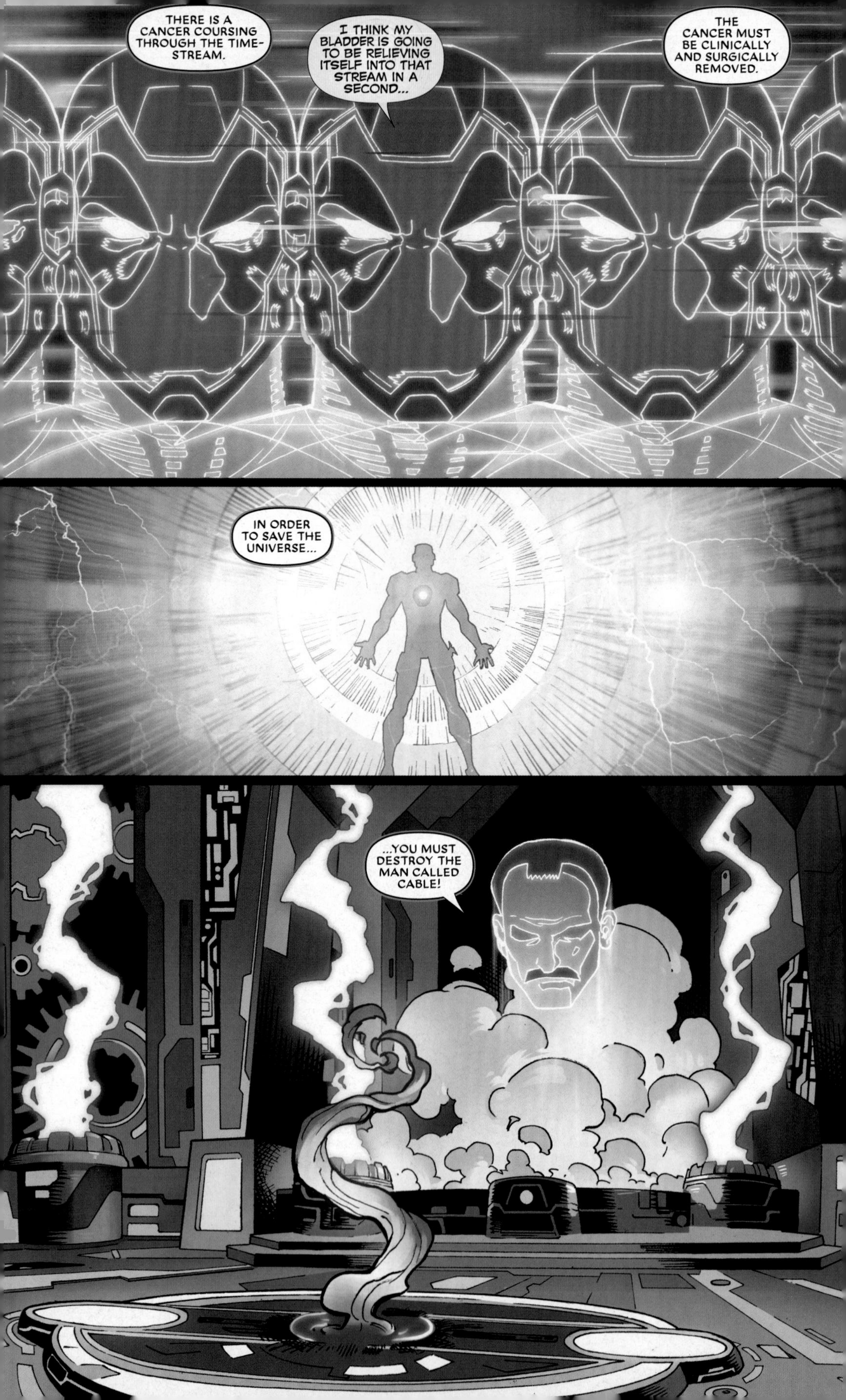
THERE IS A CANCER COURSING THROUGH THE TIME-STREAM.
I THINK MY BLADDER IS GOING TO BE RELIEVING ITSELF INTO THAT STREAM IN A SECOND...
THE CANCER MUST BE CLINICALLY AND SURGICALLY REMOVED.
IN ORDER TO SAVE THE UNIVERSE...
...YOU MUST DESTROY THE MAN CALLED CABLE!

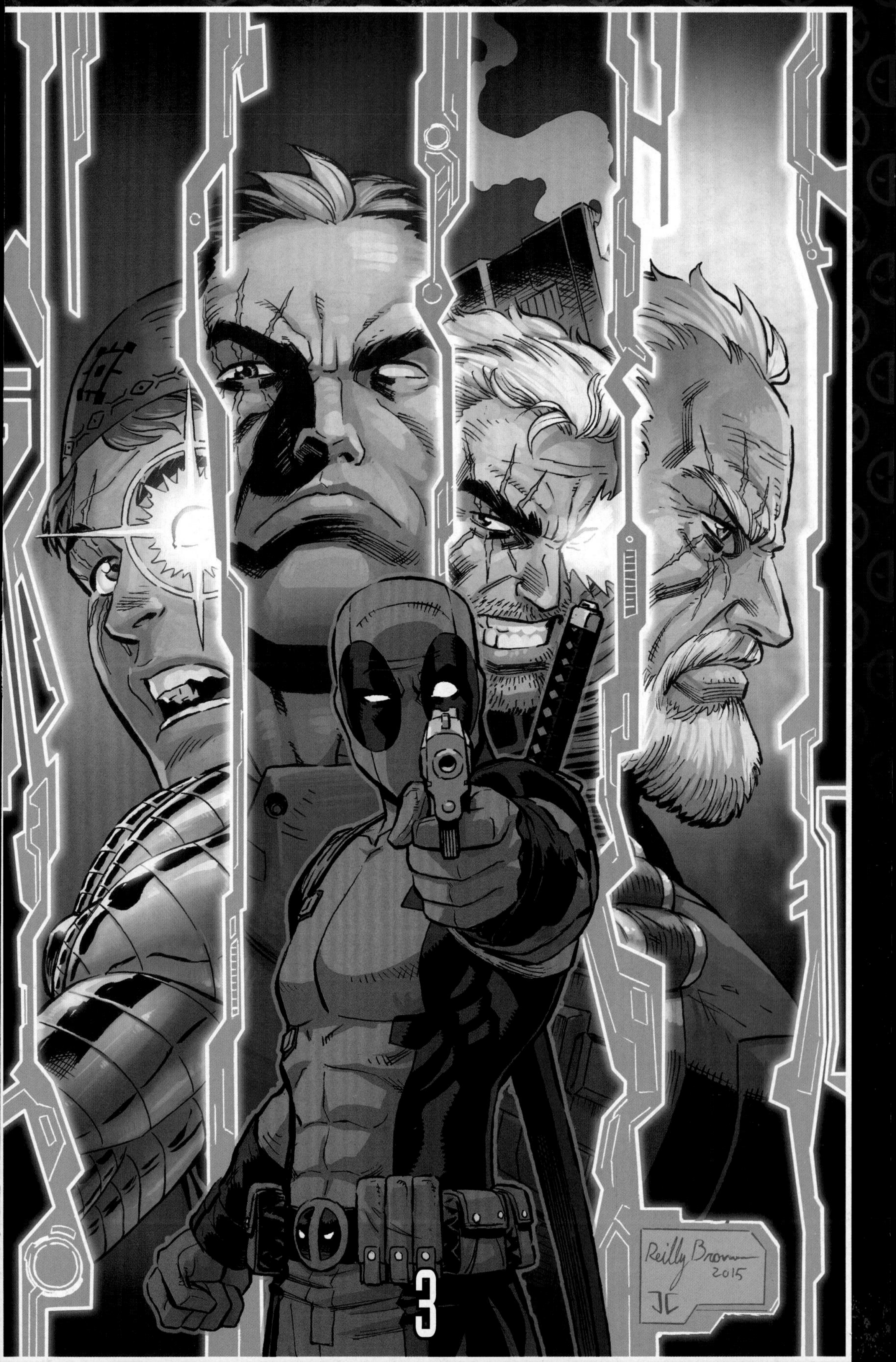
Reilly Brown
2015
JC
3

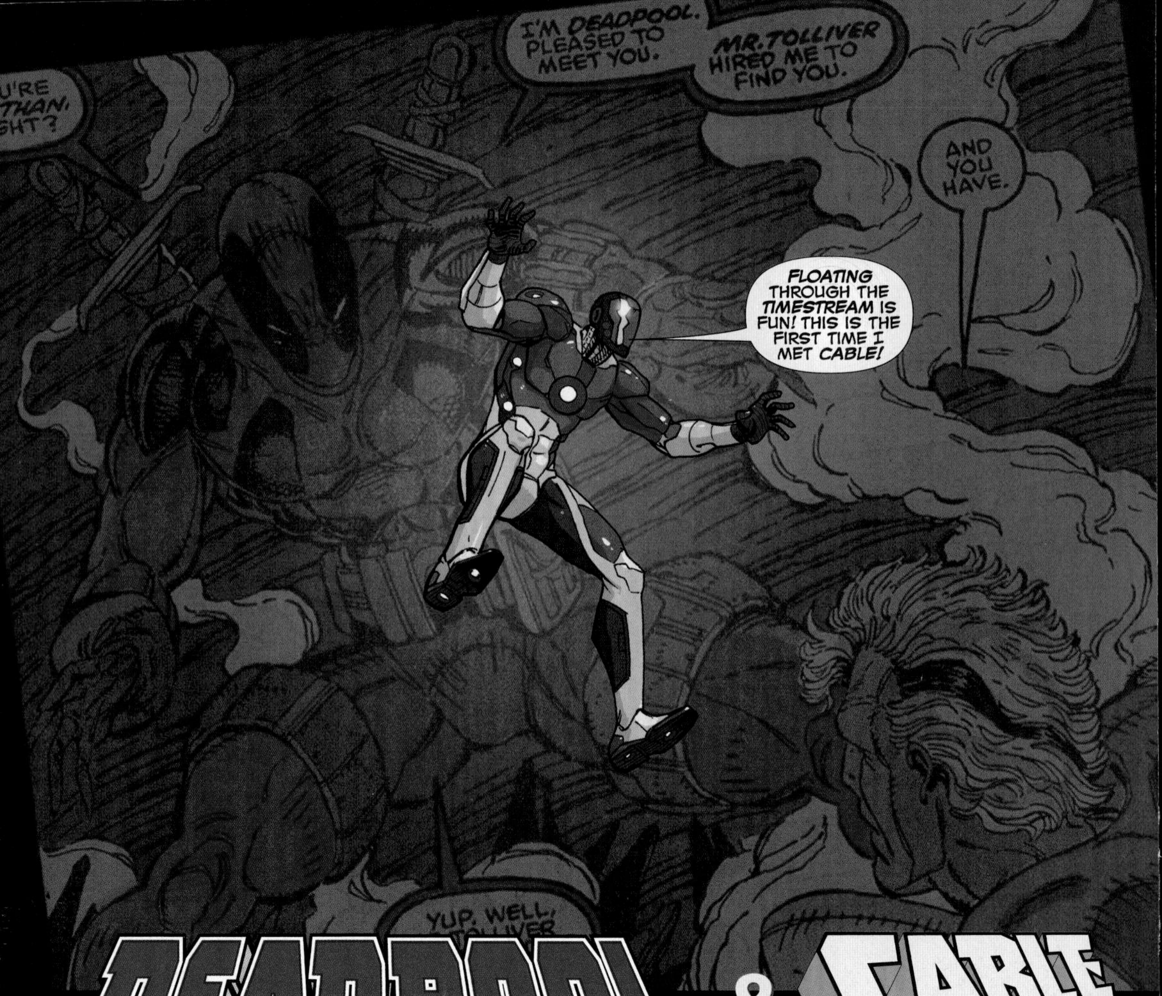
I'M DEADPOOL. PLEASED TO MEET YOU.
MR. TOLLIVER HIRED ME TO FIND YOU.
AND YOU HAVE.
FLOATING THROUGH THE TIMESTREAM IS FUN! THIS IS THE FIRST TIME I MET CABLE!

DEADPOOL & CABLE

SPLIT SECOND

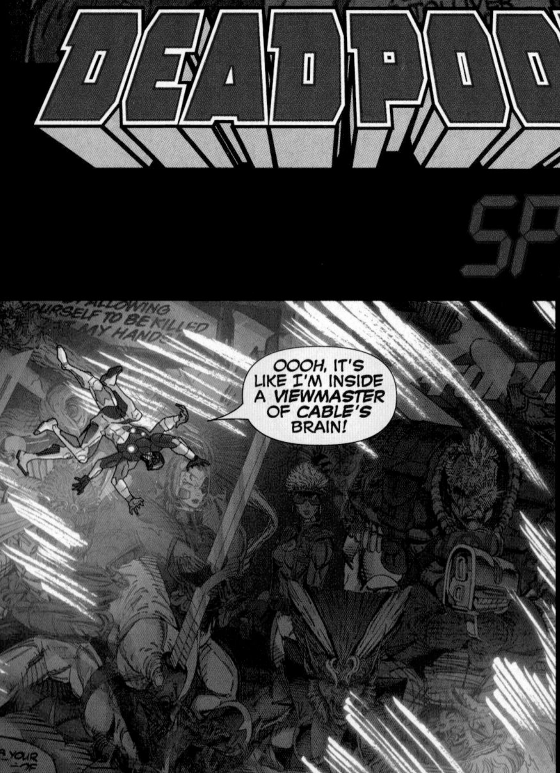
OOOH, IT'S LIKE I'M INSIDE A VIEWMASTER OF CABLE'S BRAIN!

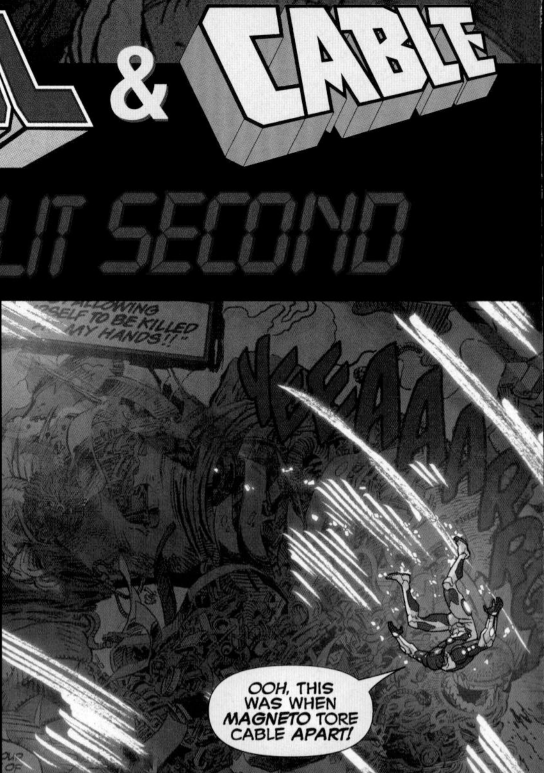
OOH, THIS WAS WHEN MAGNETO TORE CABLE APART!

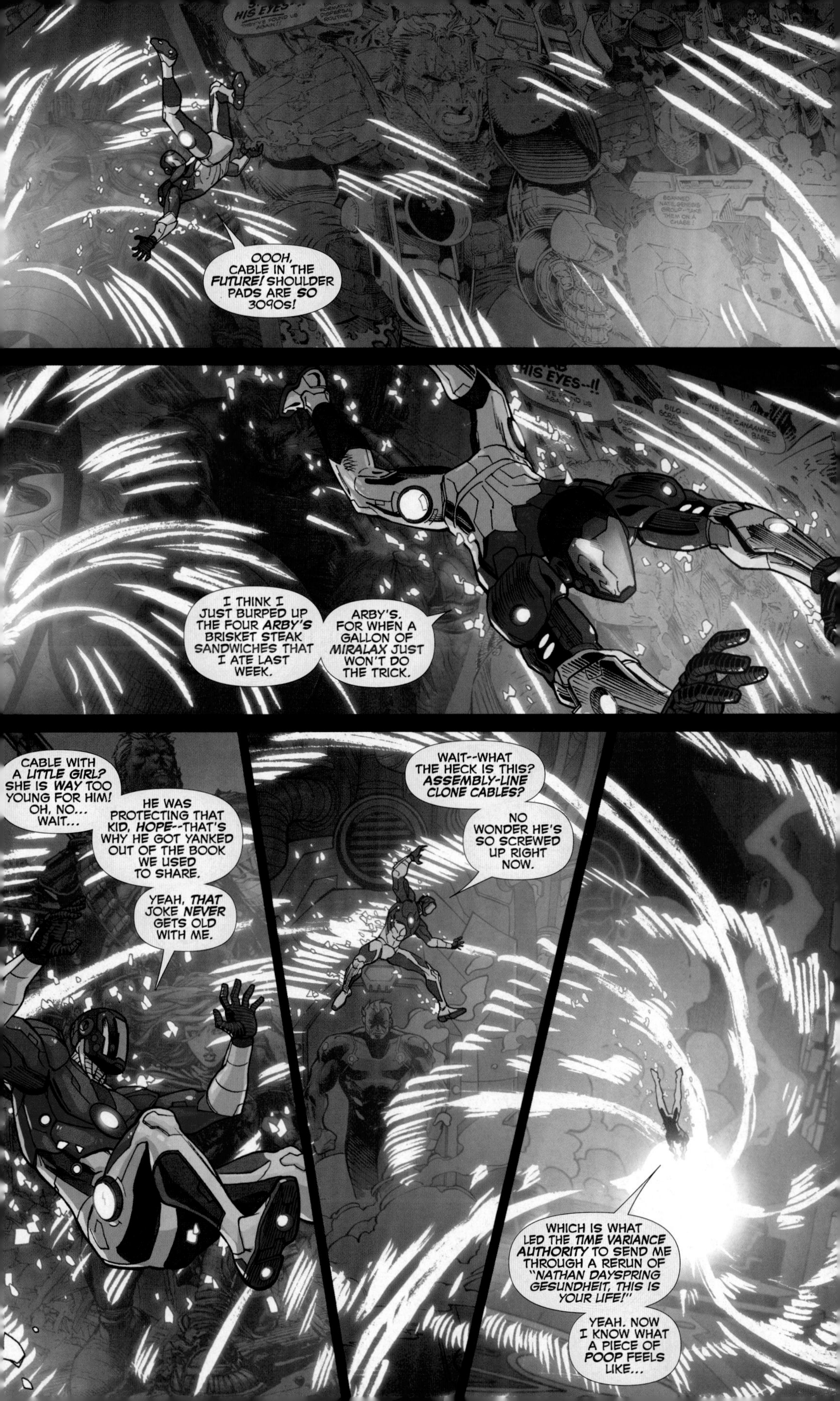
OOOH, CABLE IN THE FUTURE! SHOULDER PADS ARE SO 3090S!
HIS EYES--!!
I THINK I JUST BURPED UP THE FOUR ARBY'S BRISKET STEAK SANDWICHES THAT I ATE LAST WEEK.
ARBY'S. FOR WHEN A GALLON OF MIRALAX JUST WON'T DO THE TRICK.
CABLE WITH A LITTLE GIRL? SHE IS WAY TOO YOUNG FOR HIM! OH, NO... WAIT...
HE WAS PROTECTING THAT KID, HOPE--THAT'S WHY HE GOT YANKED OUT OF THE BOOK WE USED TO SHARE.
YEAH, THAT JOKE NEVER GETS OLD WITH ME.
WAIT--WHAT THE HECK IS THIS? ASSEMBLY-LINE CLONE CABLES?
NO WONDER HE'S SO SCREWED UP RIGHT NOW.
WHICH IS WHAT LED THE TIME VARIANCE AUTHORITY TO SEND ME THROUGH A RERUN OF "NATHAN DAYSPRING GESUNDHEIT, THIS IS YOUR LIFE!"
YEAH. NOW I KNOW WHAT A PIECE OF POOP FEELS LIKE...

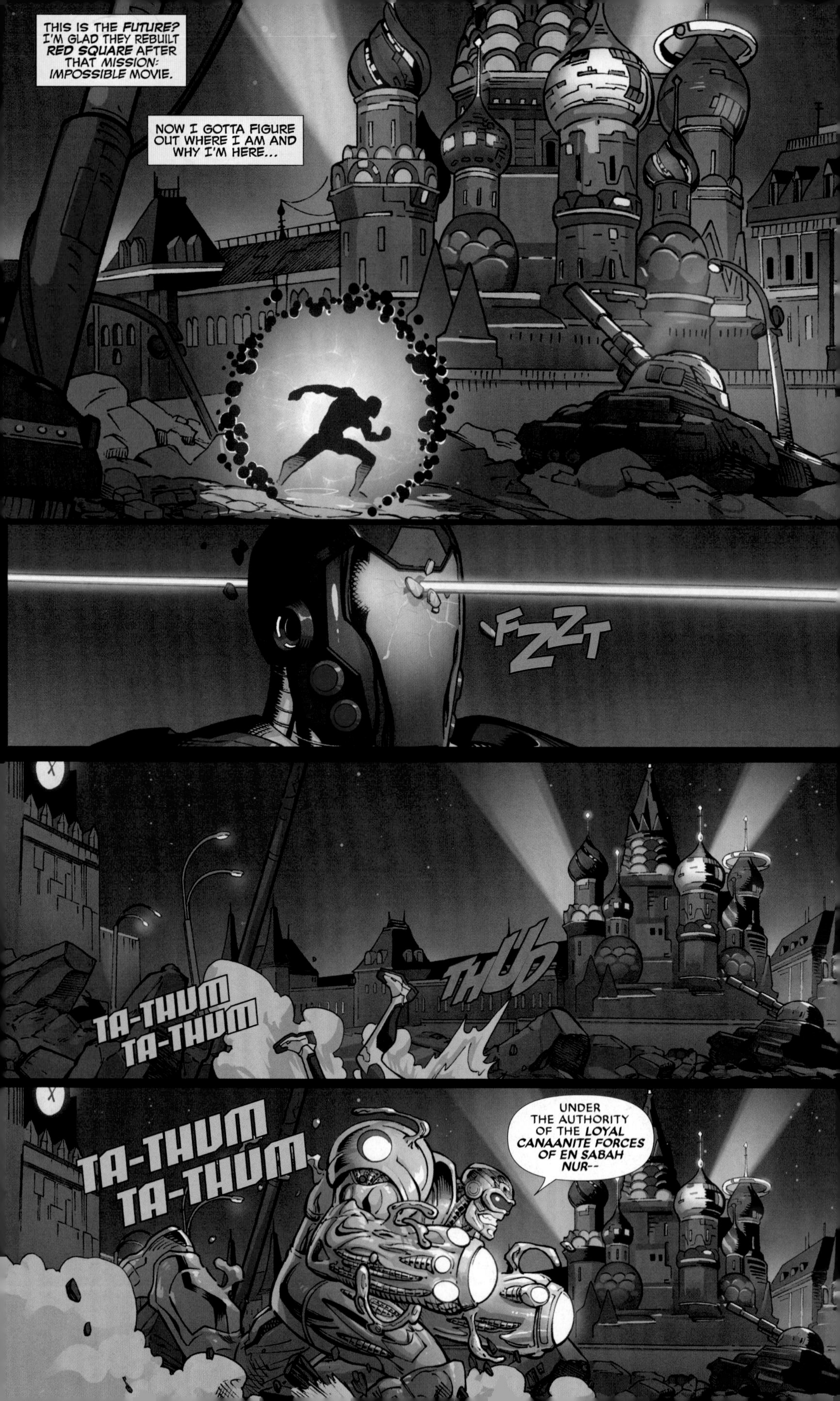

THIS IS THE FUTURE? I'M GLAD THEY REBUILT RED SQUARE AFTER THAT MISSION: IMPOSSIBLE MOVIE.
NOW I GOTTA FIGURE OUT WHERE I AM AND WHY I'M HERE...
FZZT
TA-THUM TA-THUM
THUD
TA-THUM TA-THUM
UNDER THE AUTHORITY OF THE LOYAL CANAANITE FORCES OF EN SABAH NUR--

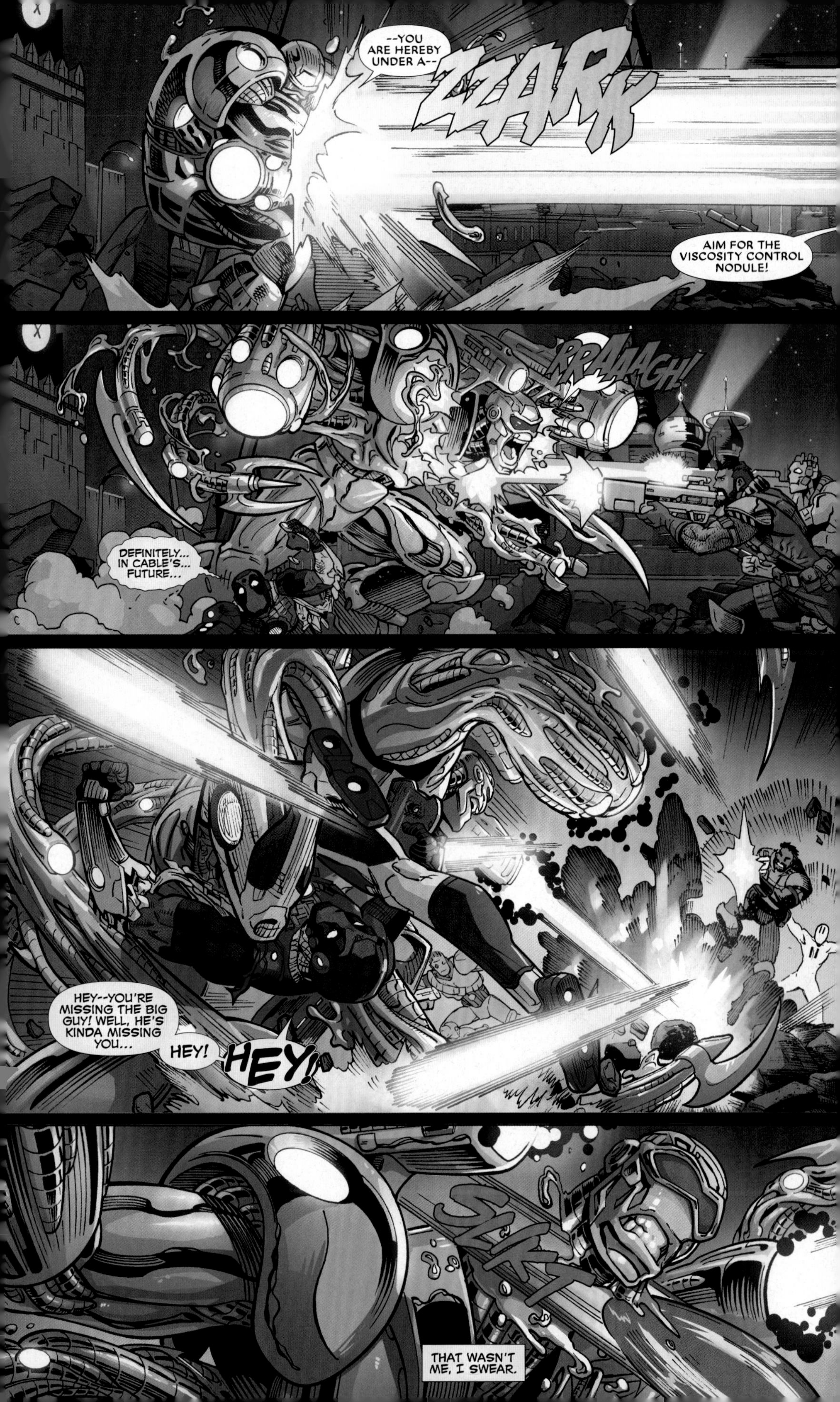
--YOU ARE HEREBY UNDER A--
ZZARK
AIM FOR THE VISCOSITY CONTROL NODULE!
RRAAAGH!
DEFINITELY... IN CABLE'S... FUTURE...
HEY--YOU'RE MISSING THE BIG GUY! WELL, HE'S KINDA MISSING YOU...
HEY!
HEY!
THAT WASN'T ME, I SWEAR.

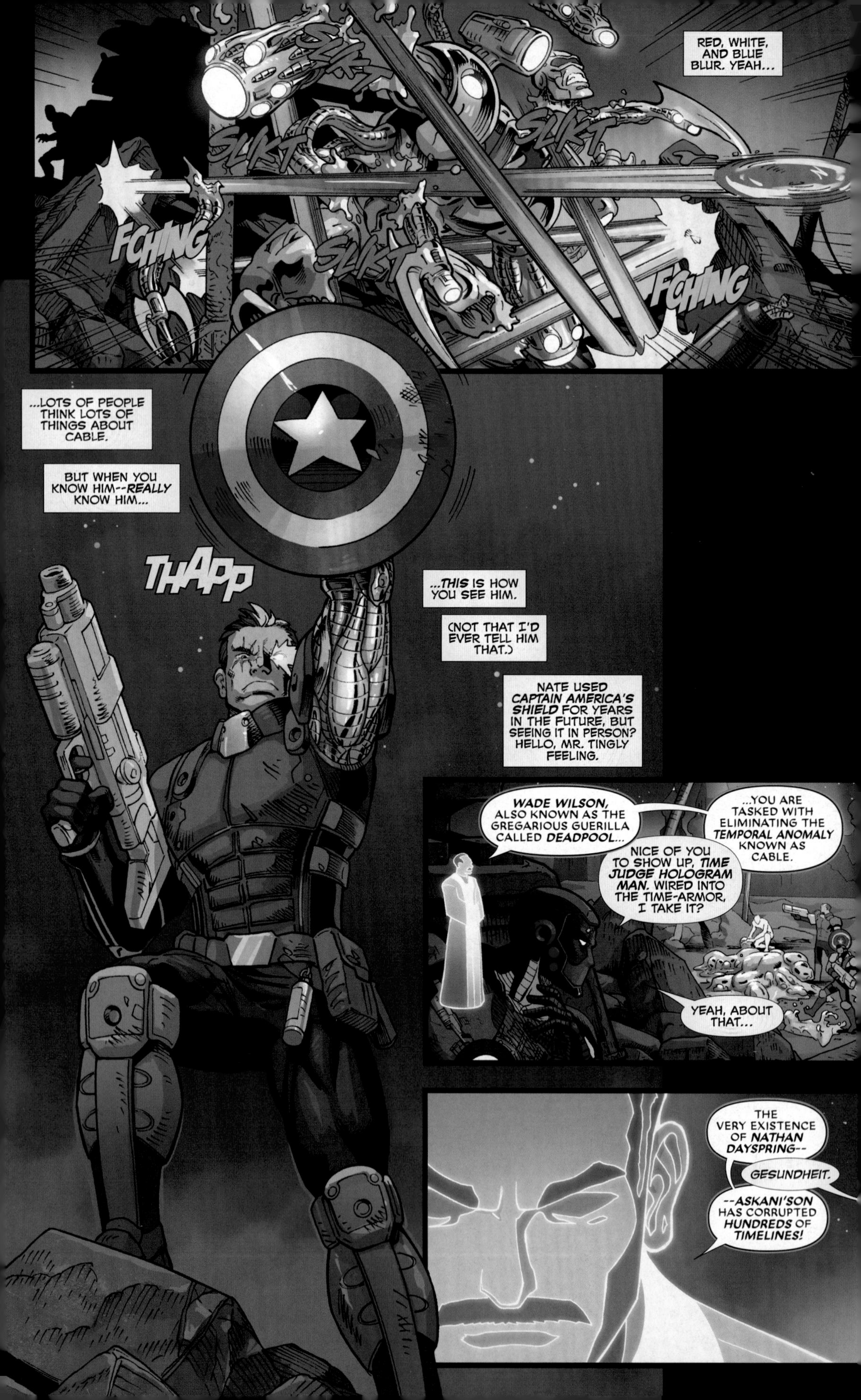
RED, WHITE, AND BLUE BLUR. YEAH...
SLIKT
SLIKT
SLIKT
SLIKT
FCHING
FCHING
...LOTS OF PEOPLE THINK LOTS OF THINGS ABOUT CABLE.
BUT WHEN YOU KNOW HIM--REALLY KNOW HIM...
THAPP
...THIS IS HOW YOU SEE HIM.
(NOT THAT I'D EVER TELL HIM THAT.)
NATE USED CAPTAIN AMERICA'S SHIELD FOR YEARS IN THE FUTURE, BUT SEEING IT IN PERSON? HELLO, MR. TINGLY FEELING.
WADE WILSON, ALSO KNOWN AS THE GREGARIOUS GUERILLA CALLED DEADPOOL...
...YOU ARE TASKED WITH ELIMINATING THE TEMPORAL ANOMALY KNOWN AS CABLE.
NICE OF YOU TO SHOW UP, TIME JUDGE HOLOGRAM MAN. WIRED INTO THE TIME-ARMOR, I TAKE IT?
YEAH, ABOUT THAT...
THE VERY EXISTENCE OF NATHAN DAYSPRING--
GESUNDHEIT.
--ASKANI'SON HAS CORRUPTED HUNDREDS OF TIMELINES!

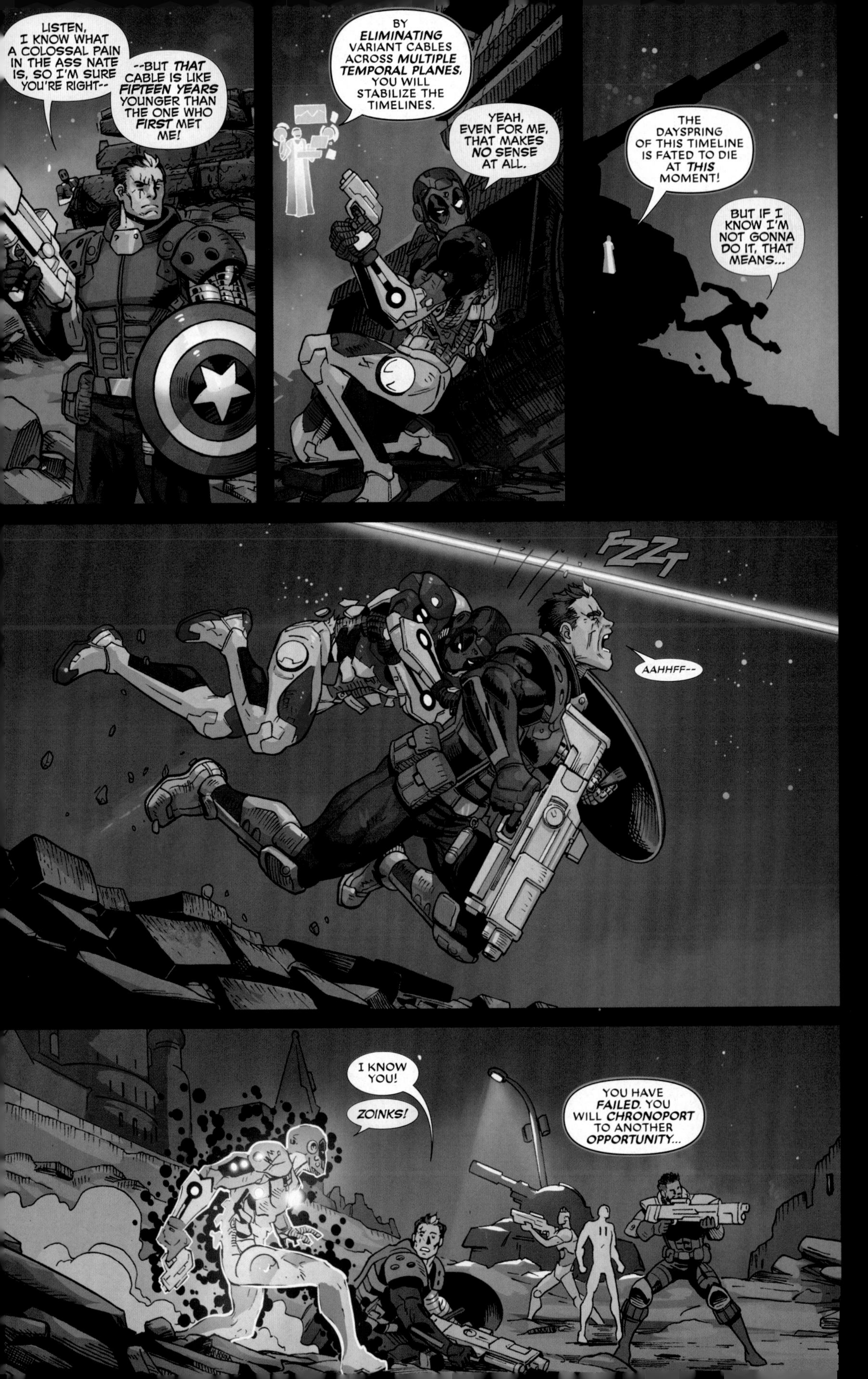

LISTEN, I KNOW WHAT A COLOSSAL PAIN IN THE ASS NATE IS, SO I'M SURE YOU'RE RIGHT--
--BUT *THAT* CABLE IS LIKE *FIFTEEN YEARS* YOUNGER THAN THE ONE WHO *FIRST* MET ME!
BY *ELIMINATING* VARIANT CABLES ACROSS *MULTIPLE TEMPORAL PLANES*, YOU WILL STABILIZE THE TIMELINES.
YEAH, EVEN FOR ME, THAT MAKES *NO SENSE* AT ALL.
THE DAYSPRING OF THIS TIMELINE IS FATED TO DIE AT *THIS* MOMENT!
BUT IF I KNOW I'M NOT GONNA DO IT, THAT MEANS...
FZZT
AAHHFF--
I KNOW YOU!
ZOINKS!
YOU HAVE *FAILED*. YOU WILL *CHRONOPORT* TO ANOTHER *OPPORTUNITY*...

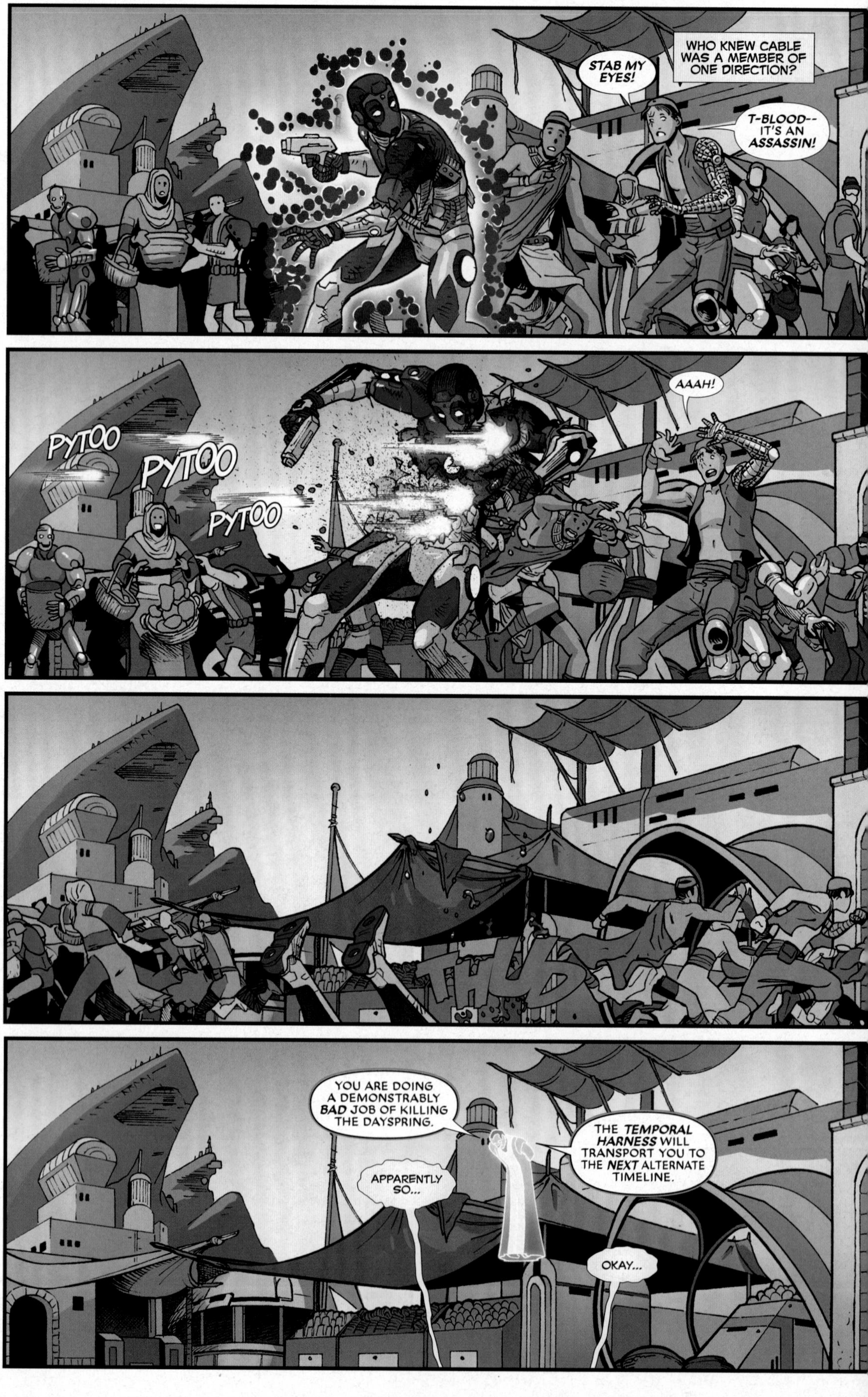
STAB MY EYES!
WHO KNEW CABLE WAS A MEMBER OF ONE DIRECTION?
T-BLOOD-- IT'S AN ASSASSIN!
AAAH!
PYTOO
PYTOO
PYTOO
THUD
YOU ARE DOING A DEMONSTRABLY BAD JOB OF KILLING THE DAYSPRING.
APPARENTLY SO...
THE TEMPORAL HARNESS WILL TRANSPORT YOU TO THE NEXT ALTERNATE TIMELINE.
OKAY...

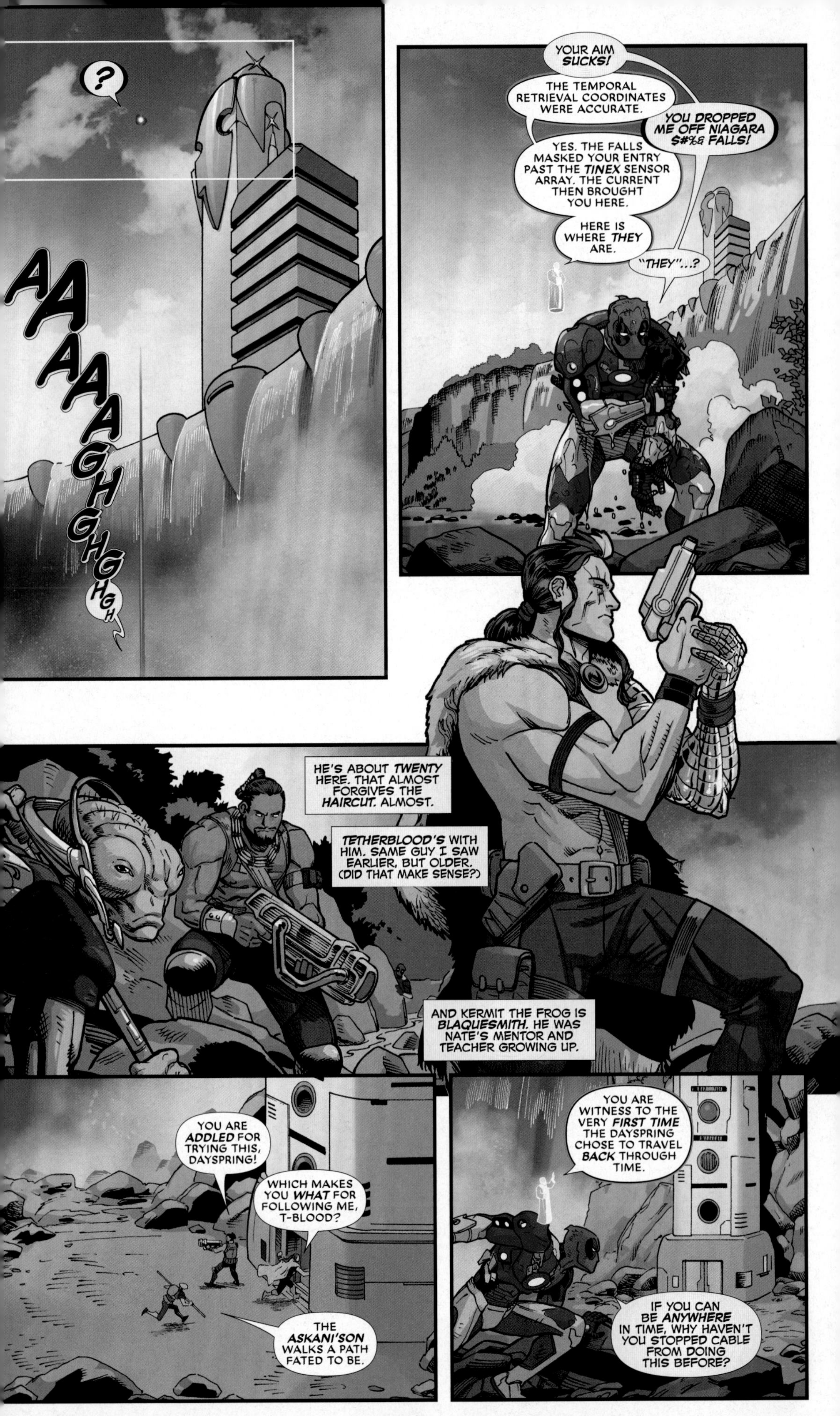
?
AAAAAAAGHGHGHGHGH
YOUR AIM SUCKS!
THE TEMPORAL RETRIEVAL COORDINATES WERE ACCURATE.
YOU DROPPED ME OFF NIAGARA $#%& FALLS!
YES. THE FALLS MASKED YOUR ENTRY PAST THE TINEX SENSOR ARRAY. THE CURRENT THEN BROUGHT YOU HERE.
HERE IS WHERE THEY ARE.
"THEY"...?
HE'S ABOUT TWENTY HERE. THAT ALMOST FORGIVES THE HAIRCUT. ALMOST.
TETHERBLOOD'S WITH HIM. SAME GUY I SAW EARLIER, BUT OLDER. (DID THAT MAKE SENSE?)
AND KERMIT THE FROG IS BLAQUESMITH. HE WAS NATE'S MENTOR AND TEACHER GROWING UP.
YOU ARE ADDLED FOR TRYING THIS, DAYSPRING!
WHICH MAKES YOU WHAT FOR FOLLOWING ME, T-BLOOD?
THE ASKANI'SON WALKS A PATH FATED TO BE.
YOU ARE WITNESS TO THE VERY FIRST TIME THE DAYSPRING CHOSE TO TRAVEL BACK THROUGH TIME.
IF YOU CAN BE ANYWHERE IN TIME, WHY HAVEN'T YOU STOPPED CABLE FROM DOING THIS BEFORE?

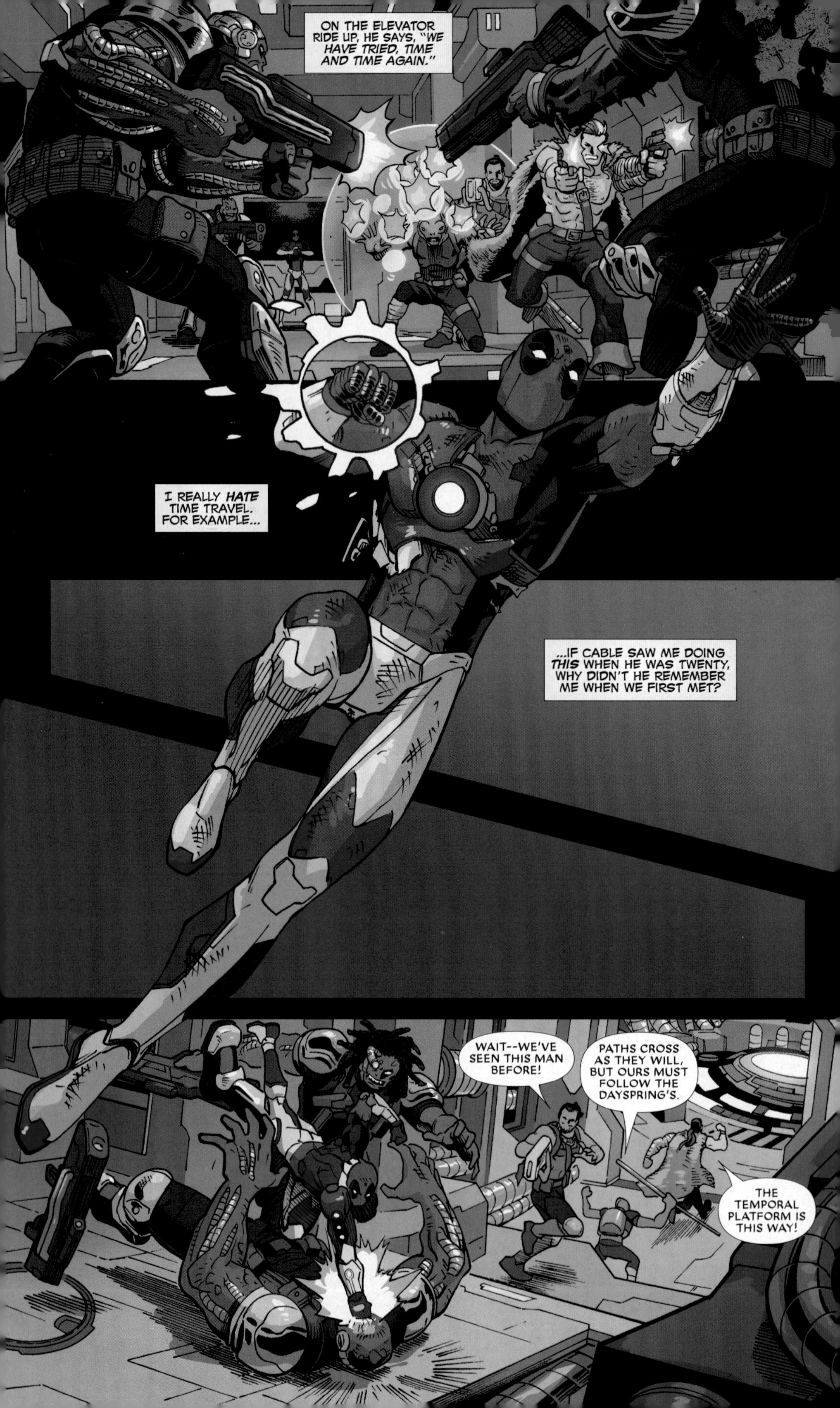
ON THE ELEVATOR RIDE UP, HE SAYS, "WE HAVE TRIED, TIME AND TIME AGAIN."
I REALLY HATE TIME TRAVEL. FOR EXAMPLE...
...IF CABLE SAW ME DOING THIS WHEN HE WAS TWENTY, WHY DIDN'T HE REMEMBER ME WHEN WE FIRST MET?
WAIT--WE'VE SEEN THIS MAN BEFORE!
PATHS CROSS AS THEY WILL, BUT OURS MUST FOLLOW THE DAYSPRING'S.
THE TEMPORAL PLATFORM IS THIS WAY!

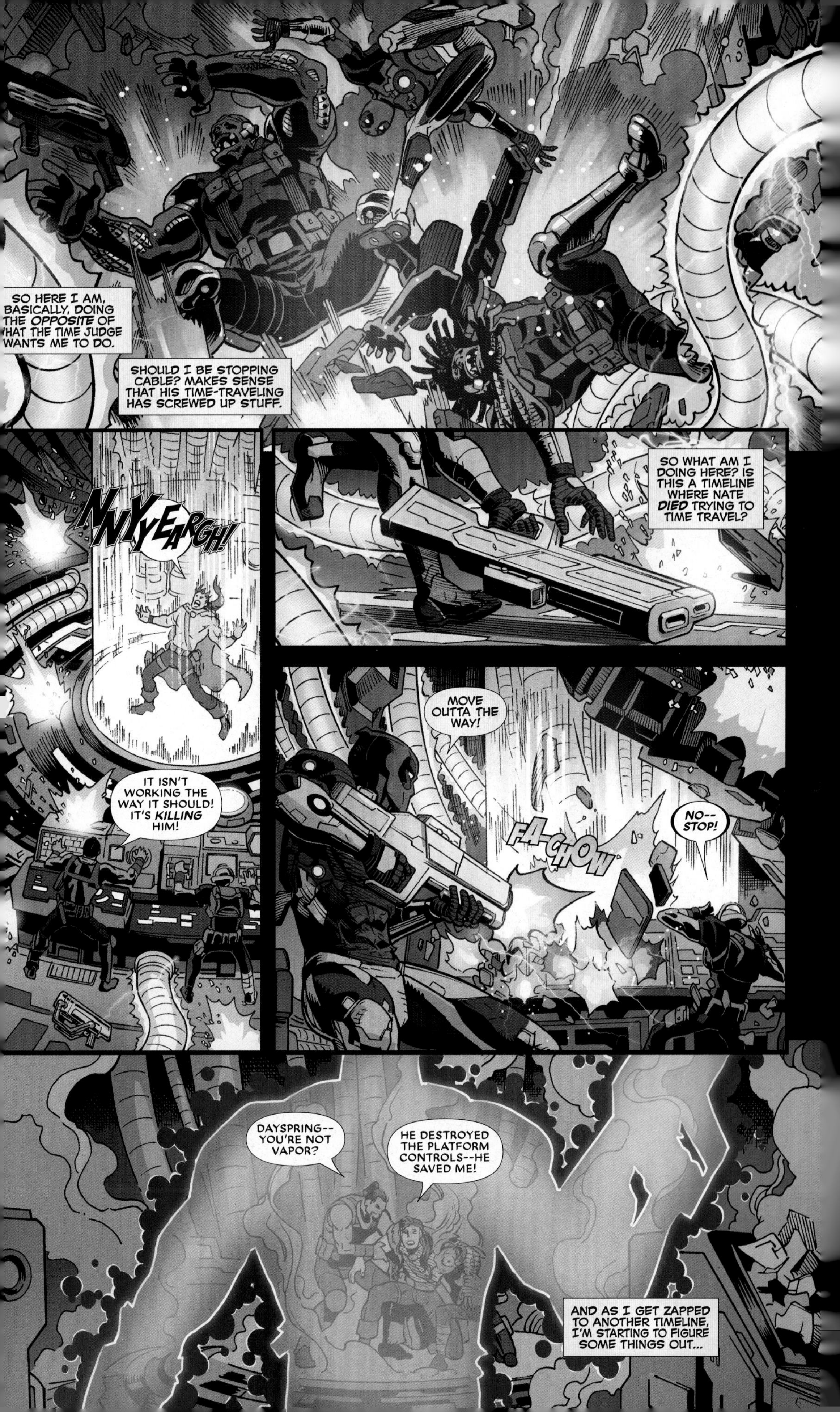
SO HERE I AM, BASICALLY, DOING THE OPPOSITE OF WHAT THE TIME JUDGE WANTS ME TO DO.
SHOULD I BE STOPPING CABLE? MAKES SENSE THAT HIS TIME-TRAVELING HAS SCREWED UP STUFF.
NNYYEARGH!
IT ISN'T WORKING THE WAY IT SHOULD! IT'S KILLING HIM!
SO WHAT AM I DOING HERE? IS THIS A TIMELINE WHERE NATE DIED TRYING TO TIME TRAVEL?
MOVE OUTTA THE WAY!
FA-CHOW
NO-- STOP!
DAYSPRING-- YOU'RE NOT VAPOR?
HE DESTROYED THE PLATFORM CONTROLS--HE SAVED ME!
AND AS I GET ZAPPED TO ANOTHER TIMELINE, I'M STARTING TO FIGURE SOME THINGS OUT...

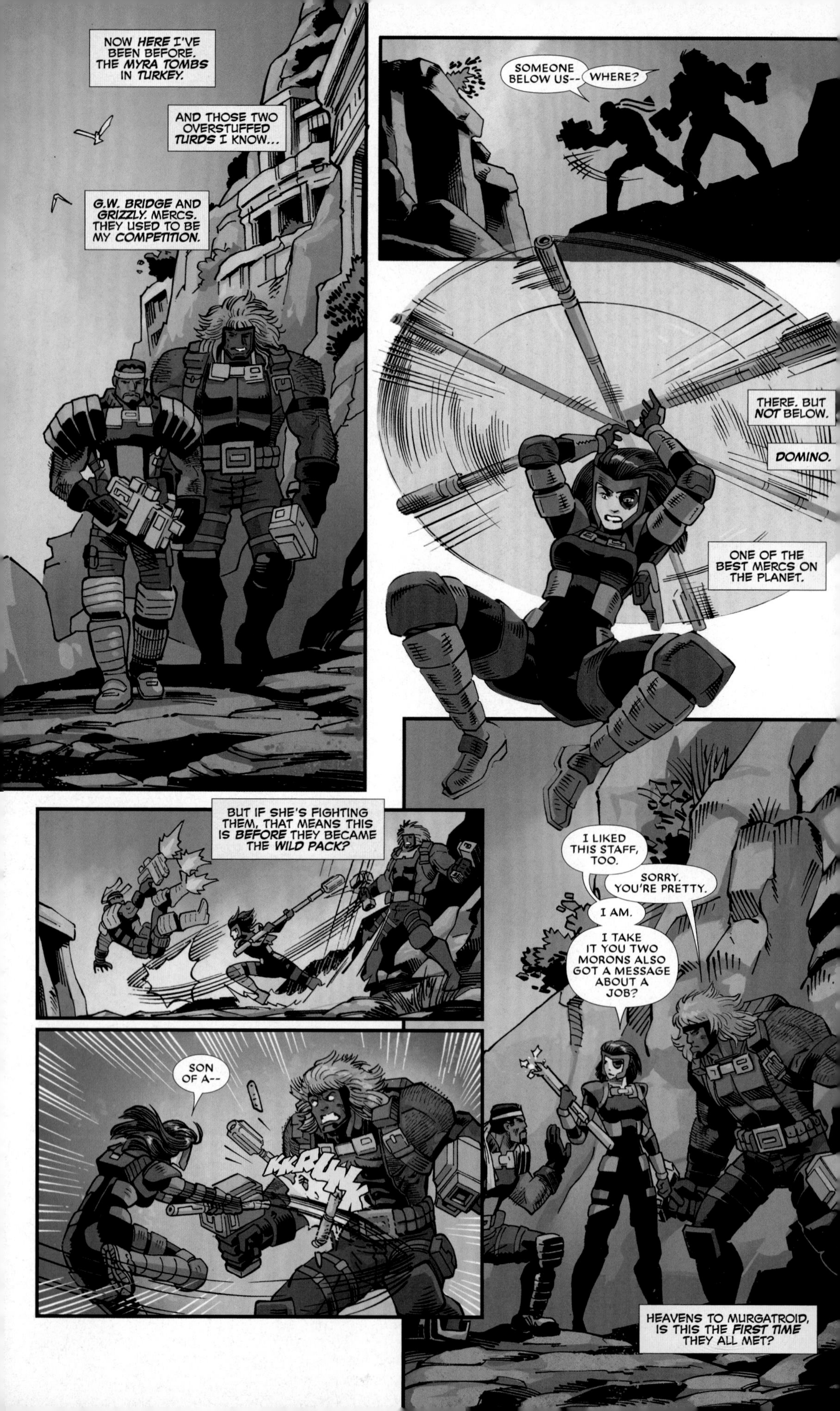

NOW HERE I'VE BEEN BEFORE. THE MYRA TOMBS IN TURKEY.
AND THOSE TWO OVERSTUFFED TURDS I KNOW...
G.W. BRIDGE AND GRIZZLY. MERCS. THEY USED TO BE MY COMPETITION.
SOMEONE BELOW US--
WHERE?
THERE. BUT NOT BELOW.
DOMINO.
ONE OF THE BEST MERCS ON THE PLANET.
BUT IF SHE'S FIGHTING THEM, THAT MEANS THIS IS BEFORE THEY BECAME THE WILD PACK?
SON OF A--
WHUNK
I LIKED THIS STAFF, TOO.
SORRY. YOU'RE PRETTY.
I AM.
I TAKE IT YOU TWO MORONS ALSO GOT A MESSAGE ABOUT A JOB?
HEAVENS TO MURGATROID, IS THIS THE FIRST TIME THEY ALL MET?

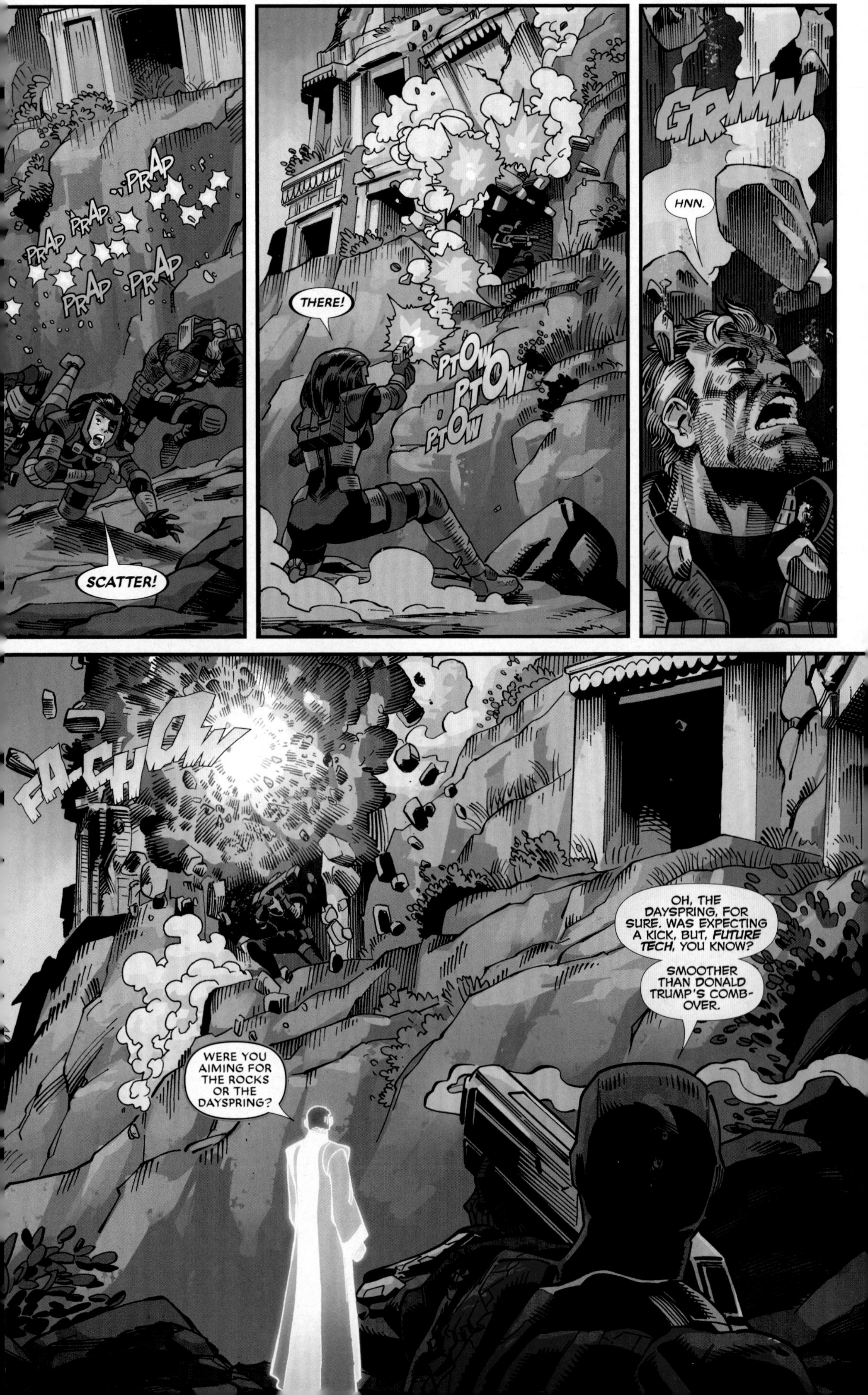

PRAP
PRAP PRAP
PRAP
PRAP PRAP
SCATTER!
THERE!
PTOW PTOW PTOW PTOW
GRMM
HNN.
FA-CHOW
WERE YOU AIMING FOR THE ROCKS OR THE DAYSPRING?
OH, THE DAYSPRING, FOR SURE. WAS EXPECTING A KICK, BUT, *FUTURE TECH*, YOU KNOW?
SMOOTHER THAN DONALD TRUMP'S COMB-OVER.

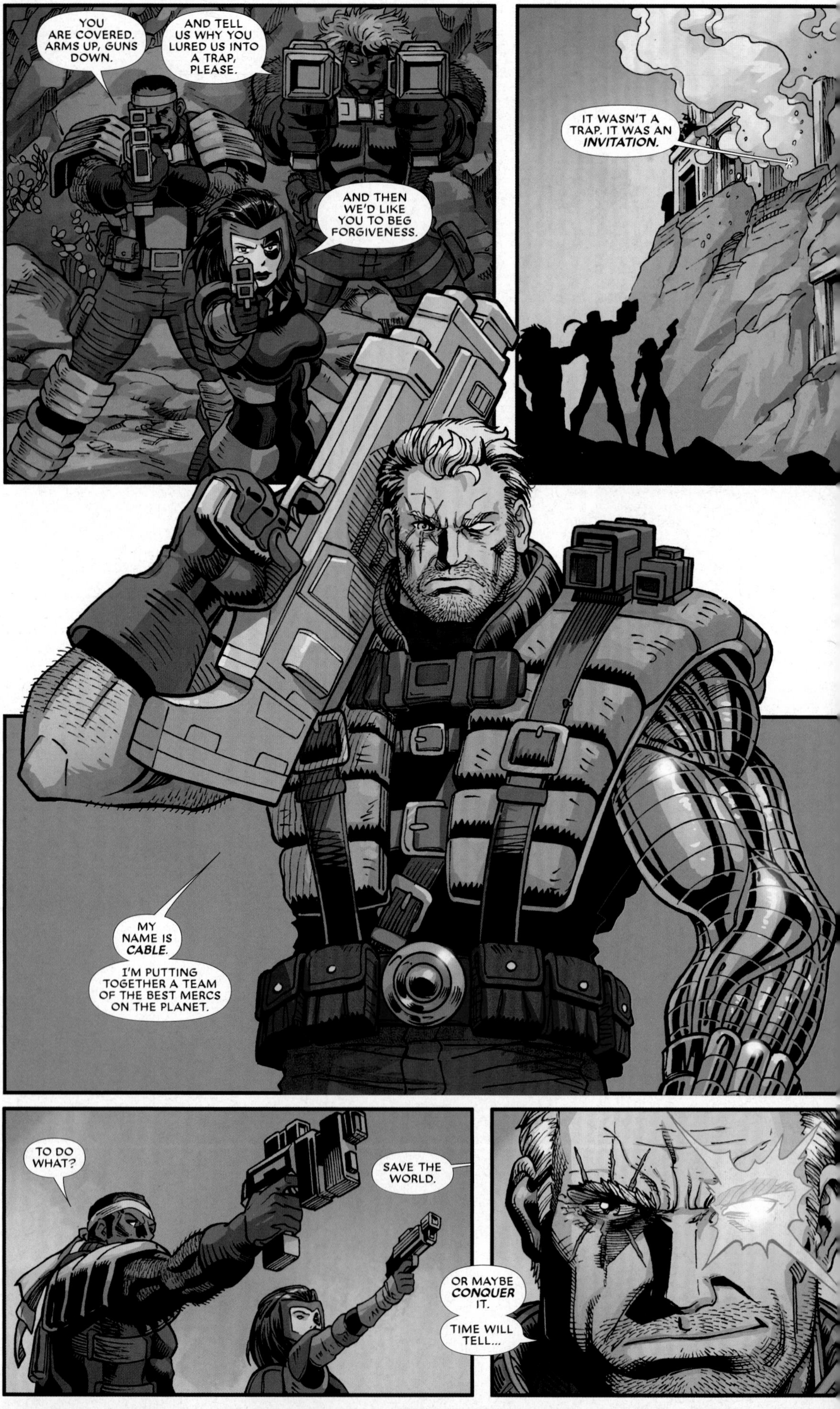
YOU ARE COVERED. ARMS UP, GUNS DOWN.
AND TELL US WHY YOU LURED US INTO A TRAP, PLEASE.
AND THEN WE'D LIKE YOU TO BEG FORGIVENESS.
IT WASN'T A TRAP. IT WAS AN *INVITATION.*
MY NAME IS *CABLE.*
I'M PUTTING TOGETHER A TEAM OF THE BEST MERCS ON THE PLANET.
TO DO WHAT?
SAVE THE WORLD.
OR MAYBE *CONQUER* IT.
TIME WILL TELL...

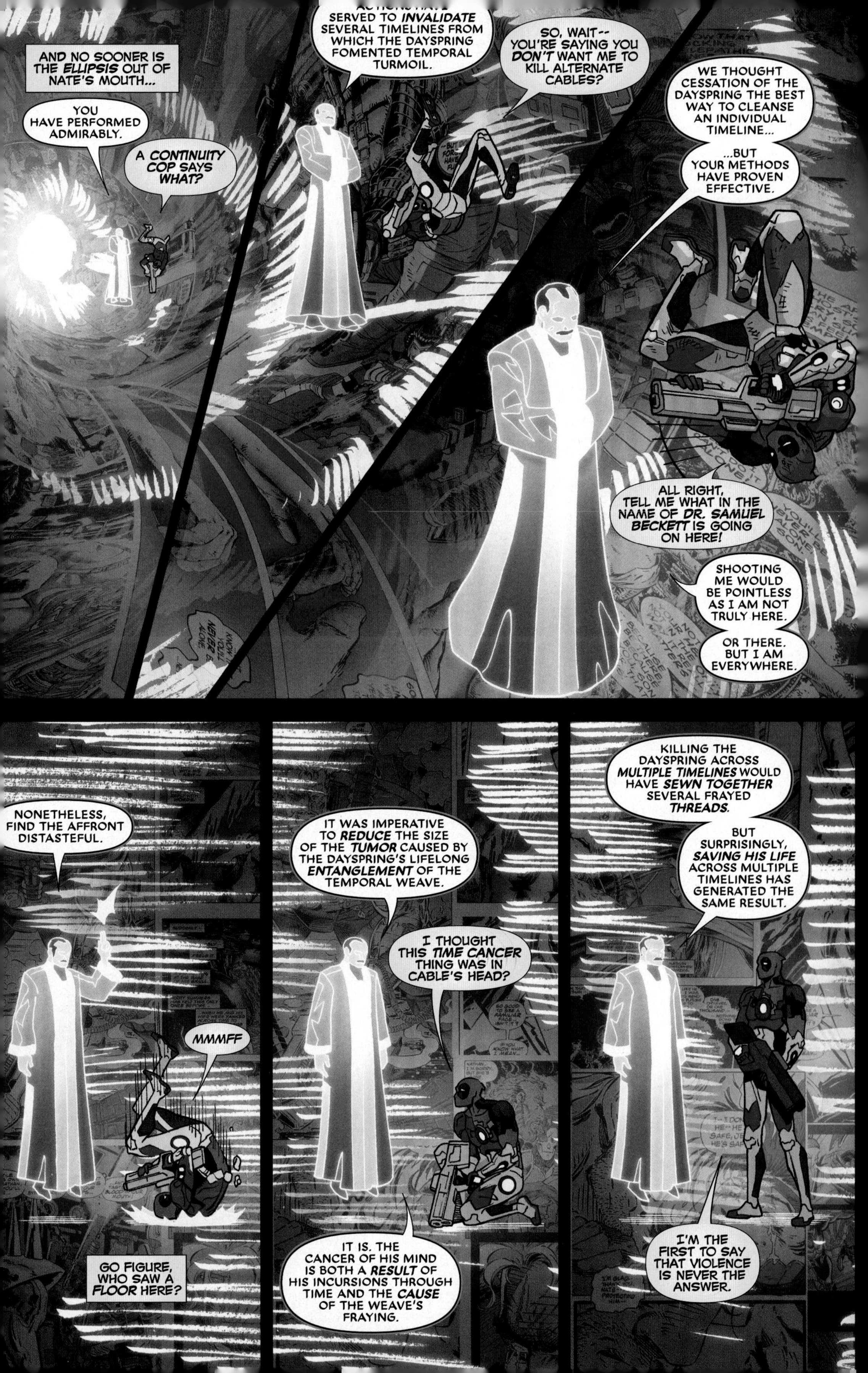

AND NO SOONER IS THE *ELLIPSIS* OUT OF NATE'S MOUTH...
YOU HAVE PERFORMED ADMIRABLY.
A *CONTINUITY COP* SAYS *WHAT?*
SERVED TO *INVALIDATE* SEVERAL TIMELINES FROM WHICH THE DAYSPRING FOMENTED TEMPORAL TURMOIL.
SO, WAIT-- YOU'RE *SAYING* YOU *DON'T* WANT ME TO KILL ALTERNATE CABLES?
WE THOUGHT CESSATION OF THE DAYSPRING THE BEST WAY TO CLEANSE AN INDIVIDUAL TIMELINE...
...BUT YOUR METHODS HAVE PROVEN EFFECTIVE.
ALL RIGHT, TELL ME WHAT IN THE NAME OF *DR. SAMUEL BECKETT* IS GOING ON HERE!
SHOOTING ME WOULD BE POINTLESS AS I AM NOT TRULY HERE.
OR THERE. BUT I AM EVERYWHERE.
NONETHELESS, I FIND THE AFFRONT DISTASTEFUL.
MMMFF
GO FIGURE, WHO SAW A *FLOOR* HERE?
IT WAS IMPERATIVE TO *REDUCE* THE SIZE OF THE *TUMOR* CAUSED BY THE DAYSPRING'S LIFELONG *ENTANGLEMENT* OF THE TEMPORAL WEAVE.
I THOUGHT THIS *TIME CANCER* THING WAS IN CABLE'S HEAD?
IT IS. THE CANCER OF HIS MIND IS BOTH A *RESULT* OF HIS INCURSIONS THROUGH TIME AND THE *CAUSE* OF THE WEAVE'S FRAYING.
KILLING THE DAYSPRING ACROSS *MULTIPLE TIMELINES* WOULD HAVE *SEWN TOGETHER* SEVERAL FRAYED *THREADS*.
BUT SURPRISINGLY, *SAVING HIS LIFE* ACROSS MULTIPLE TIMELINES HAS GENERATED THE SAME RESULT.
I'M THE FIRST TO SAY THAT VIOLENCE IS NEVER THE ANSWER.

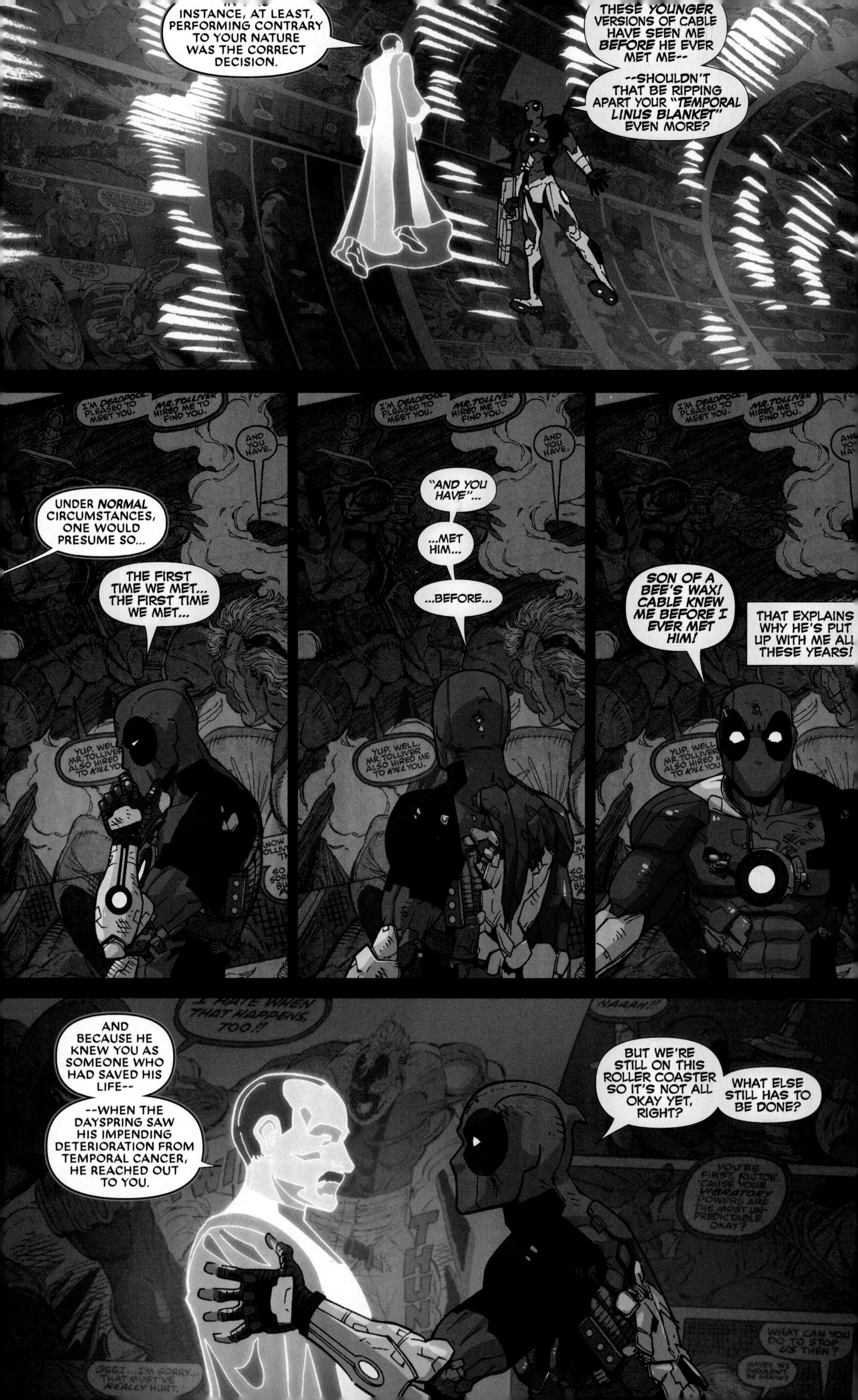

INSTANCE, AT LEAST, PERFORMING CONTRARY TO YOUR NATURE WAS THE CORRECT DECISION.
THESE YOUNGER VERSIONS OF CABLE HAVE SEEN ME BEFORE HE EVER MET ME--
--SHOULDN'T THAT BE RIPPING APART YOUR "TEMPORAL LINUS BLANKET" EVEN MORE?
I'M DEADPOOL. PLEASED TO MEET YOU.
MR. TOLLIVER HIRED ME TO FIND YOU.
AND YOU HAVE.
YUP, WELL, MR. TOLLIVER ALSO HIRED ME TO KILL YOU.
UNDER NORMAL CIRCUMSTANCES, ONE WOULD PRESUME SO...
THE FIRST TIME WE MET... THE FIRST TIME WE MET...
"AND YOU HAVE"...
...MET HIM...
...BEFORE...
SON OF A BEE'S WAX! CABLE KNEW ME BEFORE I EVER MET HIM!
THAT EXPLAINS WHY HE'S PUT UP WITH ME ALL THESE YEARS!
I HATE WHEN THAT HAPPENS, TOO.!!
NAAAH!!
AND BECAUSE HE KNEW YOU AS SOMEONE WHO HAD SAVED HIS LIFE--
--WHEN THE DAYSPRING SAW HIS IMPENDING DETERIORATION FROM TEMPORAL CANCER, HE REACHED OUT TO YOU.
BUT WE'RE STILL ON THIS ROLLER COASTER SO IT'S NOT ALL OKAY YET, RIGHT?
WHAT ELSE STILL HAS TO BE DONE?
YOU'RE FIRST, RICTOR. CAUSE YOUR VIBRATORY POWERS ARE THE MOST UN-PREDICTABLE. OKAY?
WHAT CAN YOU DO TO STOP US THEN?
GEEZ... I'M SORRY... THAT MUST'VE REALLY HURT.

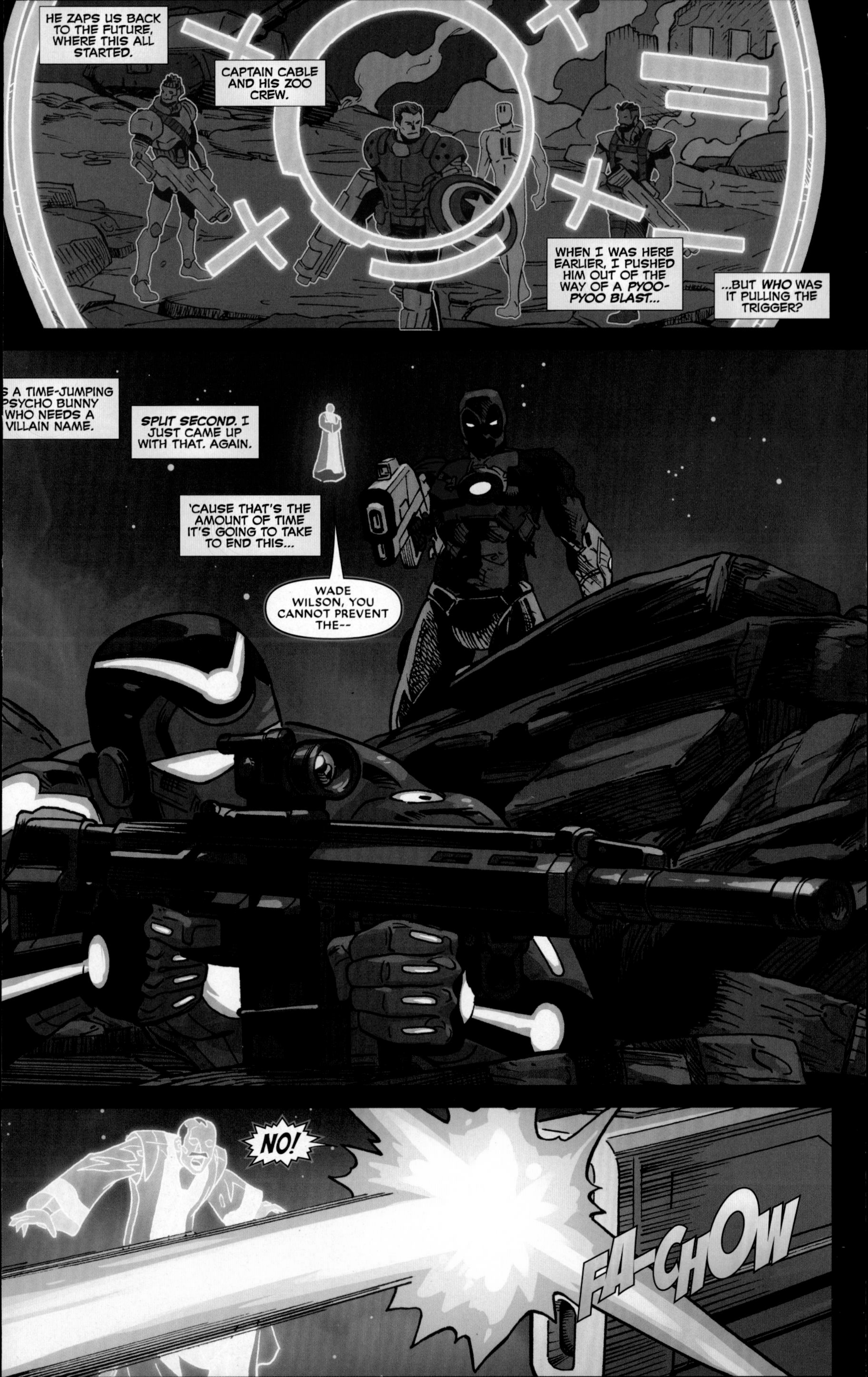
HE ZAPS US BACK TO THE FUTURE, WHERE THIS ALL STARTED.
CAPTAIN CABLE AND HIS ZOO CREW.
WHEN I WAS HERE EARLIER, I PUSHED HIM OUT OF THE WAY OF A PYOO-PYOO BLAST...
...BUT WHO WAS IT PULLING THE TRIGGER?
A TIME-JUMPING PSYCHO BUNNY WHO NEEDS A VILLAIN NAME.
SPLIT SECOND. I JUST CAME UP WITH THAT. AGAIN.
'CAUSE THAT'S THE AMOUNT OF TIME IT'S GOING TO TAKE TO END THIS...
WADE WILSON, YOU CANNOT PREVENT THE--
NO!
FA-CHOW

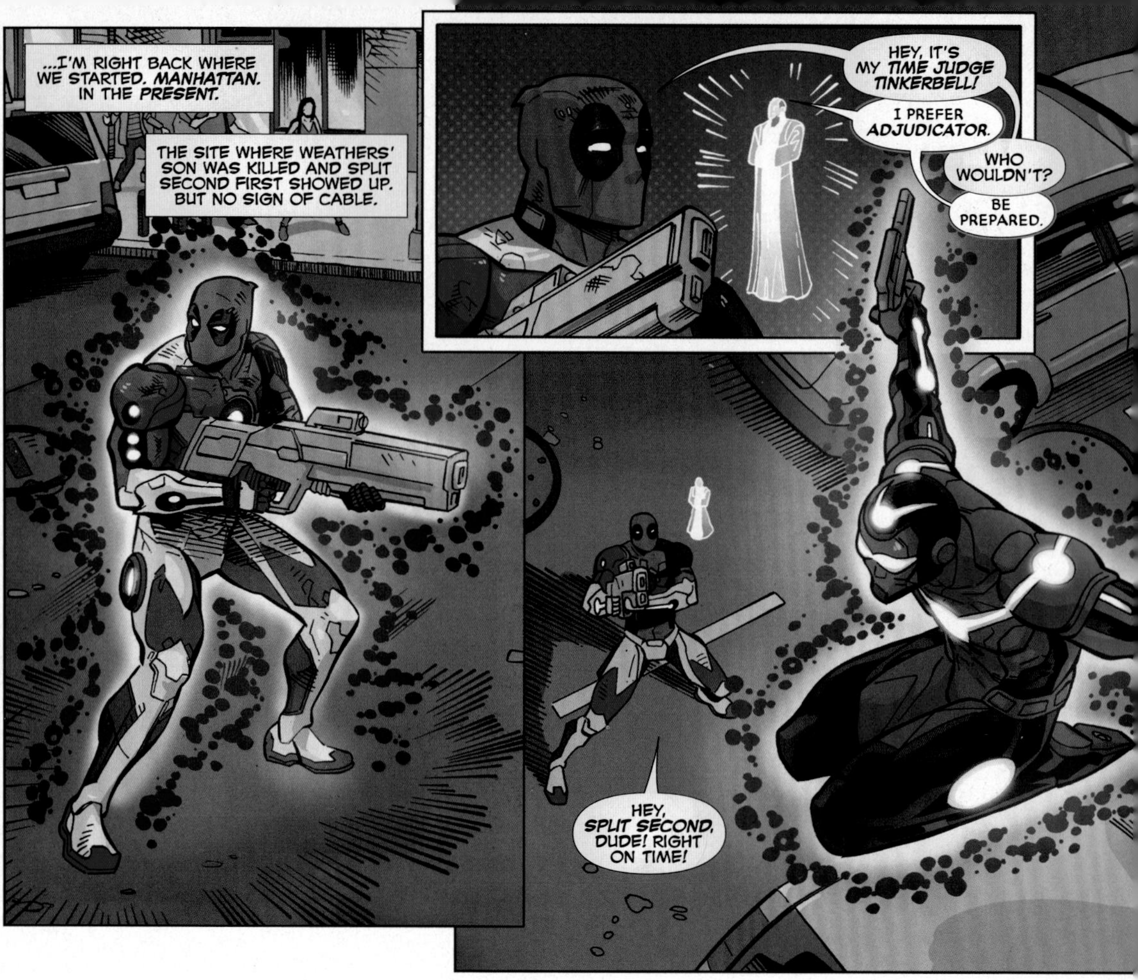
...I'M RIGHT BACK WHERE WE STARTED. MANHATTAN. IN THE PRESENT.
THE SITE WHERE WEATHERS' SON WAS KILLED AND SPLIT SECOND FIRST SHOWED UP. BUT NO SIGN OF CABLE.
HEY, IT'S MY TIME JUDGE TINKERBELL!
I PREFER ADJUDICATOR.
WHO WOULDN'T?
BE PREPARED.
HEY, SPLIT SECOND, DUDE! RIGHT ON TIME!

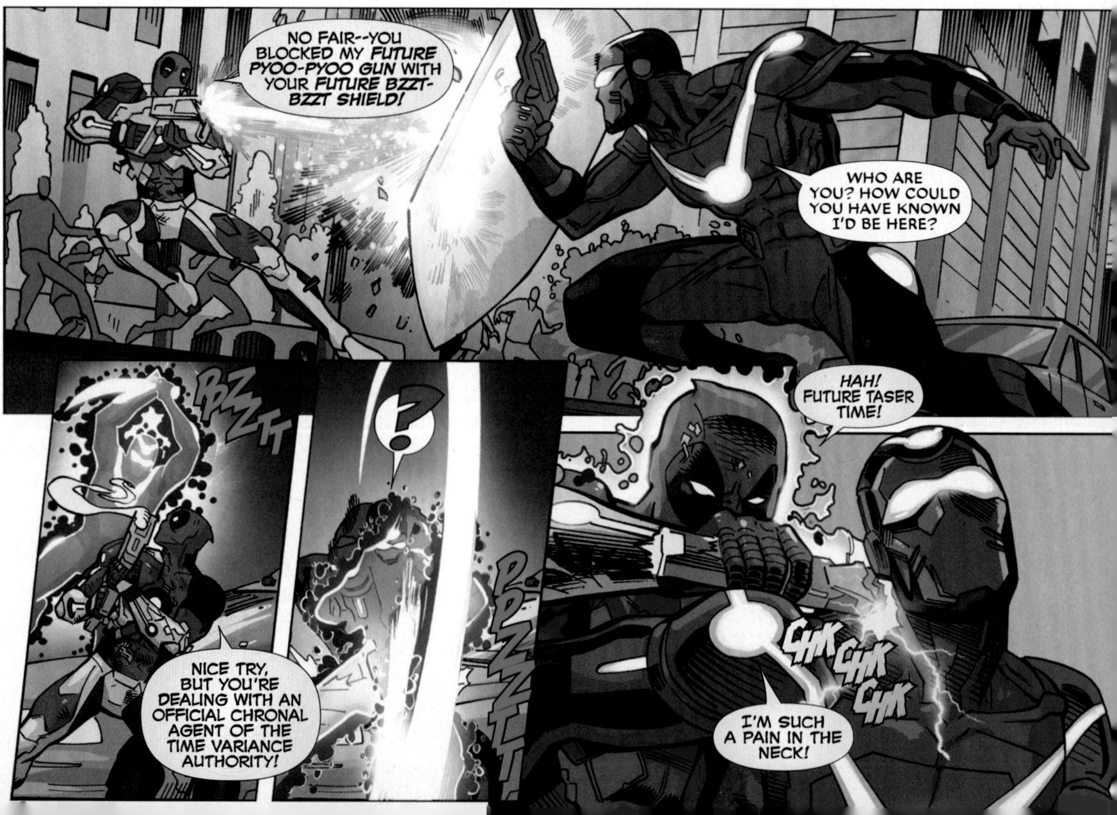
NO FAIR--YOU BLOCKED MY FUTURE PYOO-PYOO GUN WITH YOUR FUTURE BZZT-BZZT SHIELD!
WHO ARE YOU? HOW COULD YOU HAVE KNOWN I'D BE HERE?
HAH! FUTURE TASER TIME!
?!
NICE TRY, BUT YOU'RE DEALING WITH AN OFFICIAL CHRONAL AGENT OF THE TIME VARIANCE AUTHORITY!
CHK CHK CHK
I'M SUCH A PAIN IN THE NECK!

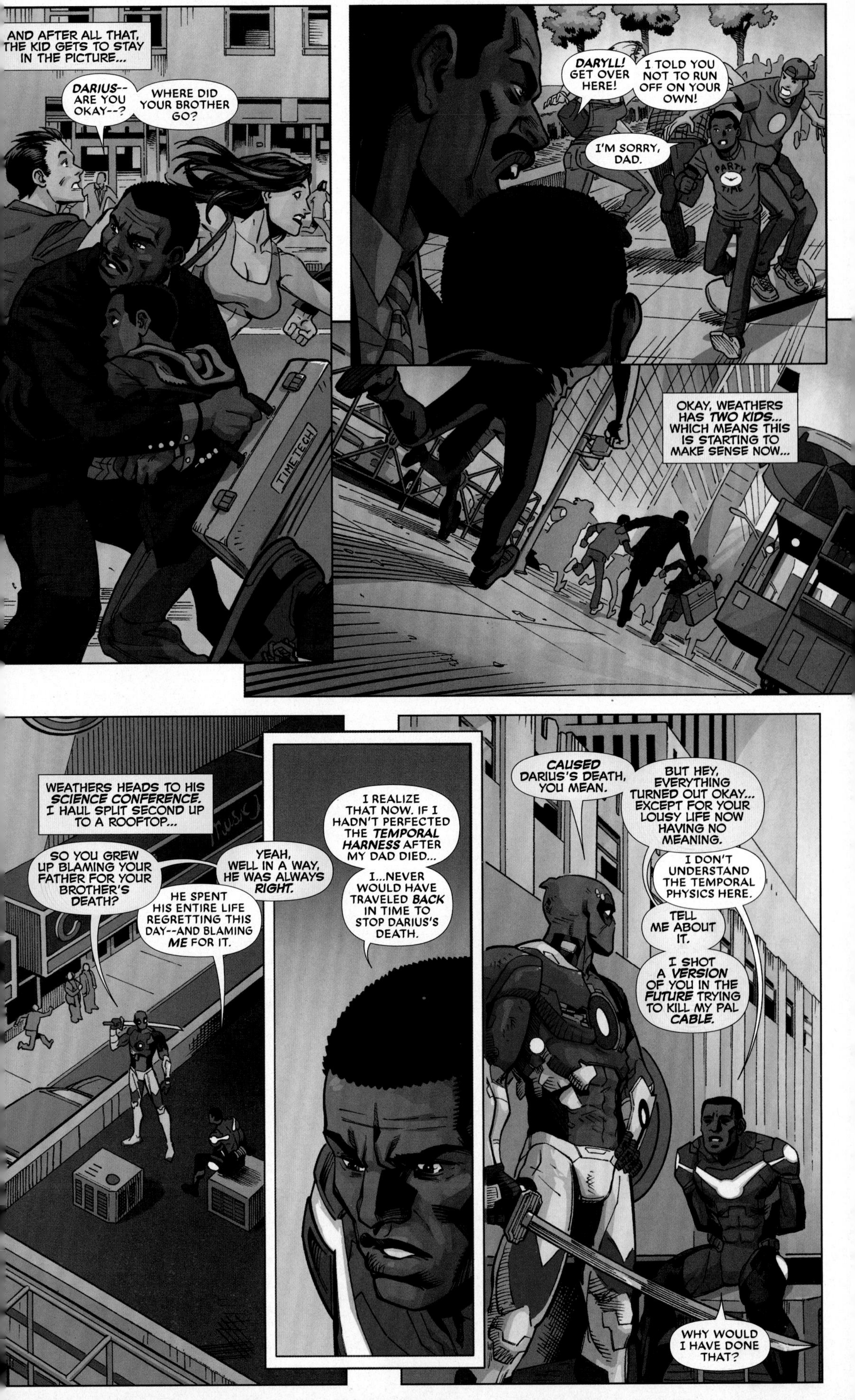
AND AFTER ALL THAT, THE KID GETS TO STAY IN THE PICTURE...
DARIUS--ARE YOU OKAY--?
WHERE DID YOUR BROTHER GO?
TIMETECH
DARYLL! GET OVER HERE!
I TOLD YOU NOT TO RUN OFF ON YOUR OWN!
I'M SORRY, DAD.
PARTY TIME
OKAY, WEATHERS HAS TWO KIDS... WHICH MEANS THIS IS STARTING TO MAKE SENSE NOW...
WEATHERS HEADS TO HIS SCIENCE CONFERENCE. I HAUL SPLIT SECOND UP TO A ROOFTOP...
SO YOU GREW UP BLAMING YOUR FATHER FOR YOUR BROTHER'S DEATH?
YEAH, WELL IN A WAY, HE WAS ALWAYS RIGHT.
HE SPENT HIS ENTIRE LIFE REGRETTING THIS DAY--AND BLAMING ME FOR IT.
I REALIZE THAT NOW. IF I HADN'T PERFECTED THE TEMPORAL HARNESS AFTER MY DAD DIED...
I...NEVER WOULD HAVE TRAVELED BACK IN TIME TO STOP DARIUS'S DEATH.
CAUSED DARIUS'S DEATH, YOU MEAN.
BUT HEY, EVERYTHING TURNED OUT OKAY... EXCEPT FOR YOUR LOUSY LIFE NOW HAVING NO MEANING.
I DON'T UNDERSTAND THE TEMPORAL PHYSICS HERE.
TELL ME ABOUT IT.
I SHOT A VERSION OF YOU IN THE FUTURE TRYING TO KILL MY PAL CABLE.
WHY WOULD I HAVE DONE THAT?

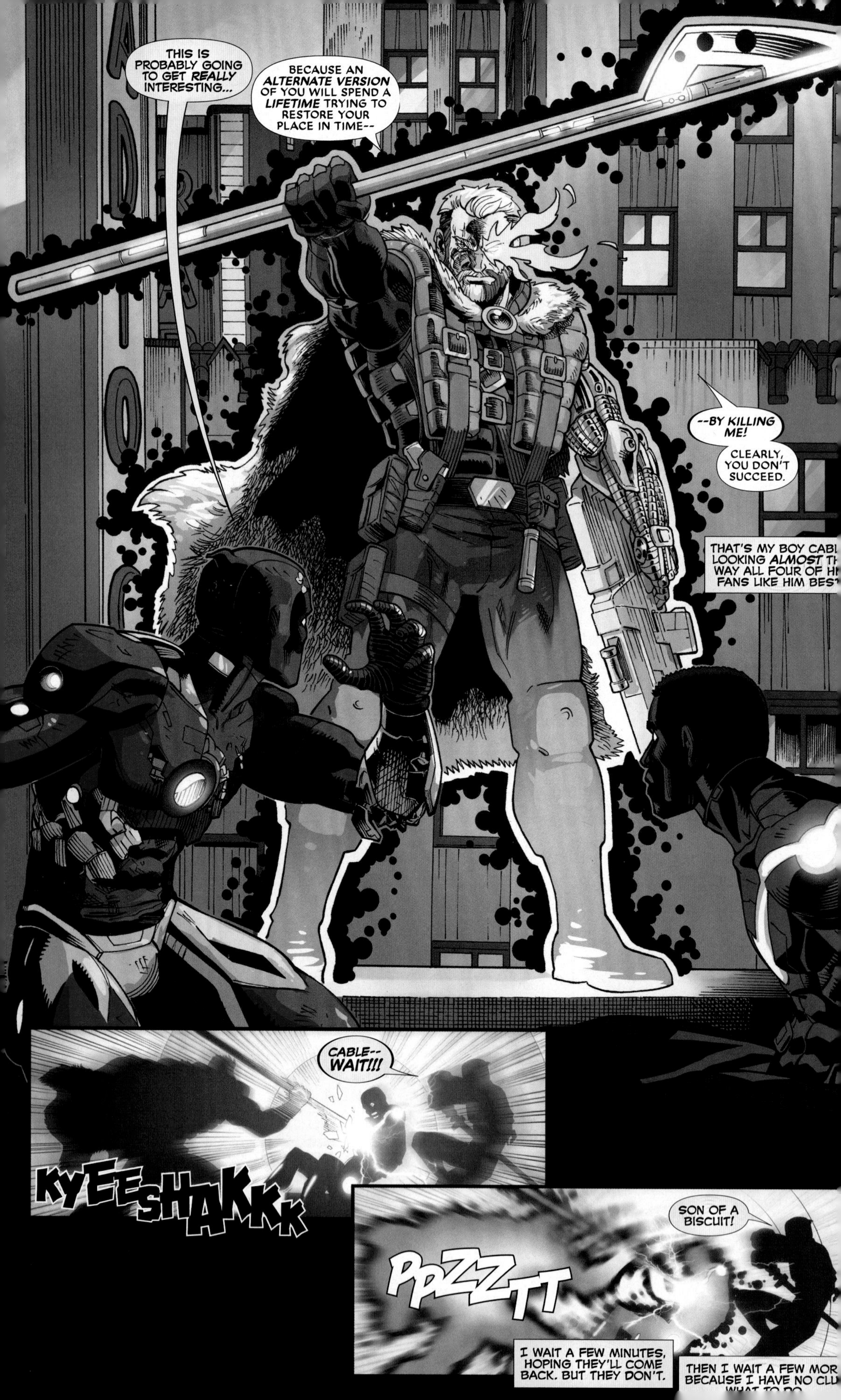

THIS IS PROBABLY GOING TO GET REALLY INTERESTING...
BECAUSE AN ALTERNATE VERSION OF YOU WILL SPEND A LIFETIME TRYING TO RESTORE YOUR PLACE IN TIME--
--BY KILLING ME!
CLEARLY, YOU DON'T SUCCEED.
THAT'S MY BOY CABL LOOKING ALMOST TH WAY ALL FOUR OF HI FANS LIKE HIM BEST
CABLE-- WAIT!!!
KYEESHAKKK
SON OF A BISCUIT!
PPZZZTT
I WAIT A FEW MINUTES, HOPING THEY'LL COME BACK. BUT THEY DON'T.
THEN I WAIT A FEW MOR BECAUSE I HAVE NO CLU

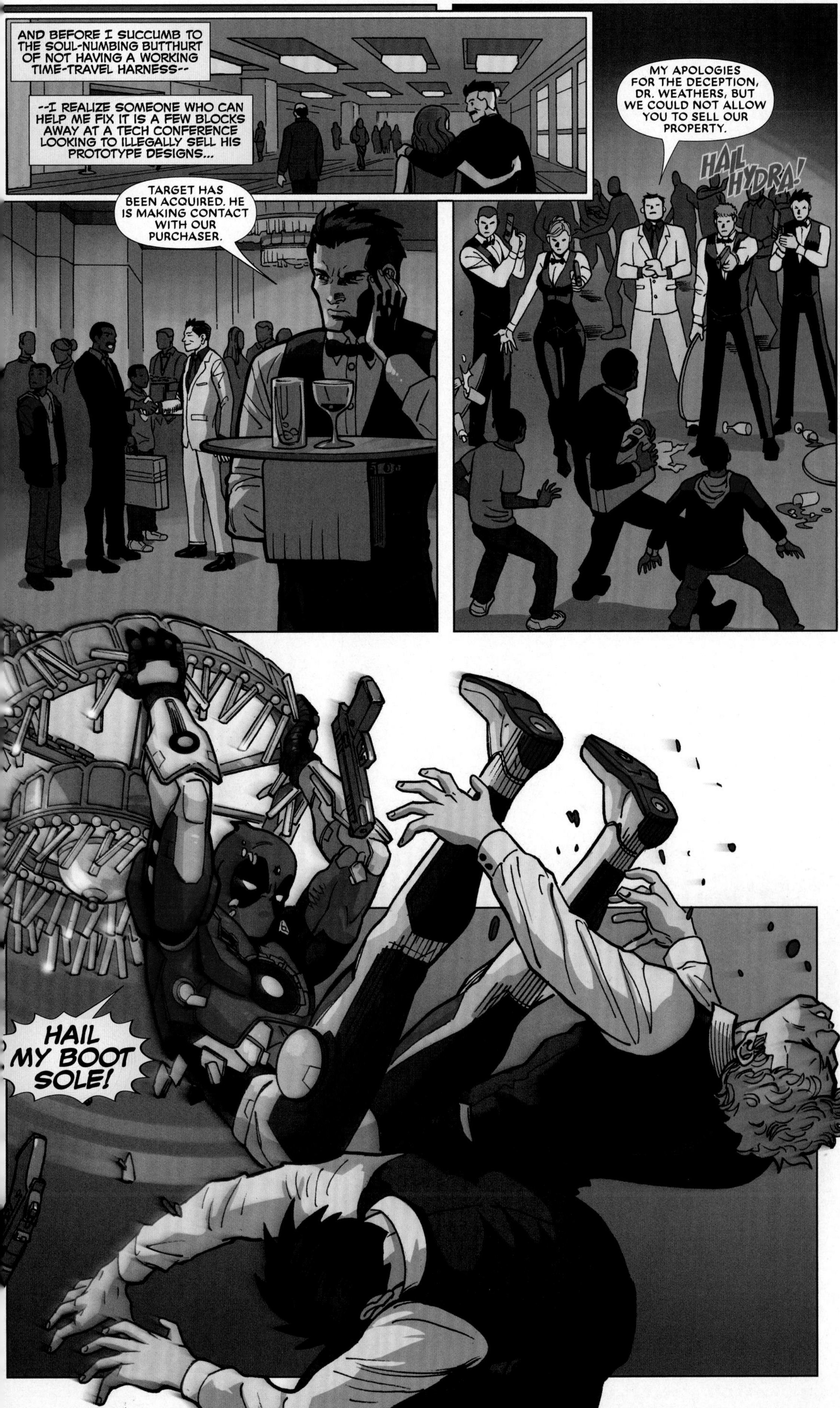
AND BEFORE I SUCCUMB TO THE SOUL-NUMBING BUTTHURT OF NOT HAVING A WORKING TIME-TRAVEL HARNESS--
--I REALIZE SOMEONE WHO CAN HELP ME FIX IT IS A FEW BLOCKS AWAY AT A TECH CONFERENCE LOOKING TO ILLEGALLY SELL HIS PROTOTYPE DESIGNS...
TARGET HAS BEEN ACQUIRED. HE IS MAKING CONTACT WITH OUR PURCHASER.
MY APOLOGIES FOR THE DECEPTION, DR. WEATHERS, BUT WE COULD NOT ALLOW YOU TO SELL OUR PROPERTY.
HAIL HYDRA!
HAIL MY BOOT SOLE!

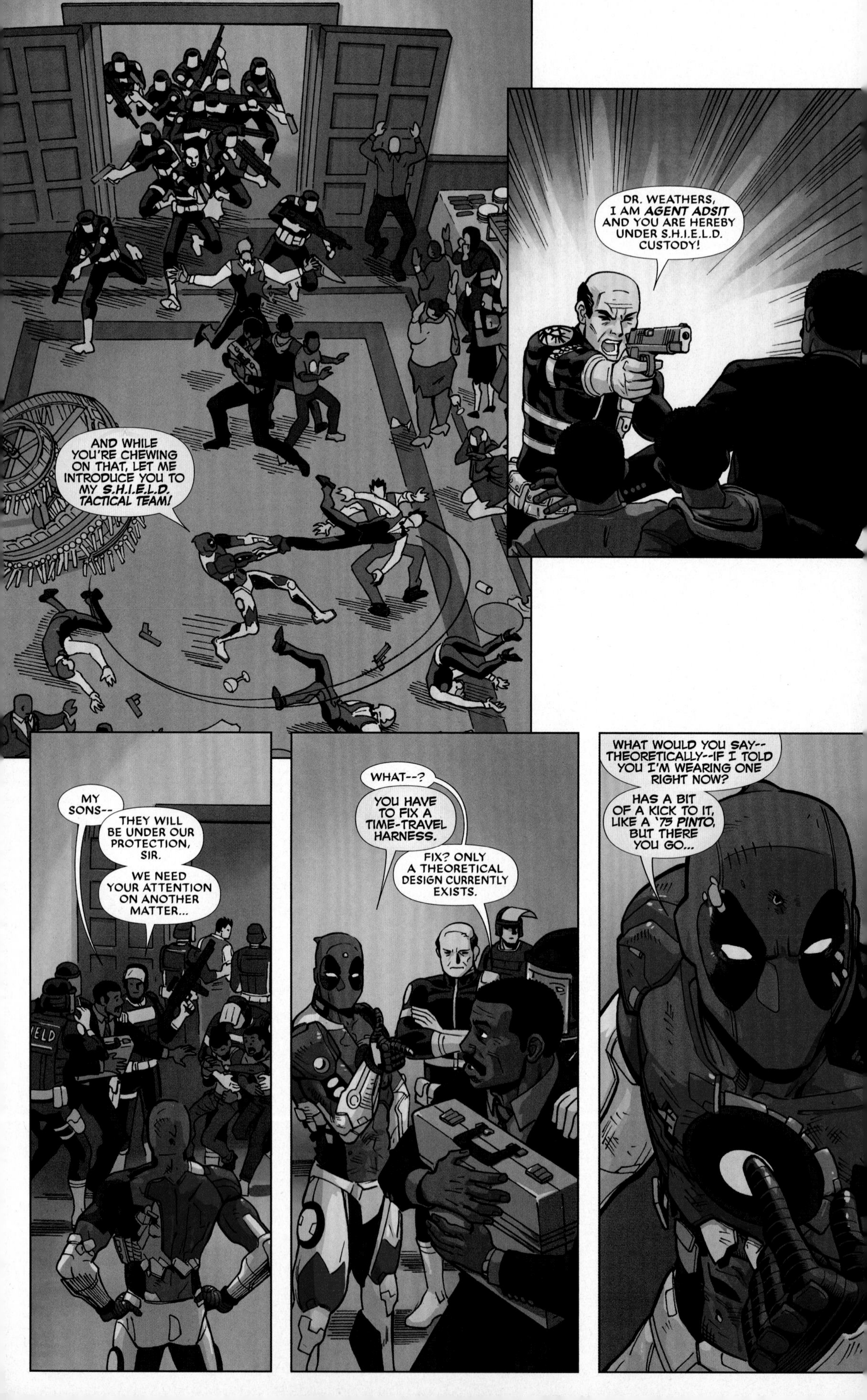
AND WHILE YOU'RE CHEWING ON THAT, LET ME INTRODUCE YOU TO MY S.H.I.E.L.D. TACTICAL TEAM!
DR. WEATHERS, I AM AGENT ADSIT AND YOU ARE HEREBY UNDER S.H.I.E.L.D. CUSTODY!
MY SONS--
THEY WILL BE UNDER OUR PROTECTION, SIR.
WE NEED YOUR ATTENTION ON ANOTHER MATTER...
WHAT--?
YOU HAVE TO FIX A TIME-TRAVEL HARNESS.
FIX? ONLY A THEORETICAL DESIGN CURRENTLY EXISTS.
WHAT WOULD YOU SAY--THEORETICALLY--IF I TOLD YOU I'M WEARING ONE RIGHT NOW?
HAS A BIT OF A KICK TO IT, LIKE A '75 PINTO, BUT THERE YOU GO...
ELD

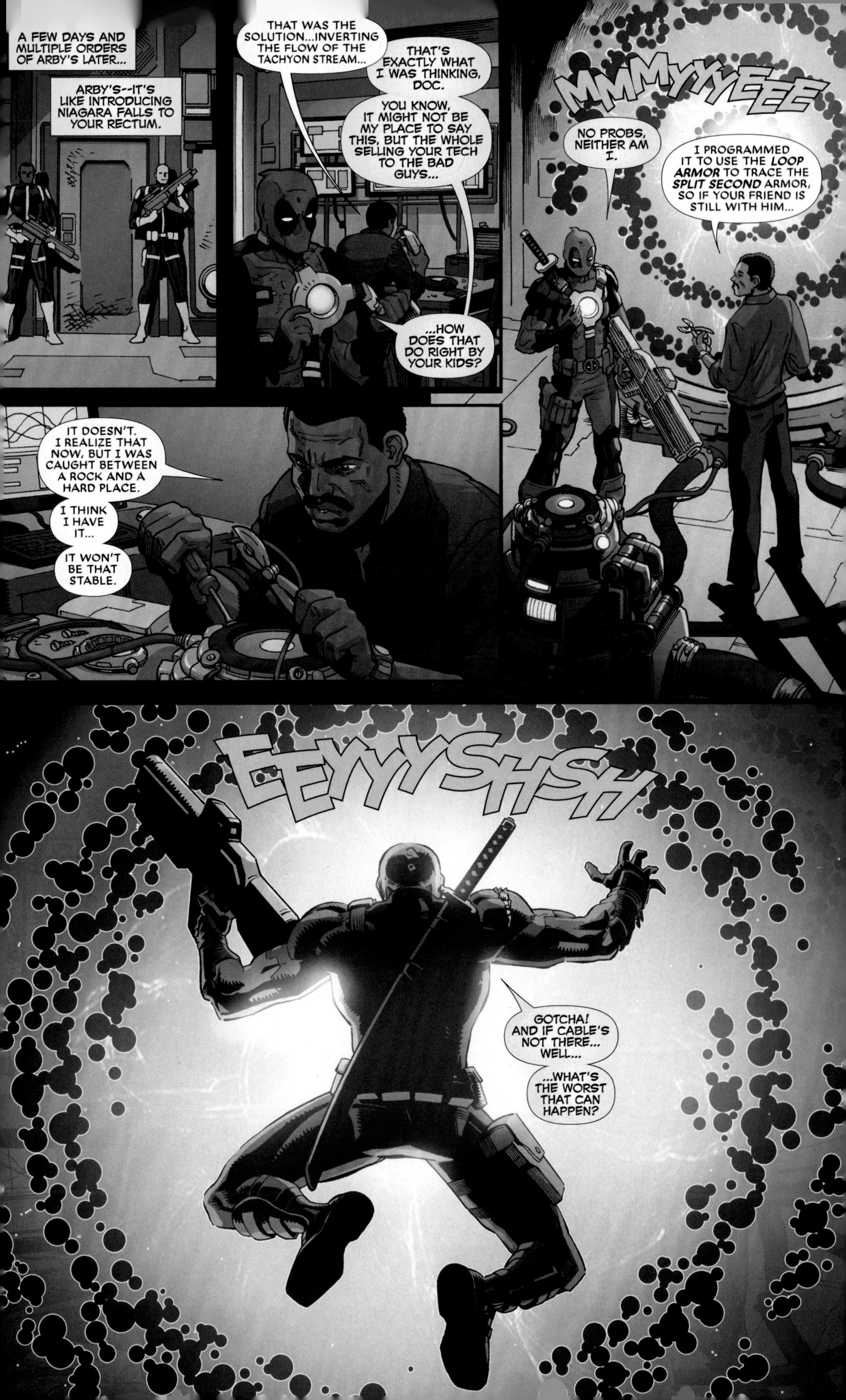
A FEW DAYS AND MULTIPLE ORDERS OF ARBY'S LATER...
ARBY'S--IT'S LIKE INTRODUCING NIAGARA FALLS TO YOUR RECTUM.
THAT WAS THE SOLUTION...INVERTING THE FLOW OF THE TACHYON STREAM...
THAT'S EXACTLY WHAT I WAS THINKING, DOC.
YOU KNOW, IT MIGHT NOT BE MY PLACE TO SAY THIS, BUT THE WHOLE SELLING YOUR TECH TO THE BAD GUYS...
...HOW DOES THAT DO RIGHT BY YOUR KIDS?
IT DOESN'T. I REALIZE THAT NOW, BUT I WAS CAUGHT BETWEEN A ROCK AND A HARD PLACE.
I THINK I HAVE IT...
IT WON'T BE THAT STABLE.
MMMYYYEEE
NO PROBS, NEITHER AM I.
I PROGRAMMED IT TO USE THE LOOP ARMOR TO TRACE THE SPLIT SECOND ARMOR, SO IF YOUR FRIEND IS STILL WITH HIM...
EEYYYSHSH
GOTCHA! AND IF CABLE'S NOT THERE... WELL...
...WHAT'S THE WORST THAT CAN HAPPEN?

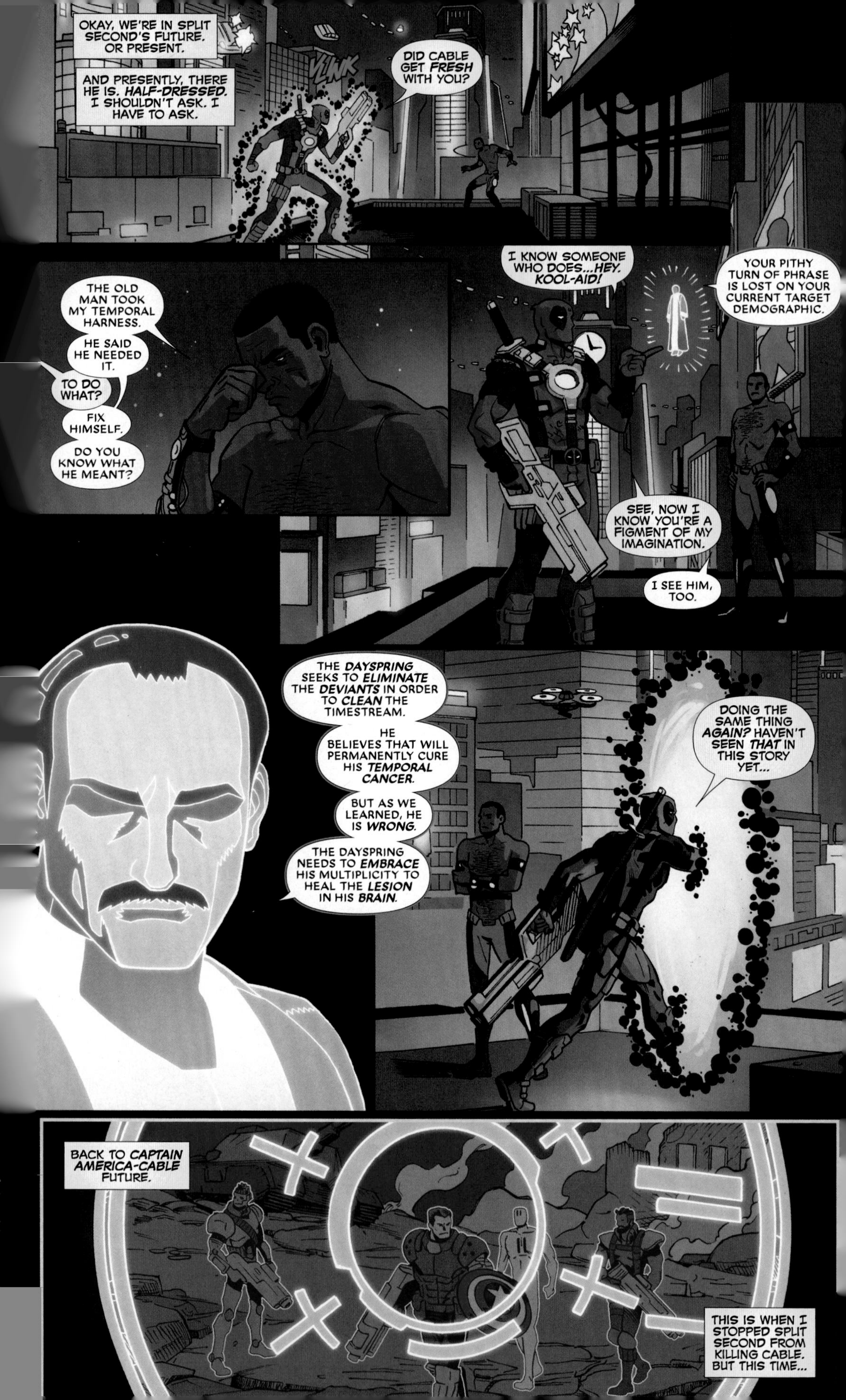
OKAY, WE'RE IN SPLIT SECOND'S FUTURE. OR PRESENT.
AND PRESENTLY, THERE HE IS. HALF-DRESSED. I SHOULDN'T ASK. I HAVE TO ASK.
VLINK
DID CABLE GET FRESH WITH YOU?
THE OLD MAN TOOK MY TEMPORAL HARNESS.
HE SAID HE NEEDED IT.
TO DO WHAT?
FIX HIMSELF.
DO YOU KNOW WHAT HE MEANT?
I KNOW SOMEONE WHO DOES...HEY. KOOL-AID!
YOUR PITHY TURN OF PHRASE IS LOST ON YOUR CURRENT TARGET DEMOGRAPHIC.
SEE, NOW I KNOW YOU'RE A FIGMENT OF MY IMAGINATION.
I SEE HIM, TOO.
THE DAYSPRING SEEKS TO ELIMINATE THE DEVIANTS IN ORDER TO CLEAN THE TIMESTREAM.
HE BELIEVES THAT WILL PERMANENTLY CURE HIS TEMPORAL CANCER.
BUT AS WE LEARNED, HE IS WRONG.
THE DAYSPRING NEEDS TO EMBRACE HIS MULTIPLICITY TO HEAL THE LESION IN HIS BRAIN.
DOING THE SAME THING AGAIN? HAVEN'T SEEN THAT IN THIS STORY YET...
BACK TO CAPTAIN AMERICA-CABLE FUTURE.
THIS IS WHEN I STOPPED SPLIT SECOND FROM KILLING CABLE. BUT THIS TIME...

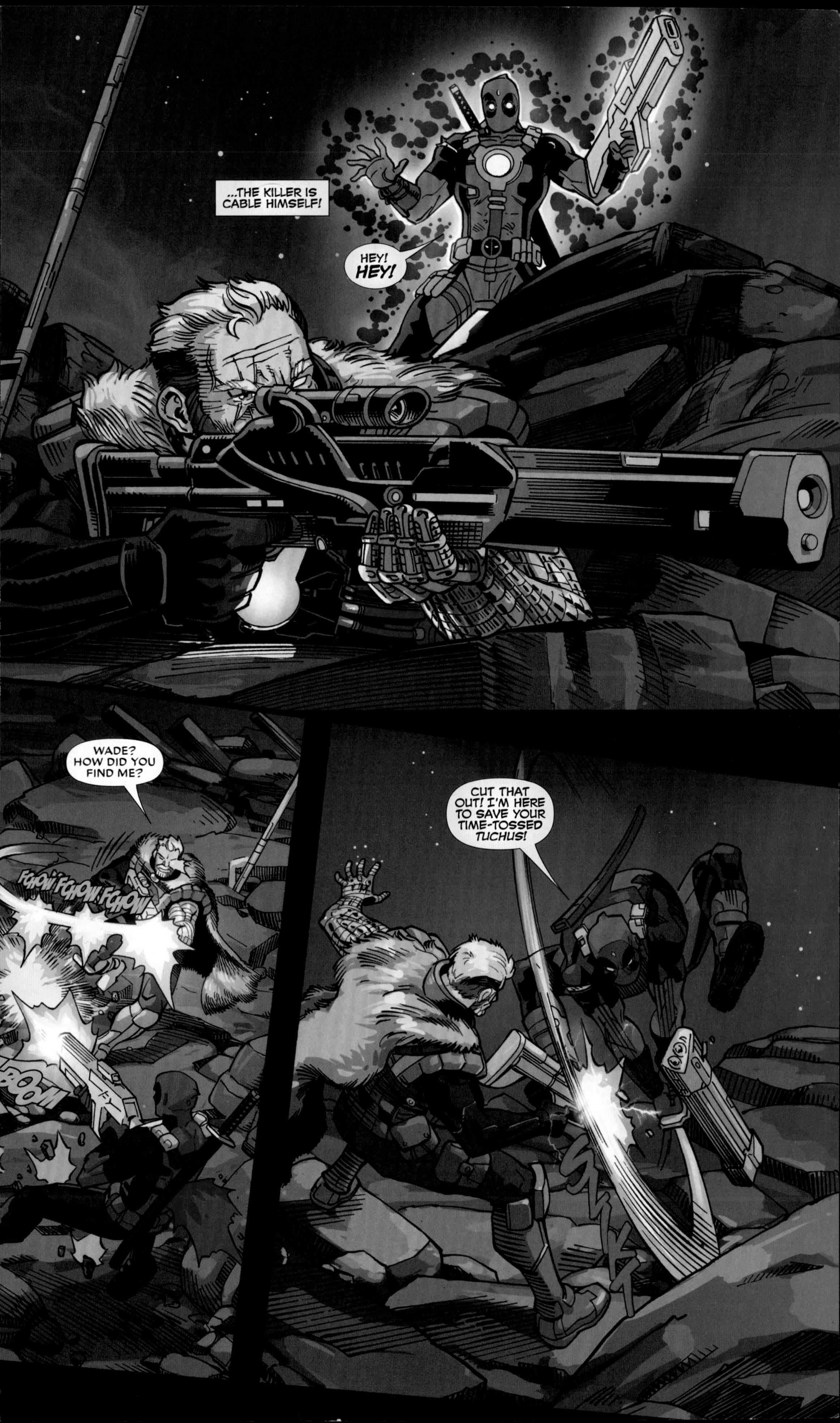
...THE KILLER IS CABLE HIMSELF!
HEY! HEY!
WADE? HOW DID YOU FIND ME?
FCHOW FCHOW FCHOW
BOOM
CUT THAT OUT! I'M HERE TO SAVE YOUR TIME-TOSSED TUCHUS!
SNIKT

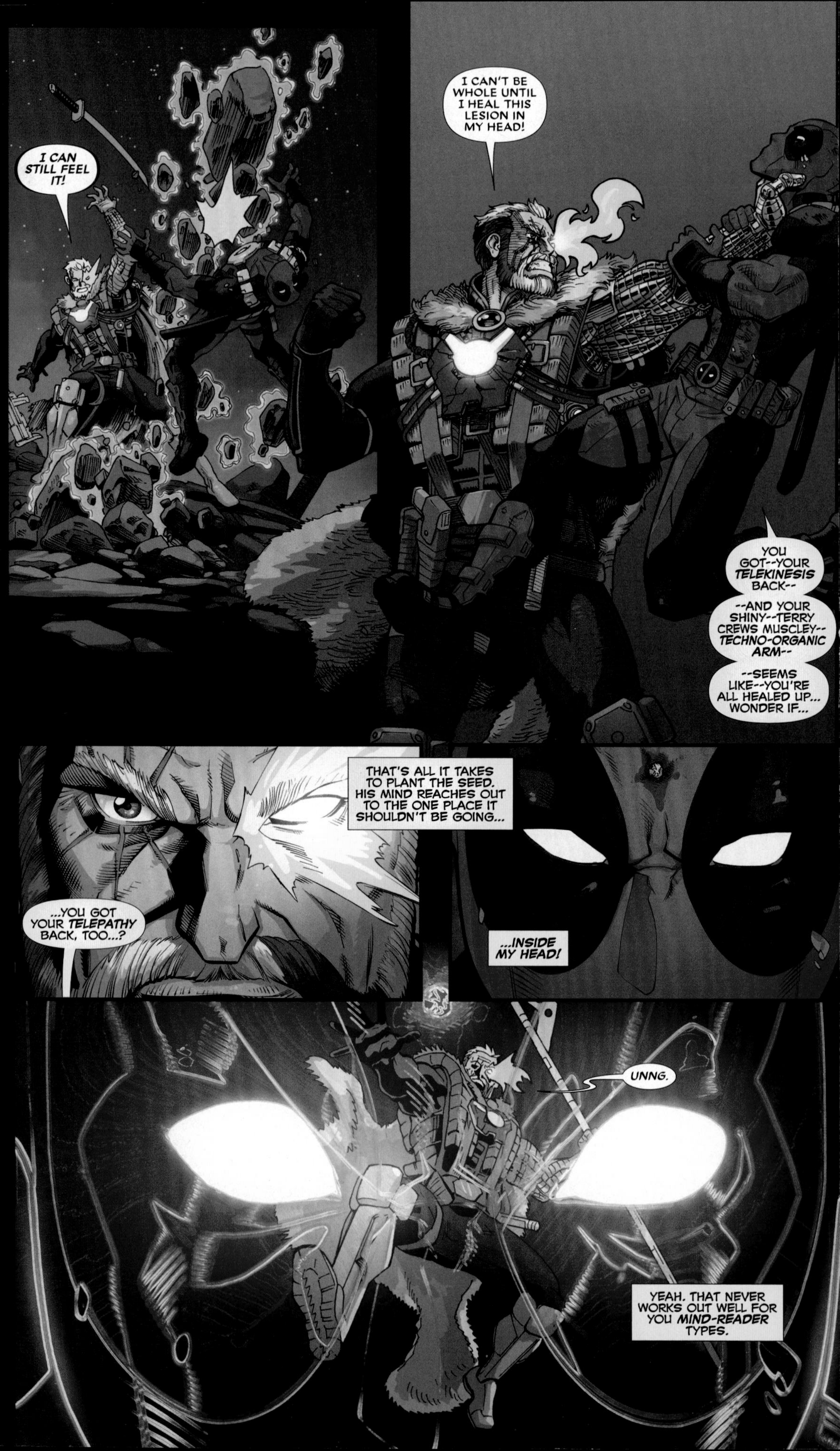
I CAN STILL FEEL IT!
I CAN'T BE WHOLE UNTIL I HEAL THIS LESION IN MY HEAD!
YOU GOT--YOUR TELEKINESIS BACK--
--AND YOUR SHINY--TERRY CREWS MUSCLEY--TECHNO-ORGANIC ARM--
--SEEMS LIKE--YOU'RE ALL HEALED UP... WONDER IF...
...YOU GOT YOUR TELEPATHY BACK, TOO...?
THAT'S ALL IT TAKES TO PLANT THE SEED. HIS MIND REACHES OUT TO THE ONE PLACE IT SHOULDN'T BE GOING...
...INSIDE MY HEAD!
UNNG.
YEAH. THAT NEVER WORKS OUT WELL FOR YOU MIND-READER TYPES.

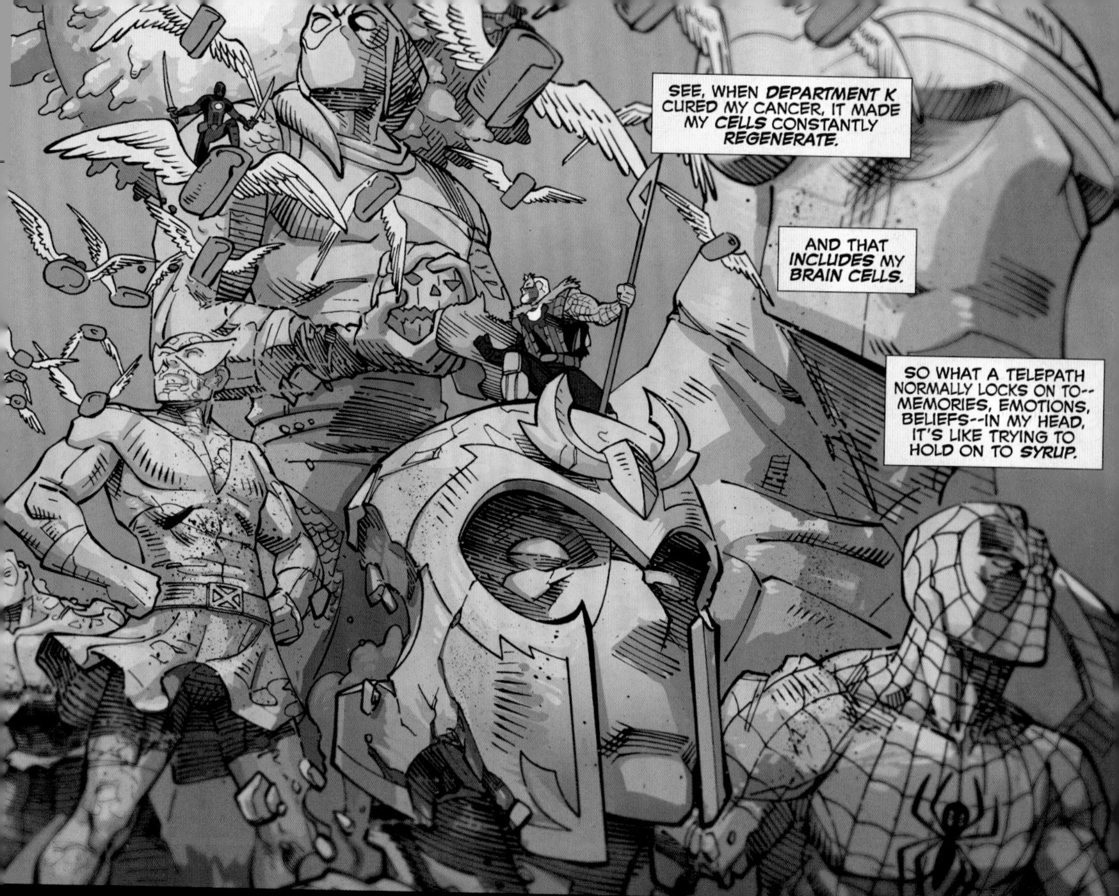
SEE, WHEN DEPARTMENT K CURED MY CANCER, IT MADE MY CELLS CONSTANTLY REGENERATE.
AND THAT INCLUDES MY BRAIN CELLS.
SO WHAT A TELEPATH NORMALLY LOCKS ON TO--MEMORIES, EMOTIONS, BELIEFS--IN MY HEAD, IT'S LIKE TRYING TO HOLD ON TO SYRUP.
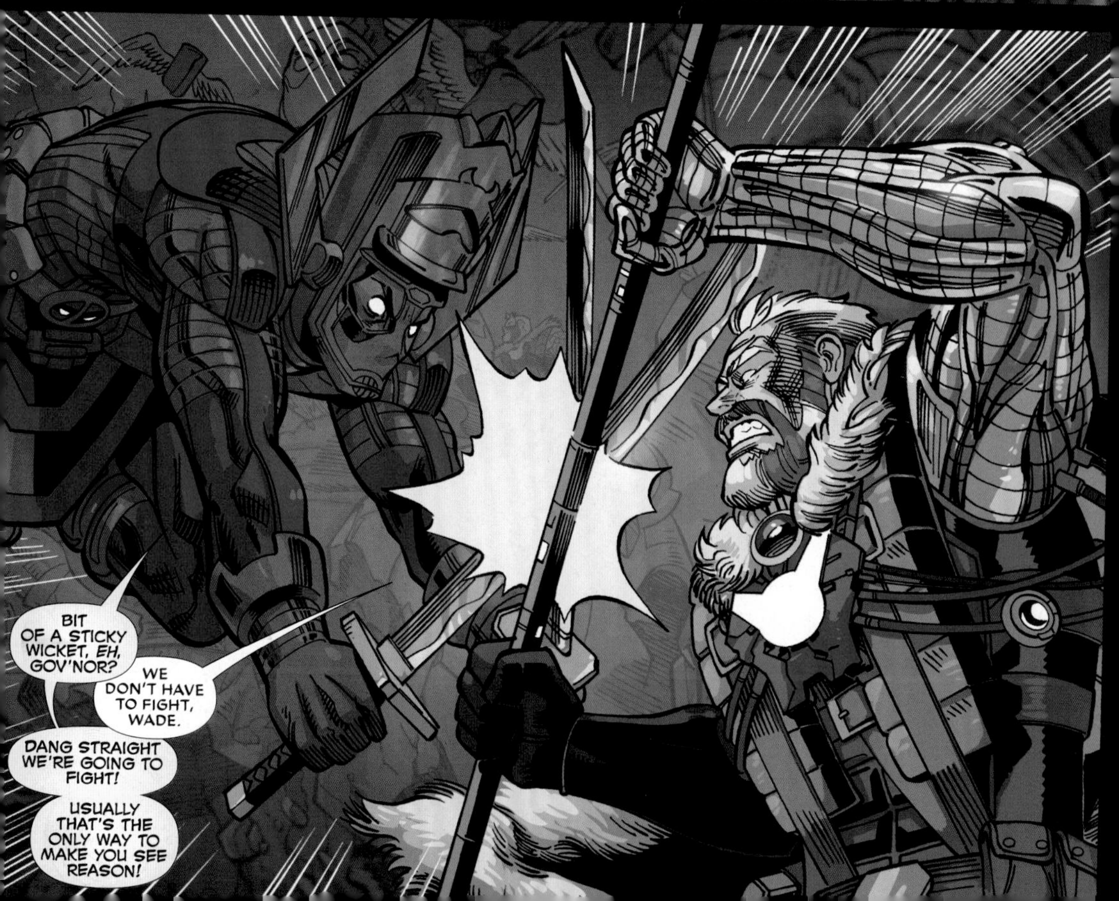
BIT OF A STICKY WICKET, EH, GOV'NOR?
WE DON'T HAVE TO FIGHT, WADE.
DANG STRAIGHT WE'RE GOING TO FIGHT!
USUALLY THAT'S THE ONLY WAY TO MAKE YOU SEE REASON!

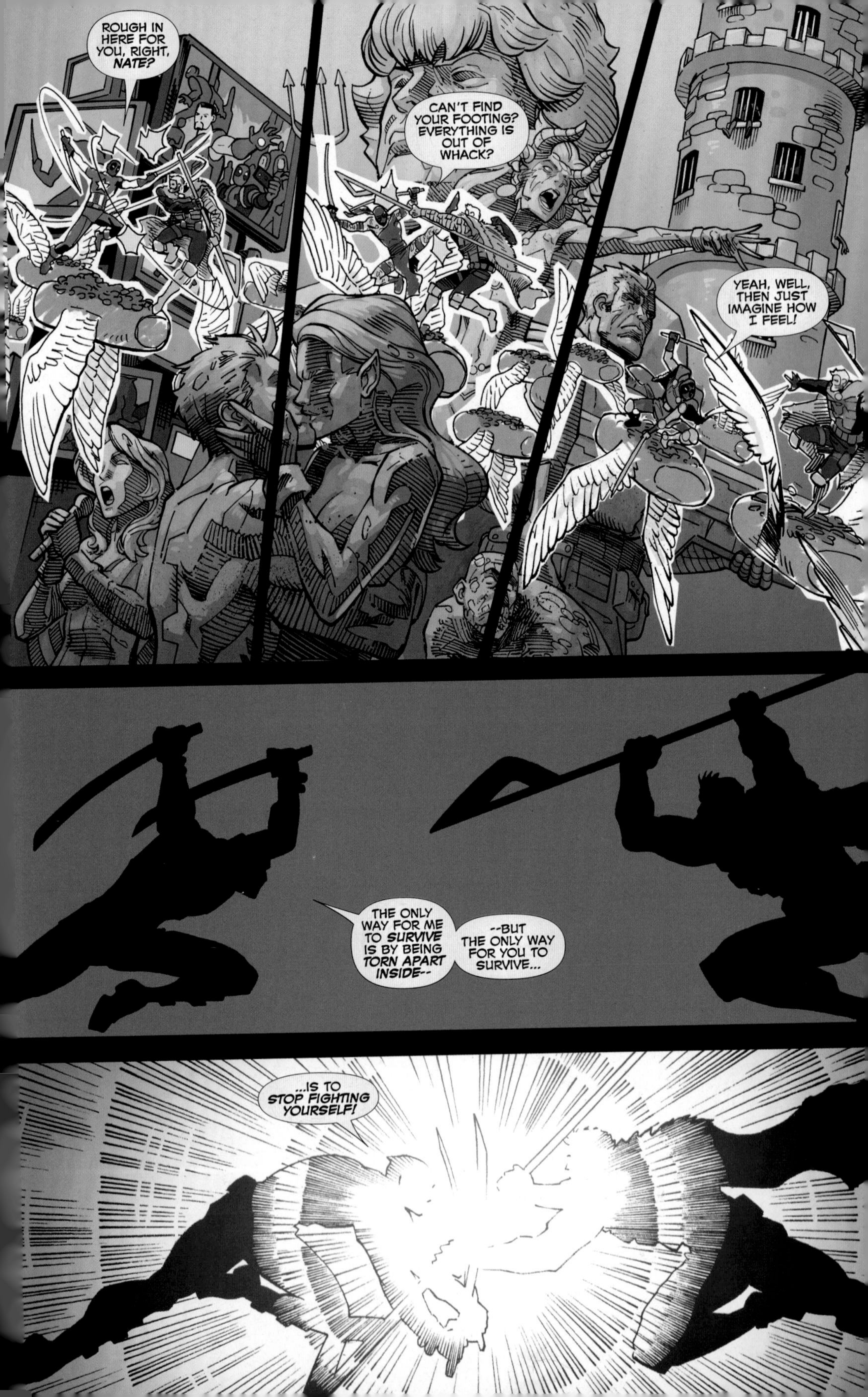
ROUGH IN HERE FOR YOU, RIGHT, *NATE?*
CAN'T FIND YOUR FOOTING? EVERYTHING IS OUT OF WHACK?
YEAH, WELL, THEN JUST IMAGINE HOW I FEEL!
THE ONLY WAY FOR ME TO *SURVIVE* IS BY BEING *TORN APART INSIDE--*
--BUT THE ONLY WAY FOR YOU TO SURVIVE...
...IS TO *STOP FIGHTING YOURSELF!*

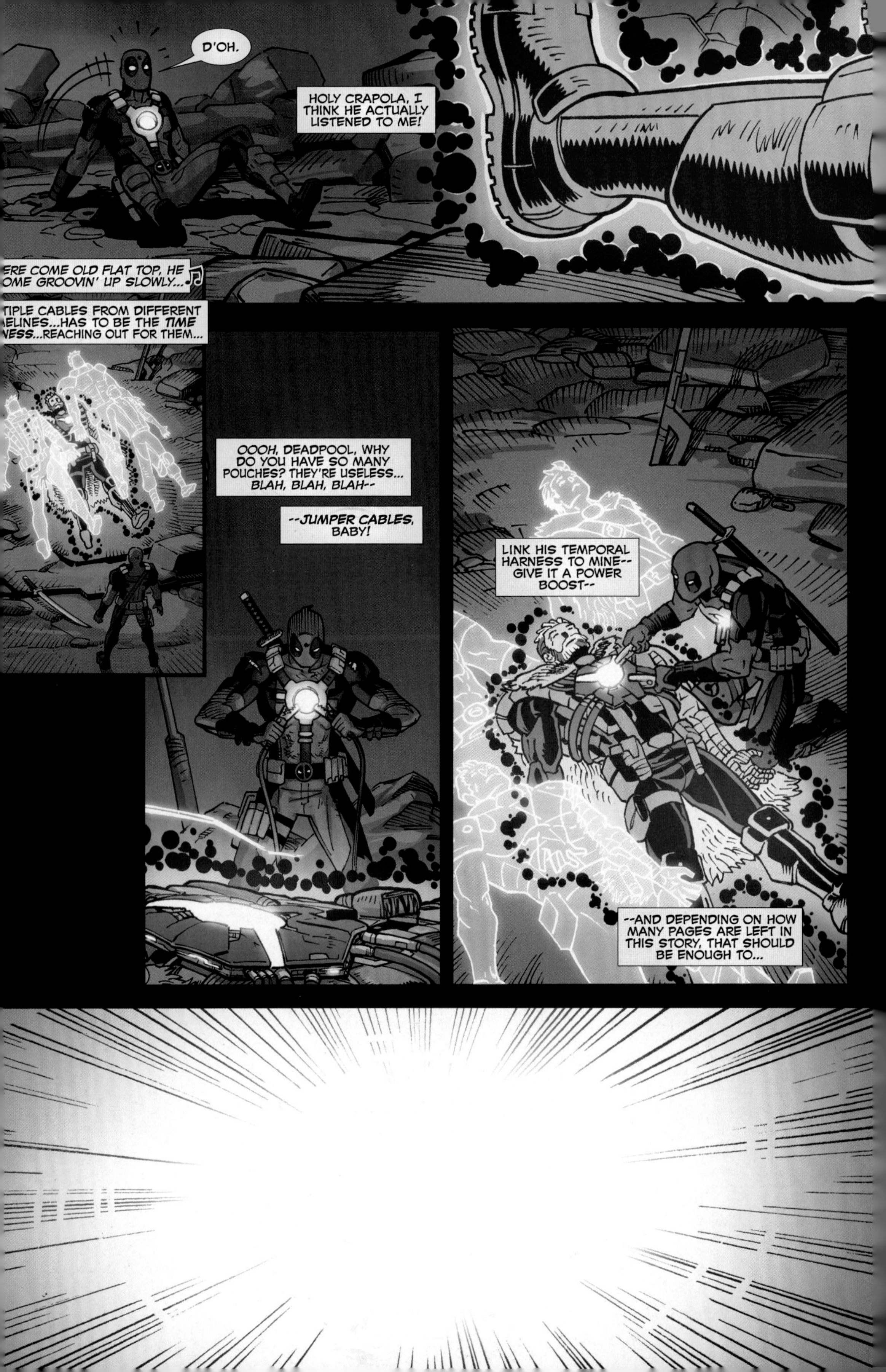
D'OH.
HOLY CRAPOLA, I THINK HE ACTUALLY LISTENED TO ME!
ERE COME OLD FLAT TOP, HE OME GROOVIN' UP SLOWLY...
TIPLE CABLES FROM DIFFERENT ELINES...HAS TO BE THE TIME NESS...REACHING OUT FOR THEM...
OOOH, DEADPOOL, WHY DO YOU HAVE SO MANY POUCHES? THEY'RE USELESS... BLAH, BLAH, BLAH--
--JUMPER CABLES, BABY!
LINK HIS TEMPORAL HARNESS TO MINE--GIVE IT A POWER BOOST--
--AND DEPENDING ON HOW MANY PAGES ARE LEFT IN THIS STORY, THAT SHOULD BE ENOUGH TO...

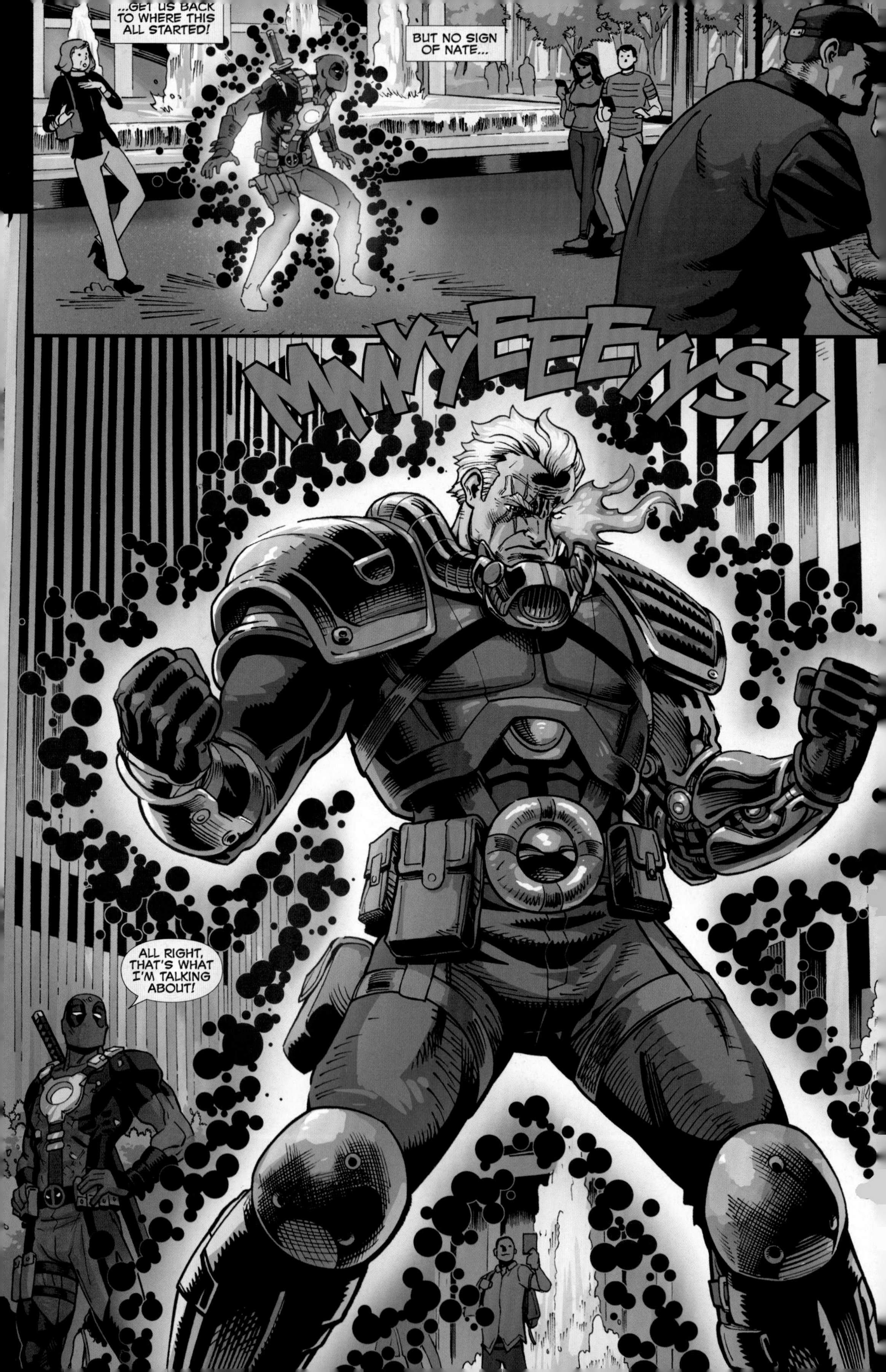
...GET US BACK TO WHERE THIS ALL STARTED!
BUT NO SIGN OF NATE...
MMMYYEEEYYSH
ALL RIGHT, THAT'S WHAT I'M TALKING ABOUT!

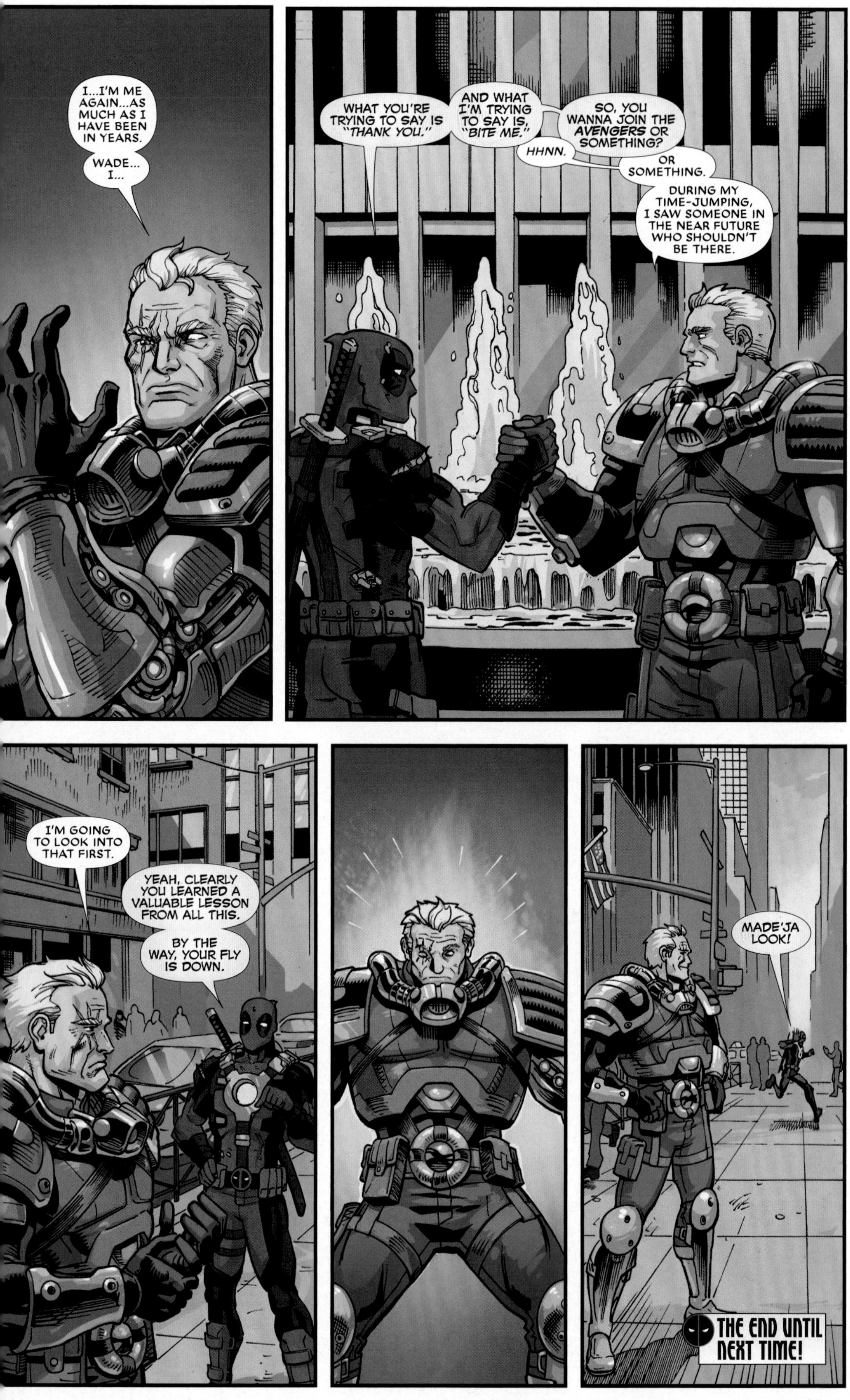
I...I'M ME AGAIN...AS MUCH AS I HAVE BEEN IN YEARS.
WADE... I...
WHAT YOU'RE TRYING TO SAY IS "THANK YOU."
AND WHAT I'M TRYING TO SAY IS, "BITE ME."
SO, YOU WANNA JOIN THE AVENGERS OR SOMETHING?
HHNN.
OR SOMETHING.
DURING MY TIME-JUMPING, I SAW SOMEONE IN THE NEAR FUTURE WHO SHOULDN'T BE THERE.
I'M GOING TO LOOK INTO THAT FIRST.
YEAH, CLEARLY YOU LEARNED A VALUABLE LESSON FROM ALL THIS.
BY THE WAY, YOUR FLY IS DOWN.
MADE'JA LOOK!
THE END UNTIL NEXT TIME!

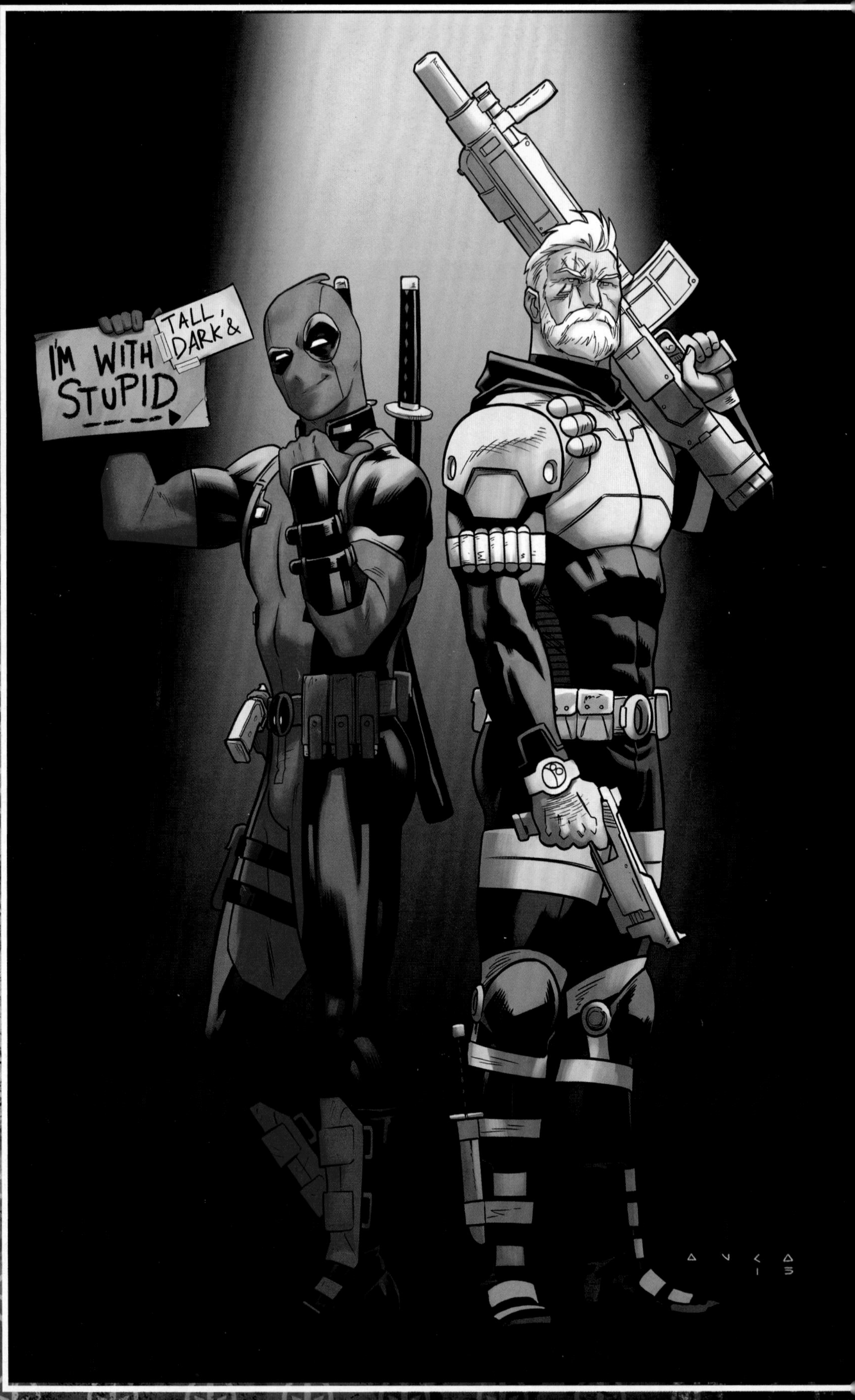
I'M WITH
TALL, DARK &
STUPID

#1 VARIANT BY **KRIS ANKA**

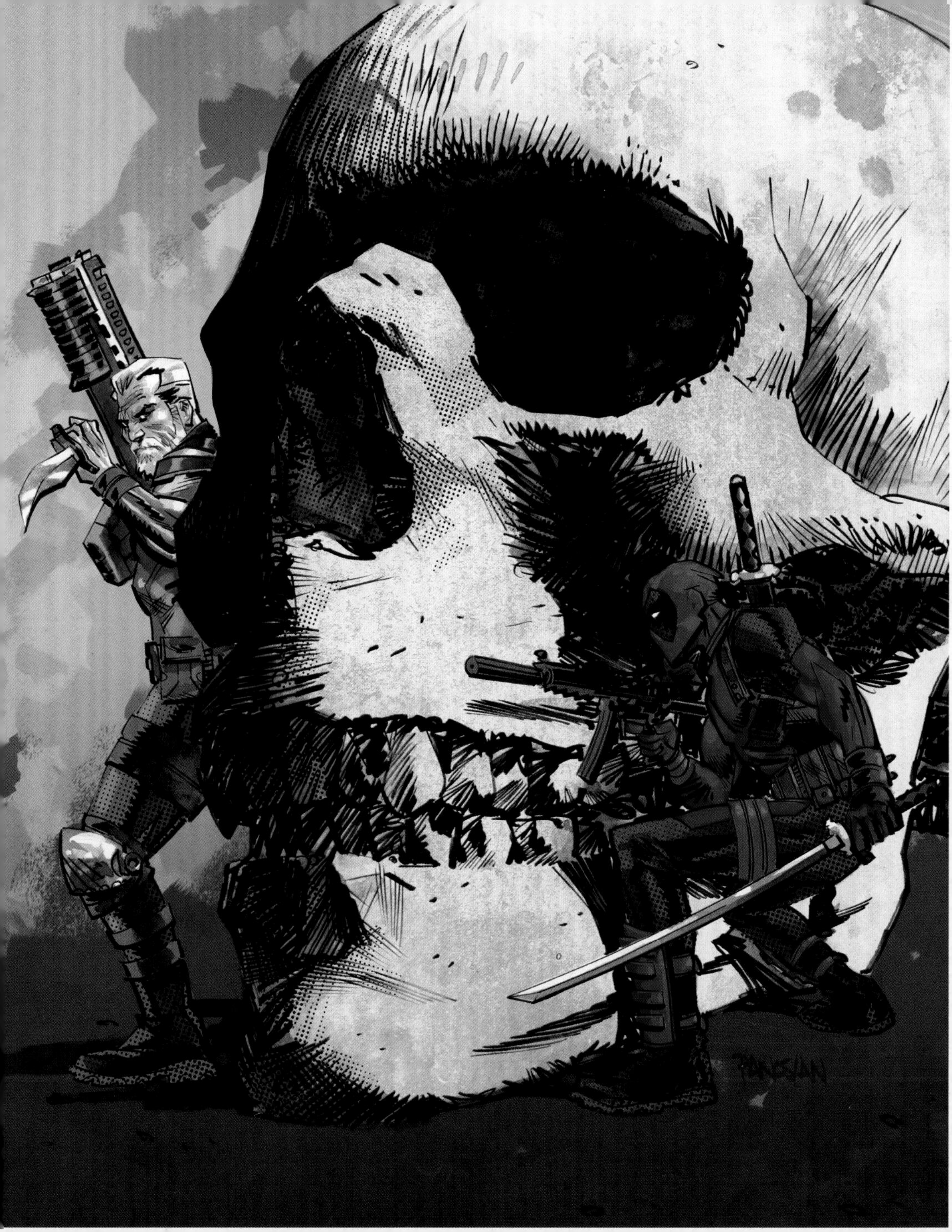

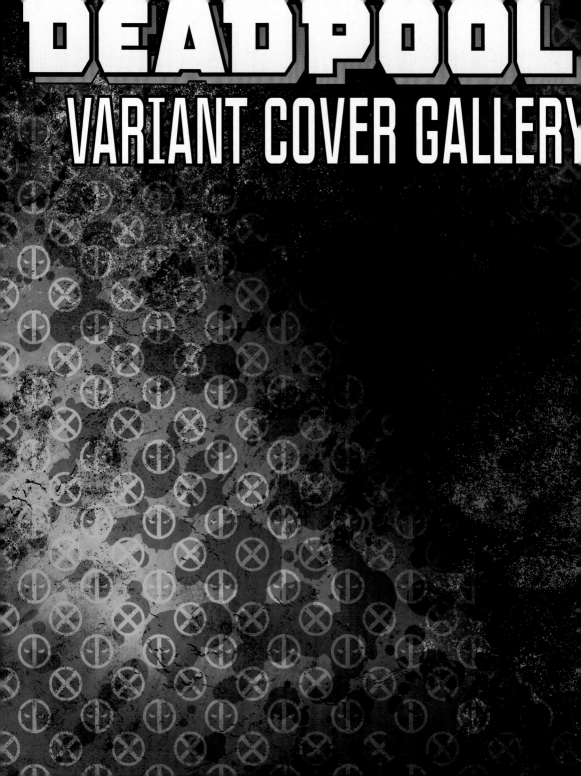

DEADPOOL

VARIANT COVER GALLERY

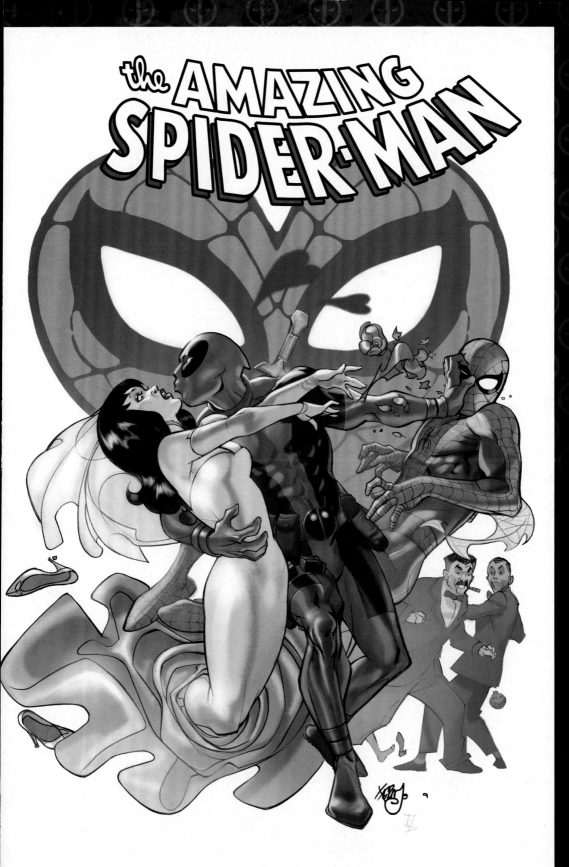

MAZING SPIDER-MAN (1999) #620 DEADPOOL VARIANT BY PASQUAL FERRY & FABIO D'AURIA

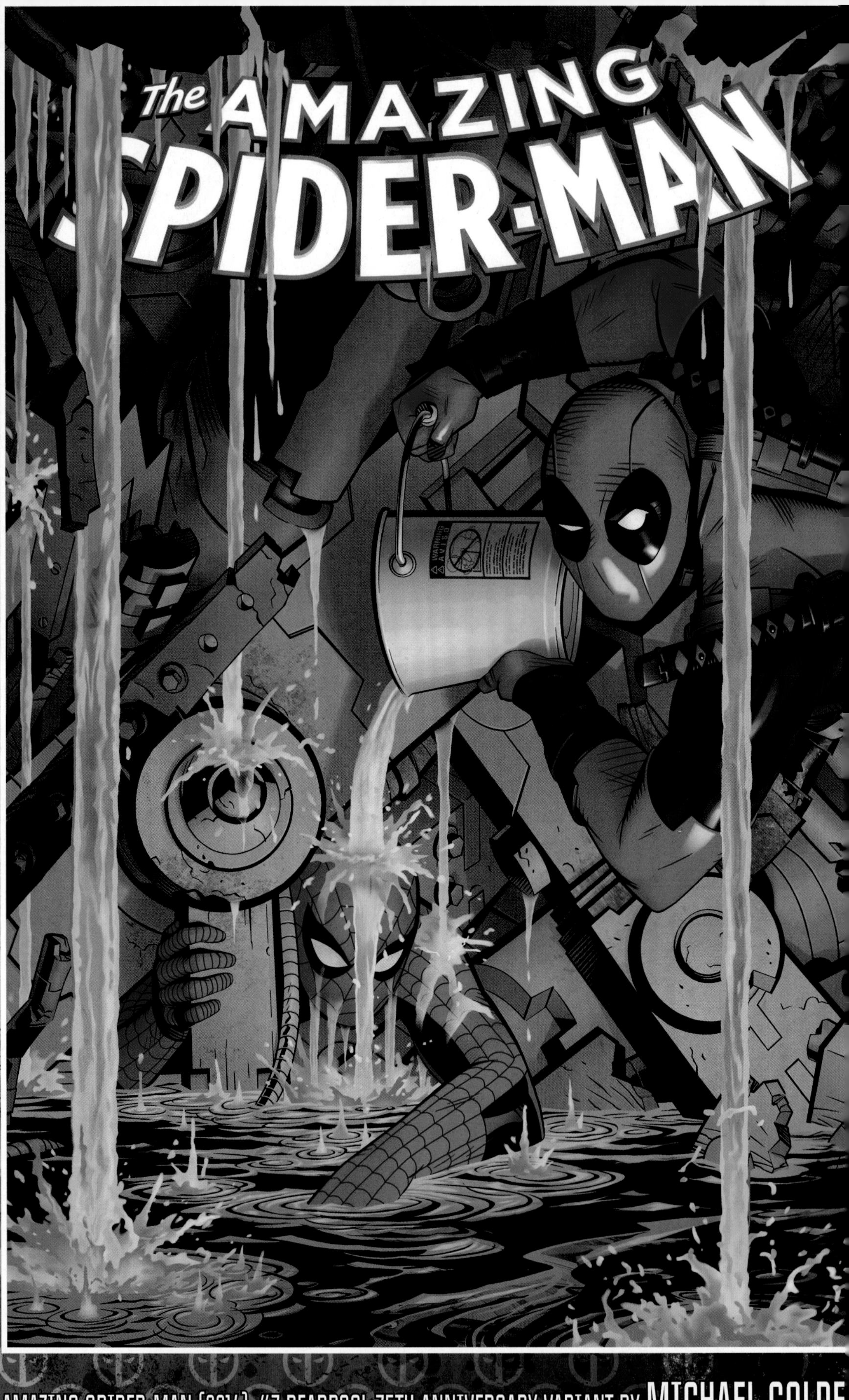

The AMAZING
SPIDER-MAN

AMAZING SPIDER-MAN (2014) #7 DEADPOOL 75TH ANNIVERSARY VARIANT BY MICHAEL GOLDE

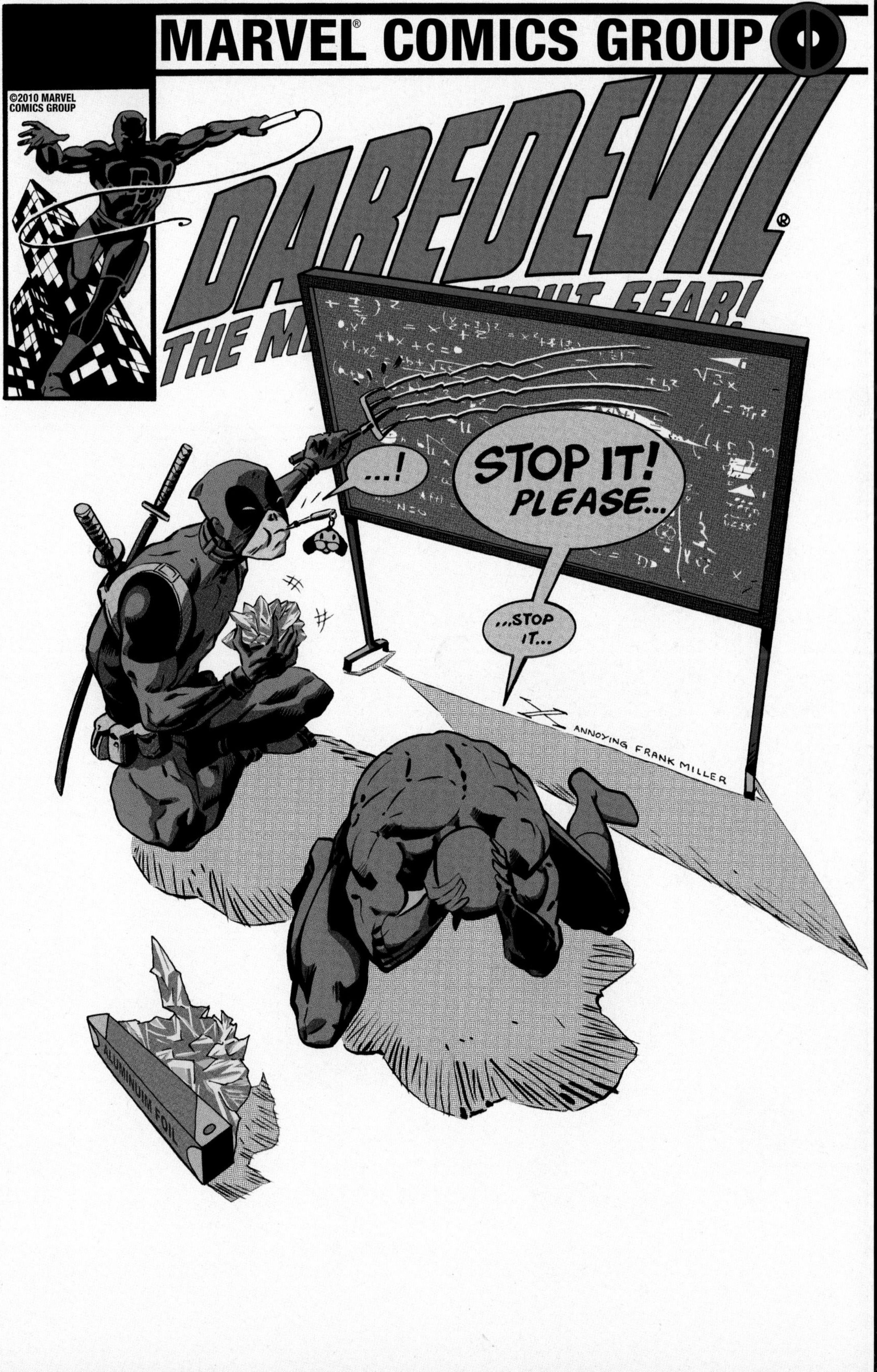

DAREDEVIL #505 DEADPOOL VARIANT BY MAX FIUMARA

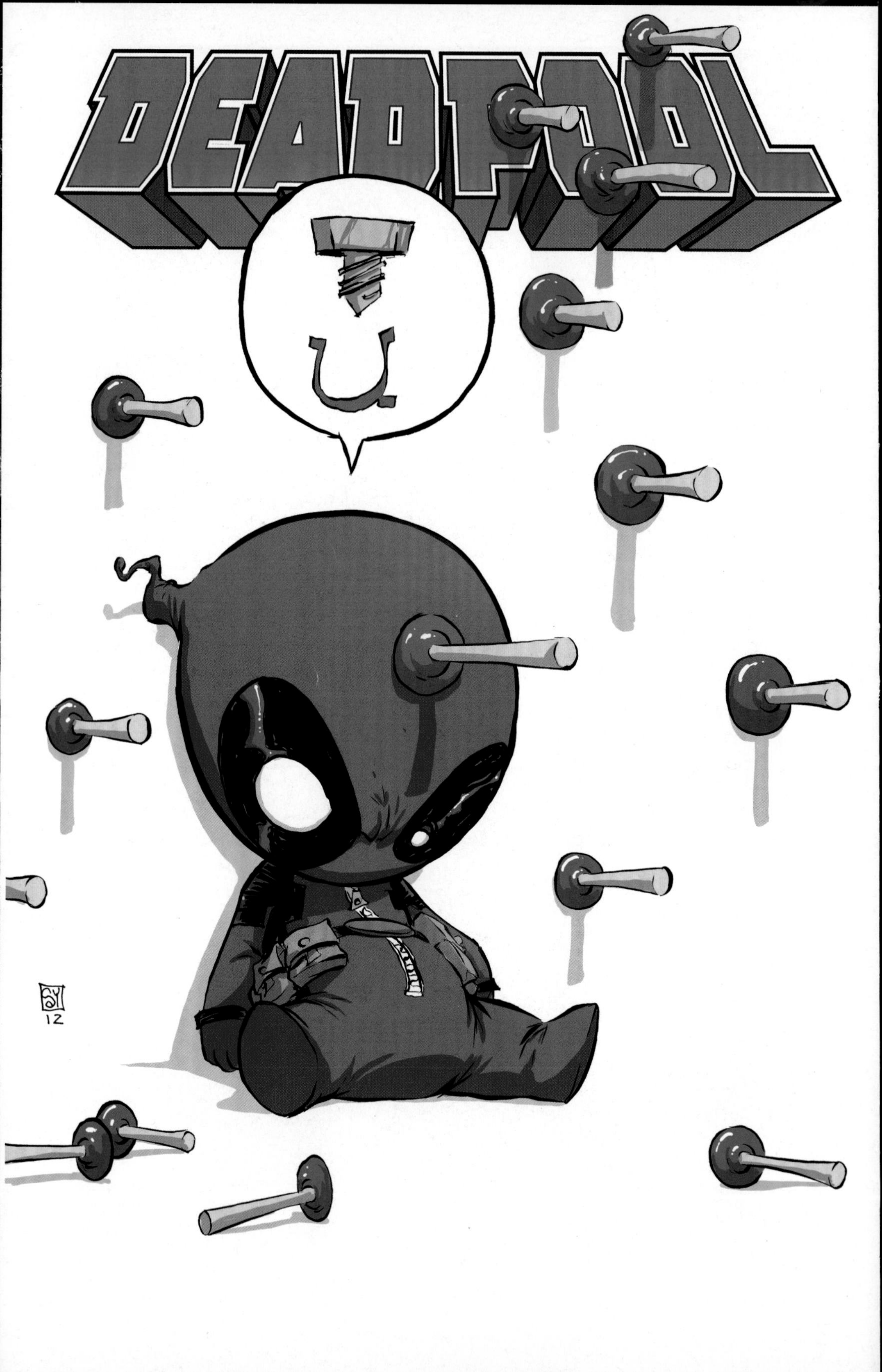
DEADPOOL

DEADPOOL (2012) #1 VARIANT BY **SKOTTIE YOUNG**

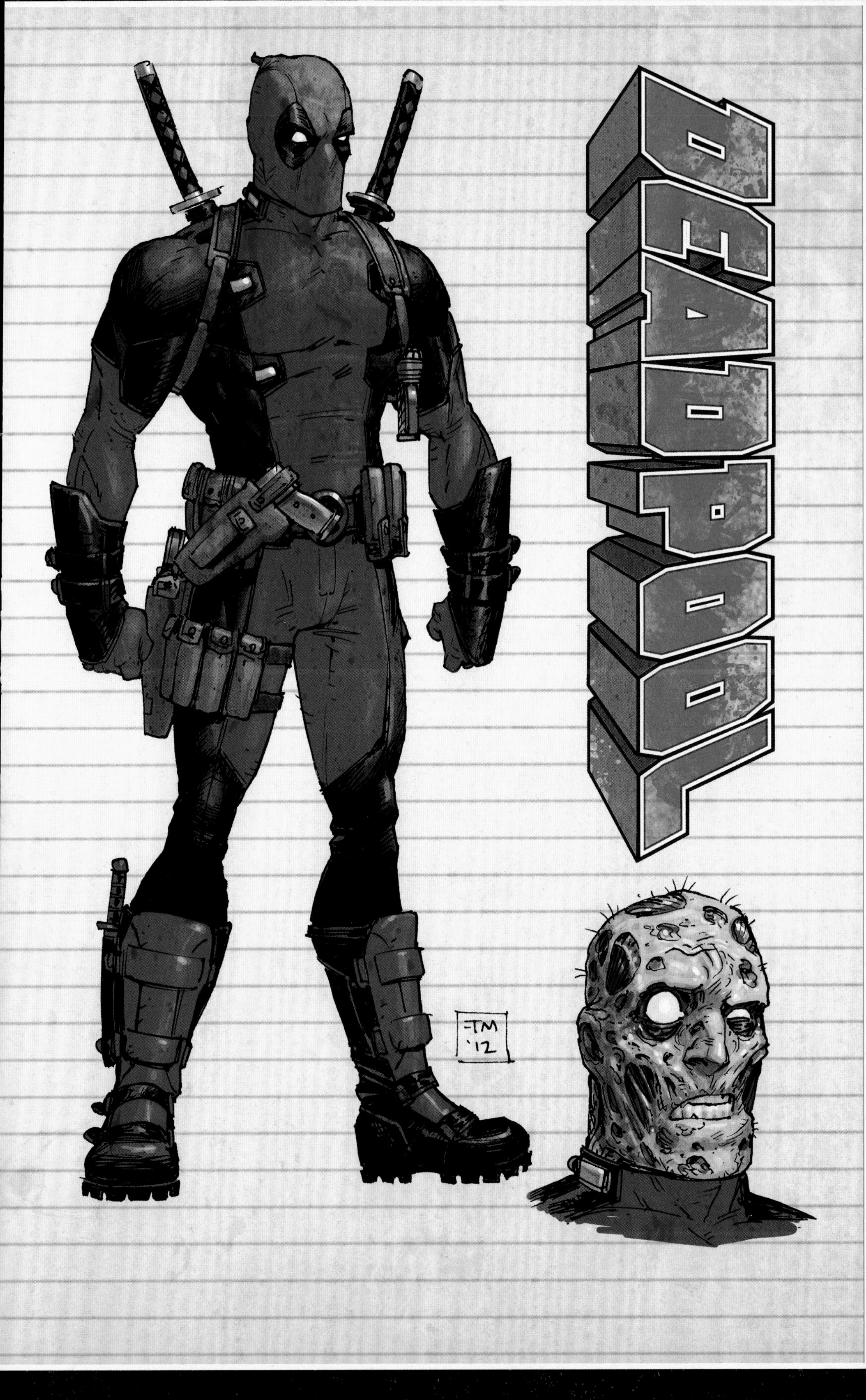
DEADPOOL
TM
'12

DEADPOOL (2012) #1 DESIGN VARIANT BY **TONY MOORE**

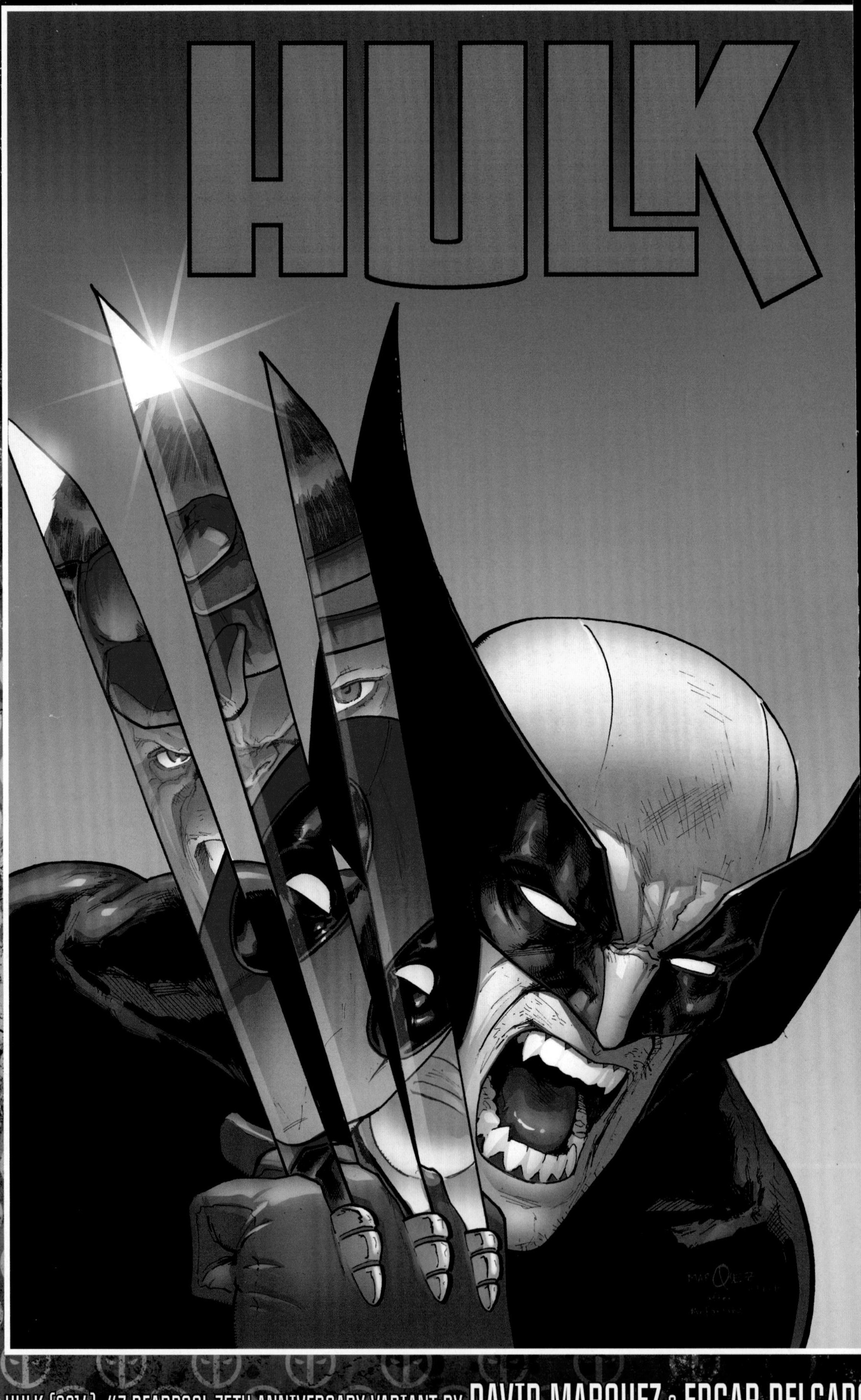
HULK

HULK (2014) #7 DEADPOOL 75TH ANNIVERSARY VARIANT BY DAVID MARQUEZ & EDGAR DELGADO

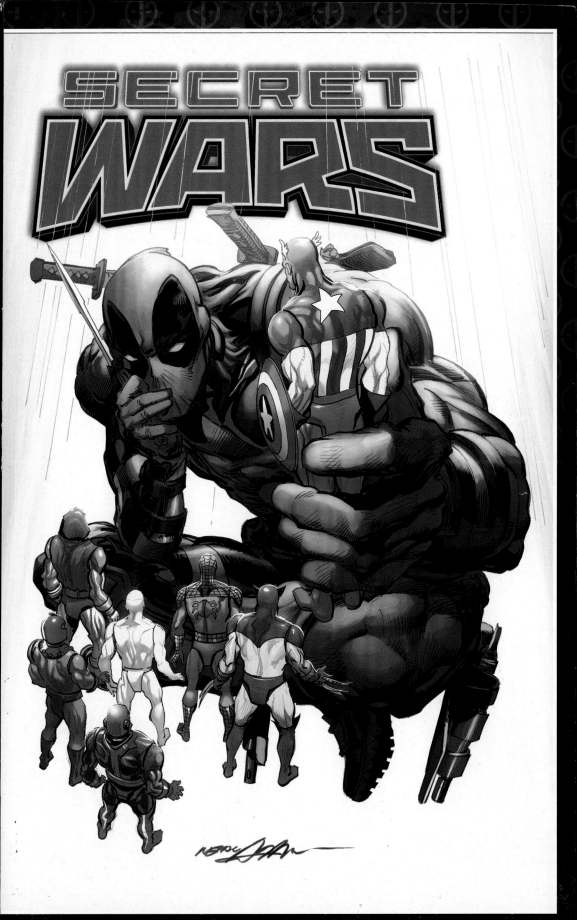

SECRET WARS #1 VARIANT BY NEAL ADAMS & FRANK MARTIN

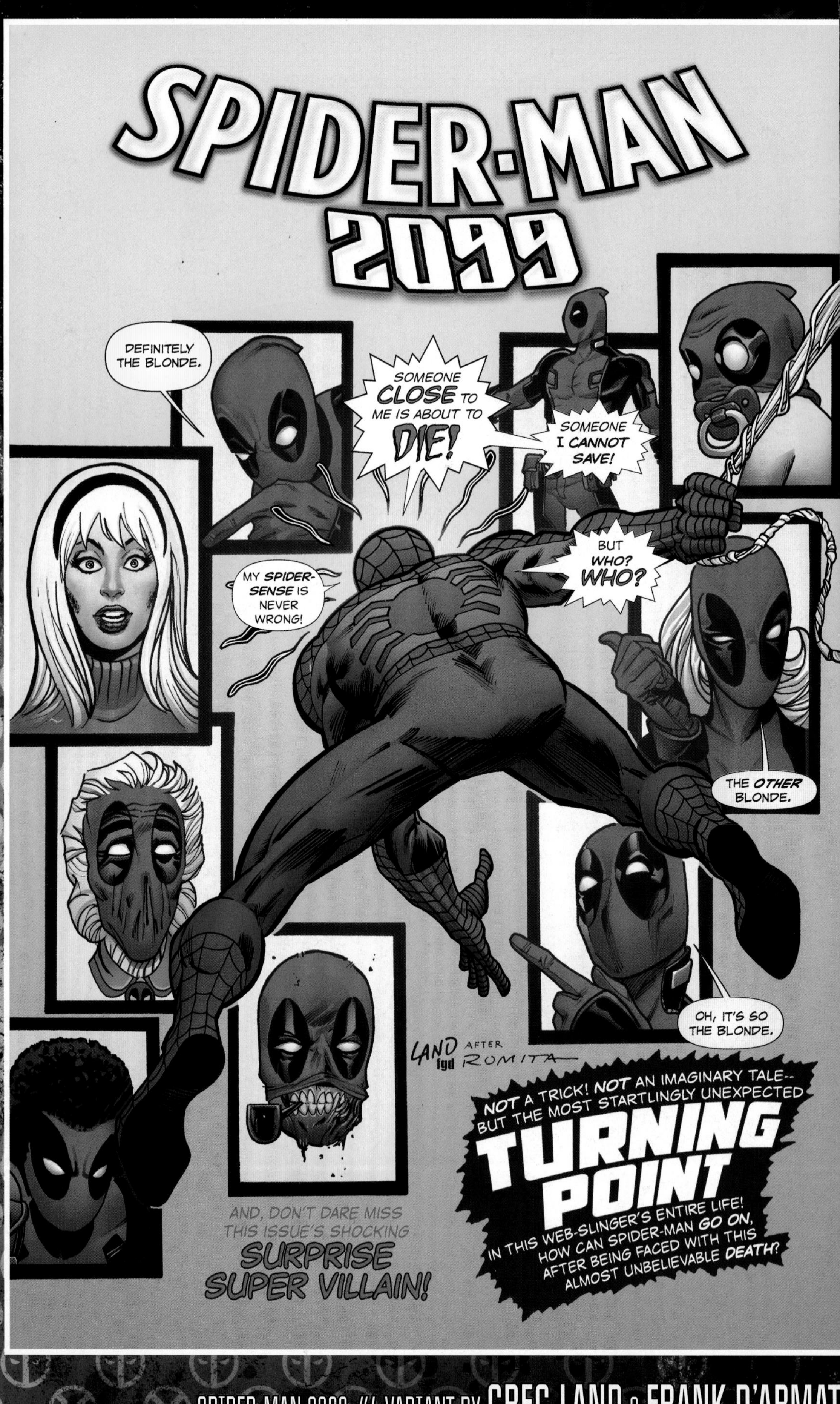
SPIDER-MAN 2099
DEFINITELY THE BLONDE.
SOMEONE CLOSE TO ME IS ABOUT TO DIE!
SOMEONE I CANNOT SAVE!
BUT WHO? WHO?
MY SPIDER-SENSE IS NEVER WRONG!
THE OTHER BLONDE.
OH, IT'S SO THE BLONDE.
LAND fgd AFTER ROMITA
NOT A TRICK! NOT AN IMAGINARY TALE-- BUT THE MOST STARTLINGLY UNEXPECTED
TURNING POINT
IN THIS WEB-SLINGER'S ENTIRE LIFE! HOW CAN SPIDER-MAN GO ON, AFTER BEING FACED WITH THIS ALMOST UNBELIEVABLE DEATH?
AND, DON'T DARE MISS THIS ISSUE'S SHOCKING SURPRISE SUPER VILLAIN!

SPIDER-MAN 2099 #4 VARIANT BY GREG LAND & FRANK D'ARMAT

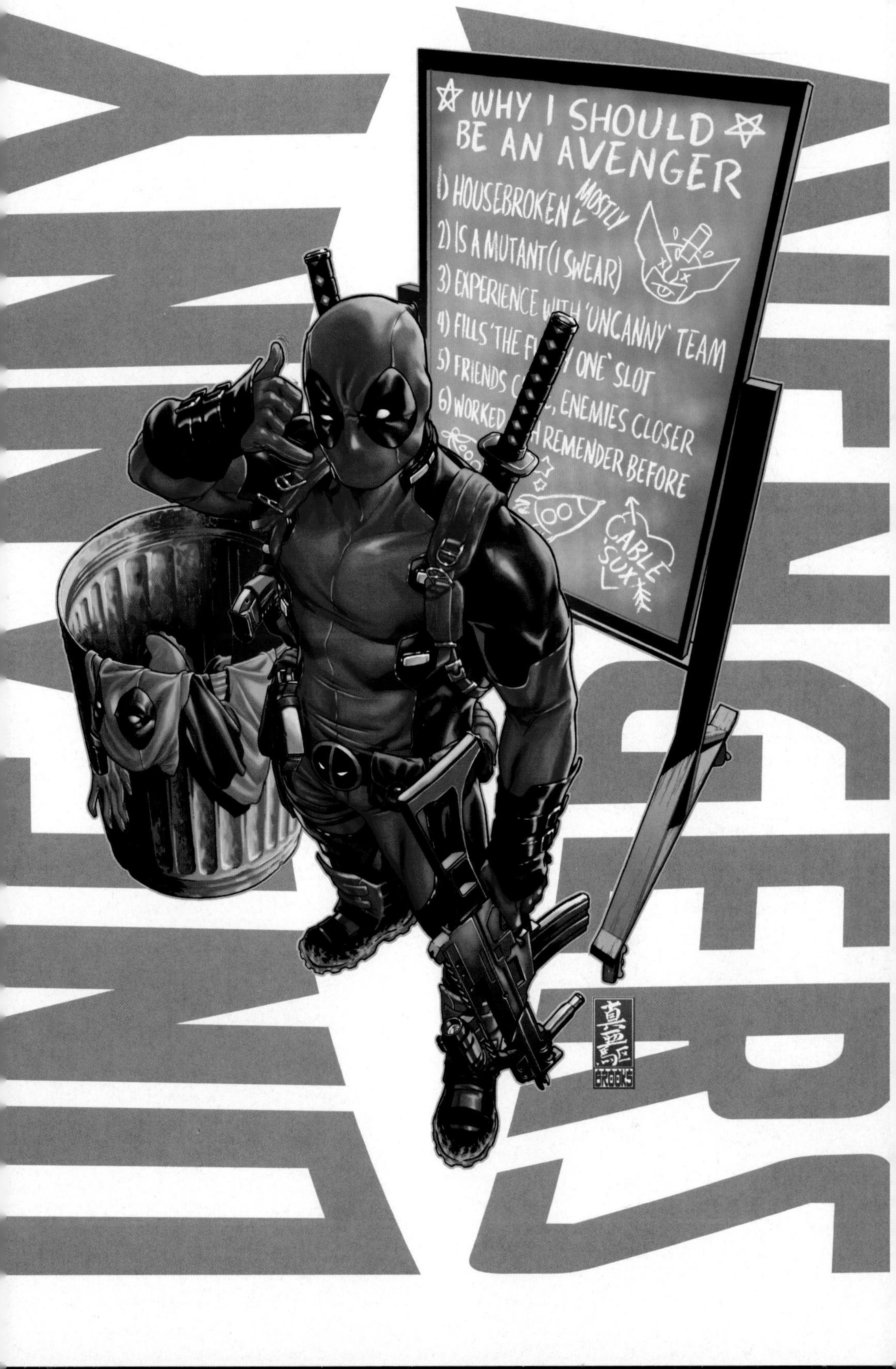
UNCANNY AVENGERS
WHY I SHOULD BE AN AVENGER
1) HOUSEBROKEN MOSTLY
2) IS A MUTANT (I SWEAR)
3) EXPERIENCE W H 'UNCANNY' TEAM
4) FILLS 'THE F Y ONE' SLOT
5) FRIENDS C , ENEMIES CLOSER
6) WORKED H REMENDER BEFORE
CABLE SUX
BROOKS

UNCANNY AVENGERS #1 DEADPOOL CALL ME MAYBE VARIANT BY **MARK BROOKS**

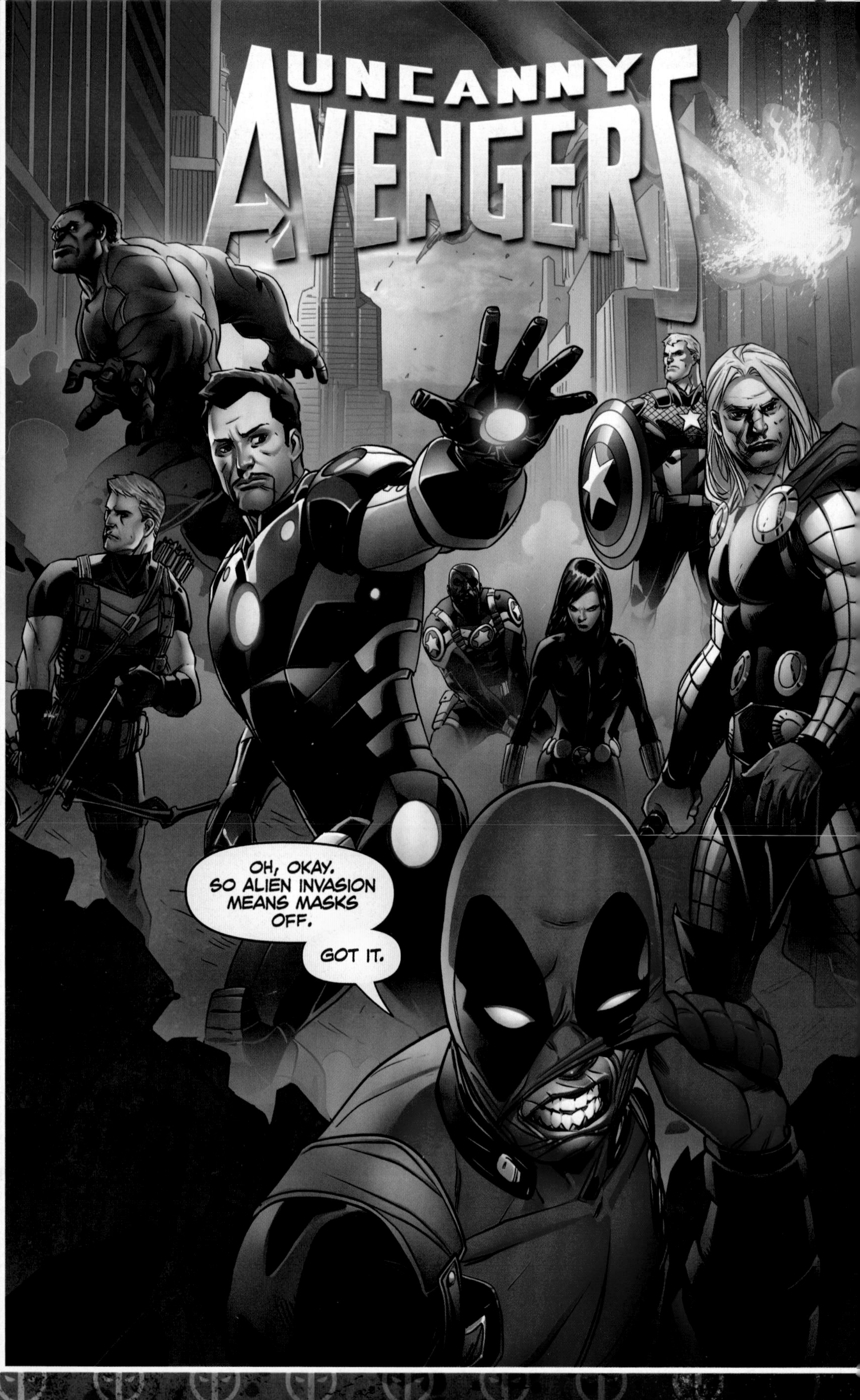
UNCANNY AVENGERS
OH, OKAY. SO ALIEN INVASION MEANS MASKS OFF.
GOT IT.

UNCANNY AVENGERS #25 DEADPOOL 75TH ANNIVERSARY VARIANT BY KHOI PHAM & FRANK D'ARMATA

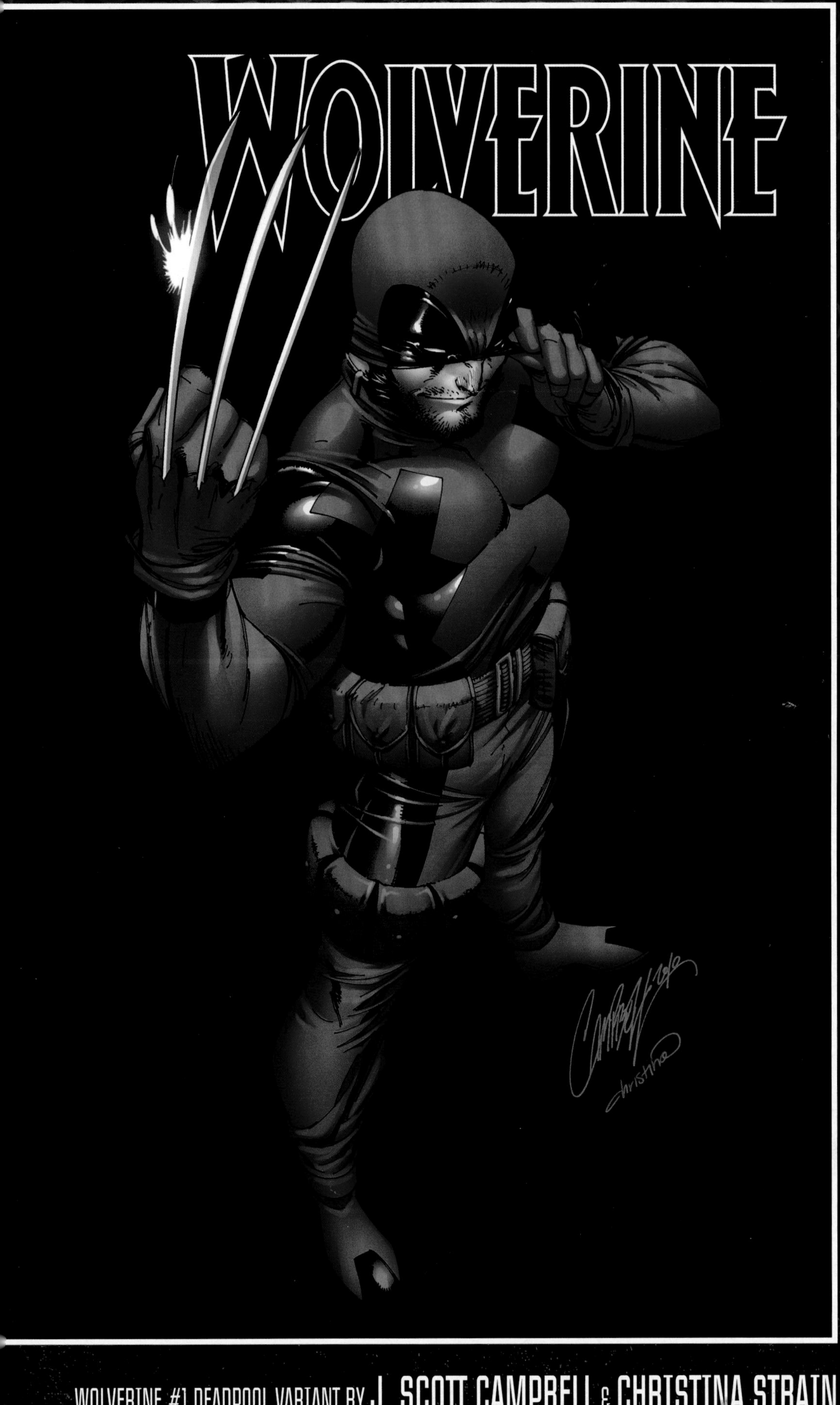
WOLVERINE

WOLVERINE #1 DEADPOOL VARIANT BY J. SCOTT CAMPBELL & CHRISTINA STRAIN

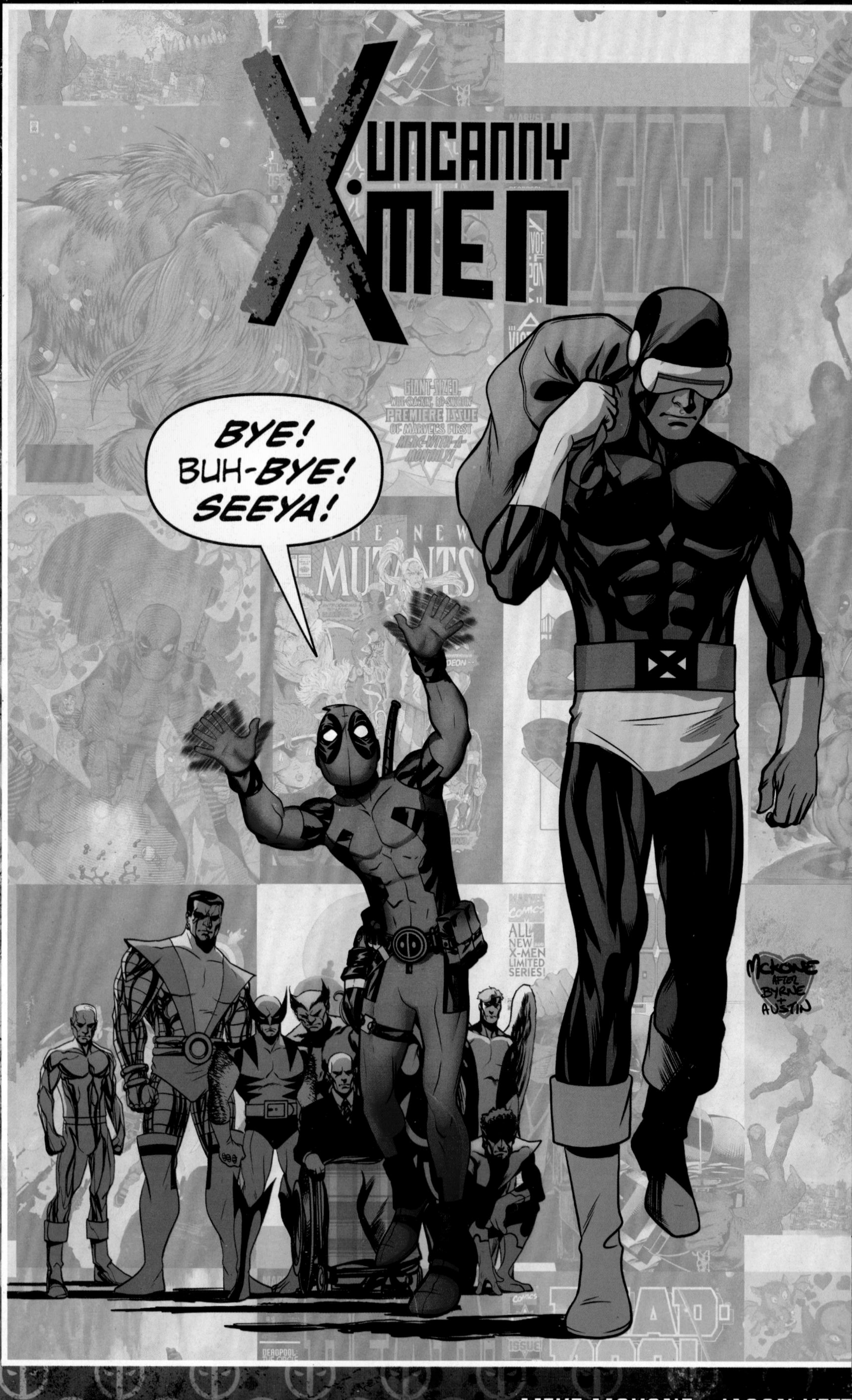
UNCANNY X-MEN
BYE! BUH-BYE! SEEYA!
THE NEW MUTANTS
ALL NEW X-MEN LIMITED SERIES!
MCKONE AFTER BYRNE + AUSTIN

UNCANNY X-MEN #27 DEADPOOL 75TH ANNIVERSARY VARIANT BY MIKE MCKONE & JASON KEIT